PROCRASTINATION

Why You Do It,
What to Do About It

Jane B. Burka, Ph.D.
&
Lenora M. Yuen, Ph.D.

ADDISON–WESLEY
*Reading, Massachusetts Menlo Park, California
London Amsterdam Sydney Don Mills, Ontario*

Library of Congress Cataloging in Publication Data

Burka, Jane B.
    Procrastination: why you do it, what to do about it.

    Includes index.
    1. Procrastination.   I. Yuen, Lenora M.   II. Title.
BF575.P95B87   1983   158'.1   83–22389

Art by Martha A. Epp, Boston, MA.
Set in 11 point Aster by Roberta J. Landi, Pleasantville, NY.

ISBN 0-201-10190-4
      0-201-10191-2

We dedicate this book to our clients.

Contents

Introduction   **ix**

PART I   UNDERSTANDING PROCRASTINATION
1   Procrastination: Nuisance or Nemesis?   **3**
2   The Procrastinator on Trial: Fear of Failure
        and Fear of Success   **19**
3   The Procrastinator in Combat: Fear of
        Losing the Battle   **43**
4   The Comfort Zone: Fear of Separation and
        Fear of Attachment   **61**
5   How You Came to Be a Procrastinator   **83**
6   Looking Ahead to Success   **105**

PART II   OVERCOMING PROCRASTINATION
7   Taking Stock: A Procrastination Inventory   **117**
8   Setting and Achieving Goals   **131**
9   Learning How to Tell Time   **147**
10   Enlisting Support from Others   **167**
11   Stress and the Procrastinator   **175**
12   Living and Working with Procrastinators   **191**

To Our Fellow Procrastinators   **219**
Further Readings   **221**
Index   **223**

Acknowledgments

No one, especially two procrastinators, can write a book alone. We wish to thank a few of the many people who have supported and sustained us throughout the process of bringing this book to completion. First, our thanks to Stuart Miller of Addison-Wesley, who initially proposed the writing of this book; to Doe Coover, Theresa Burns, Si Goodwin, and Ann Dilworth of Addison-Wesley for their editorial suggestions, their patience, and their unfailing encouragement; to our agents, Robin Straus and Susan Adler, for their advice and efforts on our behalf.

We would also like to thank our professional colleagues who offered invaluable feedback on the manuscript: Neil Brast, Hilde Burton, Elinor Caustin, Philip Cushman, Margaret Guertin, Bryan Lawton, Jeri Marlowe, Carol Morrison, Amy Schoenenberger, and Shan Steinmark. We appreciate the support provided by the staff of the Counseling Center at the University of California at Berkeley, where we first began to work professionally with procrastinators, and the help of Sharon Lucas, who assisted us with the typing of the manuscript.

For their personal encouragement from start to finish, we are grateful to Babette Bohn, Michael Freeman, Sheila Humphreys, Mitzi McCloskey, Roger Myers, Lynn Segal, Justin Simon, Bill Weber, and to our families. Their interest and reliable guidance helped us make progress even when we felt disheartened.

Finally, we would like to acknowledge our indebtedness to Federal Express, without whom we would have missed numerous last-minute deadlines.

Introduction

People who write books are supposed to be very knowledgeable about their subjects. We know procrastination from the inside out: Between us, we have been through many college all-nighters, spent long years struggling with our doctoral dissertations, paid late tax penalties, and made up elaborate stories to excuse our delays (having to visit a sick grandparent in the hospital is an all-time favorite). We're still marveling that we finished this book only two years after the original deadline! We now optimistically consider ourselves to be "moderately reformed" procrastinators.

In addition to our two lifetimes of personal experience, we have had many years of professional experience working with other procrastinators. We began when we were both on the staff of the Counseling Center at the University of California at Berkeley. In our Procrastination Groups for students we saw patterns and themes emerge again and again. While each individual's struggle was unique, there were many striking similarities among them. We learned, for example, that our plan to start the week off by holding the group on Monday mornings from nine to eleven was completely unrealistic—since no one even showed up until ten o'clock.

When we offered Procrastination Workshops for the general public, we were once again reminded of the nature of the beast. We almost cancelled our first workshop one week before the scheduled date because too few people had registered. In the end, we had to move to a larger room when two-thirds of the group signed up at the last minute.

In both our groups and workshops, we have broadened our experience through contact with many different procrastinators. In the private practice of psychotherapy we have worked with individuals in depth for extended periods of time. Our clients have opened their hearts and minds to us, and we are grateful. In this book we have given voice to many of the people with whom we've worked. To protect their confidentiality, we've changed all names and identifying information, and some of the procrastinators we describe are composites of several people we've known.

We explain the problem of procrastination in Part I of this book and suggest what you can do about it in Part II. Both components are necessary. If you don't understand why you're putting things off, then all the practical suggestions in the world aren't likely to help, because you won't let yourself use them. Yet, even if you've searched your soul and believe you thoroughly understand your reasons for procrastinating, you still won't get anywhere unless you *do* something to overcome it.

Our view of procrastination is that it serves a protective function for people. Most procrastinators are aware of the ways delaying has been working *against* them. But these same people are less familiar with how procrastination may also be working *for* them. Delaying may be a strategy that protects them from facing some difficult fears and anxieties, such as fear of failure or fear of success, fear of being controlled, fear of becoming too separate from others, or fear of being too attached to other people.

For the sake of clarity, we have separated our discussion of these fears into different chapters. But our artificial distinctions don't do justice to the complexities of human emotions. You will have to take a hard, honest look at yourself to explore the particular meanings procrastination has for you. Some of the issues we discuss will apply to you more directly than others. We've offered an overview; the particulars can only be filled in from your own personal experience.

The techniques we suggest in Part II are very effective—if you use them. Reading them may be interesting, but reading is not doing. Many procrastinators sabotage themselves by not even trying to implement these practical suggestions. Recognizing the meaning of your procrastination may help you understand your hesitation to experiment with the techniques offered in this book. We will alert you to some of the common pitfalls procrastinators are likely to encounter as they try to take the plunge. Although people who suffer usually hope for quick relief, giving up procrastination is a gradual process that takes time. For some people, in addition to self-exploration and learning practical techniques, individual or group counseling is an important and necessary step to take.

Our aim is not to do away with procrastination. We're not trying to turn our readers into efficiency experts who are relentlessly punctual and who wash every dish the moment it's used. There are plenty of times when it's in your best interest to put something aside and not attend to it. Rather, we hope that this book will help give you some freedom of choice about procrastinating, so that you will worry less and feel more in control of your life.

Part I:

Understanding Procrastination

1

Procrastination: Nuisance or Nemesis?

It's Near Year's Day—time for your annual resolutions. But after a long night of celebration, and with all the Bowl games on TV, who has time for serious reflection? By the end of January, when one friend has already lost ten pounds on her new diet and another has begun working on his taxes (who *are* these people?), you decide that the time has finally come for you to make your own resolution: "I'll never procrastinate again!"

Procrastination. The word conjures up different images for each of us. If you are among the fortunate who are not severely afflicted, you may imagine a person lying in a hammock, contentedly drinking a beer instead of mowing the lawn. But if procrastination has been a problem for you, the images are probably less pleasant: a desk so cluttered that you hardly can see it beneath the rubble; the faces of old friends you've been meaning to write for years; memories of school days that turned into all-nighters; a project that even now is waiting to be done . . . .

Procrastination plagues people of all occupations. Under the constant pressure of grades and other evaluations, a student puts off writing papers and studying for exams, only to cram for days when time has finally run out. Self-employed people have only

3

themselves to rely on to do what's necessary to stay in business—yet many find it's easy to delay when no one is watching to make sure they follow through. In a competitive office setting, some people slow down instead of trying to keep up with the fast pace. Those irritated by bureaucratic red tape may file things under "pending," rather than complete the requisite (boring) busywork. At home, the possibilities for procrastination are endless. Who isn't nagged by some unfinished project, such as cleaning out the basement or getting the kitchen painted, that has been waiting for ages to be done?

We all have had a good laugh about a situation in which we, or someone we know, put things off until it was too late or almost too late. Consider, for instance, the family who waited so long to prepare for their annual vacation that finally, at nightfall, they simply threw everything into the car and stayed in a motel in the next town!

Some classic last-minute rush situations have even been commercialized. Merchants remind us in October to shop for Christmas, but everyone knows the stores will be open on December 24 for those who insist on taking it down to the wire. Stores are only too happy to provide prewrapped, face-saving gifts for Mother's Day, Father's Day, or Valentine's Day, which, according to retailers, is the most "last-minute" of all holidays: About ten million people buy their gifts on February 14. And every year, local TV stations send their reporters to the main post office to do stories on the hordes of people lined up in their cars, all trying to mail their tax returns before midnight on April 15.

HOW CAN I TELL IF I'M PROCRASTINATING?

Anyone—young or old, brilliant or average, unemployed or professionally successful—can be a procrastinator. Procrastination does not discriminate on the basis of race, creed, sex, or ethnic origin.

People often wonder how they can differentiate between true procrastination and simply putting things off either because they don't have time to do everything or because they're naturally relaxed and low-keyed. Let's consider this important distinction.

According to the *American College Dictionary*, to procrastinate means "to defer action, delay; to put off till another day or time." Thus, whenever you put something off you are procrastinating, regardless of the reason for your delay. Strictly speaking, procrastination is the *behavior* of postponing. What distinguishes comfortable procrastination from problem procrastination is how *troublesome* your delaying is to you.

There are two ways in which procrastination can be troublesome. First, delaying may lead to external consequences ranging from innocuous (a library fine for late books) to severe (losing a job or jeopardizing a marriage). Second, people who procrastinate may suffer internal consequences, feelings that range from mild irritation and regret to intense self-condemnation and despair. Let's look at procrastination along this continuum of distress.

Some people are so busy that delay is inevitable, yet they are not distressed about it. Their lives are fast-paced, so loaded with projects and activities that something is constantly undone, waiting to be completed. They live from one deadline to the next and seem to thrive under intense pressure. They feel they are at their best when they are extremely busy, and they wouldn't choose to live any other way.

There are also people who like to take life easy. It may take them a long time to get something done, but they're in no hurry to get around to it. Although they may work hard to take care of themselves and their dependents, they aren't especially driven or pressured. They put things off, and they don't mind doing so.

At times, people deliberately *choose* to procrastinate. They might decide to put something off because it's low on their priority list or because they want to think things over before making a decision or taking action. They use procrastination to give themselves time to reflect, to clarify options, or to help themselves focus on what seems most important. Their delay is an ally, and they take better action because of it. For them, procrastination is not a problem.

We all have moments when everything seems to happen at once and we can't help but fall behind temporarily: The relatives arrive for a three-week stay; the kids are in the middle of rehearsals for the school play and need chauffeur service; the car and refrigerator break down that afternoon; and the taxes need to be at the accountant's tomorrow. At times like these, something's got to give—it would be impossible to get it all done on time. People who acknowledge their limits are not likely to feel distressed when they can't do everything. They do the best they can, but they know they can't do it all.

Some people don't suffer from their procrastination because it is limited to actions that are of little consequence to them. People who are reliably on time for everything except parties and other social engagements may see no problem in being late, especially if family and friends have adapted to it. Christmas cards may be sent out late, and the mess in the basement still has to be sorted through, but the important things get done more or less on time. Procrastination is part of their lives, but in a small way.

In contrast, there are people whose procrastinating has had significant consequences for them. To an outside observer, many of these people appear to be doing just fine. They may even be highly successful, like the lawyer who heads his own firm or the woman who is able to manage five children and a full-time job. But inside they feel miserable. They are frustrated and angry with themselves because their procrastinating, which may be a well-kept secret, has prevented them from doing all they think they are capable of. Thus, although they appear to be doing well, they suffer.

For other people, procrastination has led not only to internal suffering, but to significant external consequences as well—they have endured major setbacks at work, at school, in relationships, or at home. They may have lost much that is important to them. In some cases, they never were able to achieve something they truly wanted. For people who feel they are at the mercy of procrastination, delaying is neither a minor irritant nor a joke.

Procrastination was tragic for Henry, a forty-five-year-old accountant. Because of his continual delays, Henry has lost two jobs and is in danger of losing a third. On his last job, he waited so long to begin a complex audit that in order to get an extra week's time, he told his client that his wife was ill in the hospital. The client, anxious about the audit, called Henry at home, where his wife answered the phone. Unaware of Henry's fabrication, she responded to the client's concern for her health with great surprise. The stunned client reported the discrepancy to Henry's supervisor, who fired him.

Or consider the plight of Brian, whose wife, Linda, filed for divorce after fourteen years of marriage. Linda said that she finally had gotten tired of waiting for him to get his life on track. For years, Brian had been saying that he would soon be able to spend time with her and their children, but it never happened. He was always busy thinking up new ideas that would get him further as a self-employed salesman, though he never put any of them into practice. He had enough trouble just keeping up with his existing accounts. Often, planned family activities had to be deferred or forgotten altogether because of some project Brian had started but not quite completed. Linda finally got fed up when they had to put off their long-awaited anniversary trip to Hawaii—Brian just *had* to make some sales calls he'd been putting off. "It was the last straw," Linda said. "I realized then that things were never going to change as long as I lived with Brian."

A final example is Susan, a lawyer who is being sued by a client because she didn't have the client's case prepared in time for the court appearance. "I don't know what came over me," she said. "I knew when the court date was, but I just kept putting off gathering material. Finally, that morning, I scribbled a few notes, but I hadn't done a bit of background research." Because Susan has had similar trouble with other clients, she is now in danger of being disbarred and may never practice law again.

Like Henry, Brian, and Susan, some procrastinators find that their delaying seems to have a life and will of its own. They want to make progress, but are unable to move—so they spin their wheels, until the pressure is so great or the deadline so imminent that they somehow extract themselves from the mire, though not always successfully.

THE CYCLE OF PROCRASTINATION

Many people compare the experience of procrastination to living on an emotional roller-coaster. Their moods rise and fall as they attempt to make progress and predictably slow down. When they anticipate starting a project and then work toward its completion, procrastinators undergo a sequence of thoughts, feelings, and behaviors that is so common we have called it the Cycle of Procrastination. There are, of course, individual variations of this sequence. The cycle may be drawn out over a period of weeks, months, or even years, or it may occur so rapidly that one moves from the beginning to the end in a matter of moments.

1. *"I'll start early this time."*

At the outset, procrastinators are usually very hopeful.

When a project is first undertaken, the possibility exists that *this* time it will be done in a sensible and systematic way. Although they feel unable or unwilling to start *right now*, procrastinators often believe that this start will somehow spontaneously occur, with no planned effort on their part. It is only after some time has elapsed and it becomes apparent that this time may *not* be different after all that their hope changes into apprehension.

2. *"I've got to start soon."*

The time for an early start has passed, and illusions of doing the project right *this* time are fading. Anxiety builds and the pressure to begin intensifies. Having almost lost hope for the spontaneous start, the procrastinator now begins to feel pushed to make some effort to do something soon. But the deadline is not yet in sight, so some hope remains.

3. *"What if I don't start?"*

As the time continues to pass, and the procrastinator *still* hasn't made a start, it is no longer a question of the ideal beginning, or even of the push to get going. By now, any remaining optimism has been replaced by foreboding. The procrastinator, imagining that he or she may *never* start, may have visions of horrible consequences that will ruin life forever. At this point the person may become paralyzed, a number of thoughts circling around in his or her head, until they seem almost dizzying:

a. *"I should have started sooner."* This conclusion reflects guilt, a constant companion to most procrastinators. They look back over the time they have lost and realize that it's irretrievable. The pressure of the circumstances is such that soon they'll have no choice but to begin. Looking back, they regret the behavior that has brought them to the edge of the precipice, knowing they could have prevented it if only they had started sooner. As one procrastinator put it, "I have the experience of constant lament."

b. *"I'm doing everything but...."* It is extremely common for procrastinators at this stage to do everything and anything *except* the avoided project. The urge to reorganize the desk, clean the apartment, or try out all of Julia Child's new recipes suddenly becomes irresistible. Previously avoided but less onerous tasks cry out to be done now. So the procrastinator writes overdue letters, calls friends after months of silence, or unpacks the boxes from last year's move. In no time the procrastinator is busy accomplishing things, happily absorbed in any activity that is not *it*. He or she is soothed by the rationalization, "Well, at least I'm getting *something* done!" Sometimes distracting activity seems so productive that the procrastinator actually believes he or she is making progress on The Project. Eventually, however, it becomes clear that *it* still isn't done.

    c. *"I can't enjoy anything."* Many procrastinators try to distract themselves with pleasurable, immediately rewarding activities. They go to the movies, get together with friends, or spend the weekend sailing. Although they *try* hard to enjoy themselves, the shadow of the unfinished project looms dark before them. Any enjoyment they felt rapidly disappears and is replaced by guilt, apprehension, or disgust.

    d. *"I hope no one finds out."* As time drags on and nothing is done, some procrastinators begin to feel ashamed. They don't want anyone to know of their predicament, so they create ways to cover up their inactivity. They try to look busy even when they're not working; they present the illusion of progress even if they haven't taken the first step; they invent elaborate lies to justify their delay. Some literally hide—avoiding office, people, phone calls, and any other contact that might reveal their awful secret. As the cover-up continues, the procrastinator usually feels increasingly fraudulent. In response to your excuse about the "family emergency" that delayed your report, people may offer condolences on your grandmother's death, but you know that she's alive and well, playing bridge in Florida. This sense of fraudulence only adds to the internal and external pressures that intensify with each passing day.

    4. *"There's still time."*

    Though feeling guilty, ashamed, or fraudulent, the procrastinator continues to hold on to the hope that somehow there's still time to get the project done. The ground may be crumbling away underfoot, but the procrastinator desperately tries to remain optimistic and waits for the magical reprieve that rarely comes.

    5. *"There's something wrong with me."*

    By now the procrastinator is desperate. Good intentions to start early didn't work; shame, guilt, and suffering didn't work; the faith in magic didn't work. The procrastinator's worry about getting the project done is replaced by a far more frightening fear: "It's *me*.... There's something *wrong* with me!" You may entertain the notion that you're lacking something fundamental that everyone else has—self-discipline, courage, brains, or luck. After all, they could get this done!

    6. *The Final Choice: To Do or Not to Do.*

    At this point the procrastinator makes a decision either to

carry on to the bitter end or to abandon the sinking ship. He or she thus takes one of the two following paths:

Path 1: *Not to Do*

a. *"I can't do this!"* The tension has become unbearable. Time is now so short that the project seems totally impossible to do in the minutes or hours remaining. Because you've reached your level of intolerance, the effort required to pull through seems beyond your capability. Thinking, "I can't stand this anymore!" you may decide that the pain of trying to finish would be too great for you. You give up.

b. *"Why bother?"* At this late stage in the game, some procrastinators look ahead at all there is left to do and decide that it's simply too late to pull it off this time. There's no way in the world they could complete the project as they had initially planned—it can't be done well with so little time remaining. Any efforts made now wouldn't really make a difference in the final outcome. Now that there's no point in working hard, why bother even trying? They've messed up again, and that's all there is to it. So they don't do anything more.

Path 2: *To Do—On to the Bitter End*

a. *"I can't wait any longer."* By now, the pressure has become so great that you can't stand waiting another minute. The deadline is too close or your own inertia has become so painful that it's finally worse to do nothing than it is to take action. So, like a prisoner on a death row, you resign yourself to your unavoidable fate... and you begin.

b. *"This isn't so bad. Why didn't I start sooner?"* At last, the project is under way. To your own amazement, it's not as bad as you had feared. Even if it is difficult, painful, or boring, at least it's getting done—and that's a tremendous relief. There may even be times when it is actually a pleasure to do! Procrastinators are sometimes unnerved by this stage, unable to reconcile the discrepancy between their dreadful anticipation and the relatively benign experience of the action itself. Puzzled, they may also feel a tinge of regret for all the needless suffering they have endured. "I could have actually enjoyed doing this, or gotten it over with so much more easily. Why didn't I just do it sooner?"

c. *"Just get it done!"* The end is almost at hand. There's not a second to spare as you begin to race the clock in order to finish. When you play the perilous game of brinksmanship, you no longer have the luxury of extra time to plan, refine, or improve what's done. Your focus is no longer on how well you could have done it, but on whether you can get it done at all.

7. *"I'll never procrastinate again!"*

When the project is finally either abandoned or finished, the procrastinator usually collapses with relief and exhaustion. It's been a difficult ordeal. But at long last, rest is possible...at long last, life can be enjoyed. The idea of going through this process even once more is so abhorrent that the procrastinator resolves never to get caught in the cycle again. Next time you'll start early, be more organized, stay on schedule, control your anxiety. And your conviction is firm—until the next time.

So the Cycle of Procrastination comes to an end with an emphatic promise to renounce this behavior forever. In spite of their sincerity and determination, however, most procrastinators find themselves repeating the cycle over and over again.

THE ROOTS OF PROCRASTINATION

Although it may be tempting to attribute your procrastination to a genetic aberration, unfortunately there's no such thing as a procrastination gene! Instead we must look to some of the environmental factors that have influenced us—the events, situations, and attitudes that have shaped our lives.

When we ask procrastinators to speculate about the factors that have led them down the path of delay, they often tell us, "We live in a competitive society! Everyone is expected to perform perfectly all the time. You just can't keep up with all that pressure."

Competition is indeed pervasive in our culture. In fact, we are urged not only to compete—we are urged to win. Despite the old adage, "It's not whether you win or lose, it's how you play the game," few people strive to come in second. It is the winner who reaps the harvest of prestige, money, glamour, or fame. It is the winner who gets the attention and who is considered a "success."

And how do we define "success"? Advertisements tell us that success means having lots of money, power, prestige, beauty—and, preferably, all of the above. If you do not have any or all of these things in abundance, you can still be successful if you have a perfectly spotless floor, drive the right car, feed your dog or cat the most nutritious pet food, raise perfect children, and at least attempt to get rid of all your personal flaws like dandruff and cellulite. Magazines entice us with the lines: "You can plan a perfect Christmas party," "How to find the perfect lover," "The perfect job is waiting for you." In short, success is most often defined in terms of perfection. The message we hear is, "You, too, can have it all!" But what it really means is: "If you don't have it all, there's something wrong with you."

Confronted with such impossibly high standards, no wonder so many of us run for the cover of procrastination. But there must be more to becoming a procrastinator than simply being exposed to a high-pressured, perfection-conscious society. If that were all there is to it, then everyone would have trouble with procrastination. There are many people who respond to cultural pressures by exhibiting signs of distress other than the inability to produce— among them overworking, depression, psychosomatic illnesses, alcoholism, drug addictions, and phobias.

To understand how we have chosen procrastination as our primary strategy for coping, we must look to the more personal dimensions of our lives. The remainder of Part I of this book is devoted to an in-depth examination of these personal issues in an effort to understand the reasons for our behavior. But as a way to begin this understanding, we'd like you to consider when it all got started.

Earliest Memories

Do you remember the first time you procrastinated? What were the circumstances? Did you put off doing something for school or was it something your parents told you to do? How old were you? High school...elementary school? Even earlier than that? How did the situation turn out, and how did you feel about it?

Some people recall, with startling clarity, the first time they procrastinated. Others have vague, fleeting images, or recall events that on the surface bear little resemblance to procrastination as they currently practice it. Here are a few examples of some early memories that procrastinators have described to us:

I remember it was in the second grade, when we were given our first paper to do. We had to write two paragraphs about mountains and hand it in the next day. As soon as the teacher assigned it, I remember feeling scared—what was I going to say? All that night, I worried about it, but I didn't do it. Finally the next morning over breakfast, my mother wrote it for me. I copied it over and handed it in. At the time, I felt relieved. But I also felt like a liar. I got an "excellent" on the paper.

I don't remember any incident exactly. It's more a fuzzy sense of my mom telling me to do something, and my feeling, "I won't do it!"

The summer between high school and college. My father died of cancer that summer. He'd been a wonderful father to me. I was visiting him in his hospital room, and he looked so frail and weak, it scared me terribly. I wanted him to be strong and healthy again, to be my father again. Here I was, going off to college in the fall, my first time away from home. I needed him to help me face it. And he said to me, "Do it for me, Sugar. Be a success for me. I know you can do it." Those were practically his last words to me. Since then, throughout college and graduate school, I have never handed anything in on time.

I used to hurry through my homework so I could go out and play. My father checked over it before I could leave. He would always find something wrong with how I'd done it, and I'd have to do it over. Or else he'd give me something else to do before I could go out. Finally I realized that it didn't matter how fast or how well I did my homework—he just wanted to keep my busy, so that I couldn't leave until he was ready to let me. After that, I stopped trying to finish fast. I just daydreamed and dawdled around.

Fifth grade. I'd always done well in school, and all the teachers liked me. That year, a group of girls in my class formed a club, and they wouldn't let me join because I was the teacher's pet. They called me a goody two-shoes. I felt as though I was contaminated. And I remember making a conscious decision that I would never be a teacher's pet again. So I stopped working, and started procrastinating. Just like that.

For many, the earliest symptoms of procrastination occurred in school—the first formal introduction of a young child to our larger, competitive society. The tracking systems of most schools emphasize academic ability as the major factor for distinguishing between students. You probably knew whether you were an "A,"

"C," or "F" kid. The social cliques that form in school are often based on these distinctions as well. The "brains," the "jocks," and the "partyers" may mock the children in the other groups in order to establish their own distinct places in the hierarchy. Experiences at the hands of one's peers can have a powerful effect on a person's academic and social confidence. Long after school years have passed, many adults still think of themselves in terms of how they were labeled as children.

In the fourth grade, Anton, accustomed to being near the top of his class, became bored by the material and stopped doing his work. Dismayed by his poor performance, the school administration put him back into a third-grade class for a two-week period to see if he would fare better among "the little kids." When he complained to his father about being put back, his dad told him this was what he deserved for not paying attention. Jolted and humiliated by the demotion, Anton vigorously reapplied himself to his schoolwork and was returned to the fourth grade at the end of two weeks. In one way, since he began to produce and achieve again, the intervention was successful. But years later as an adult, Anton is still haunted by the memory of those two weeks. In his job as a stockbroker he relives daily the fear of being humiliated by poor performance. The experience has become one of the driving forces of his personality and his procrastination: he is so determined to prove himself that he is never satisfied with his work and, consequently, has trouble finishing anything.

Unfortunately, people sometimes forget that grades do not measure intellect alone. They also measure a child's ability to concentrate, to cooperate, and to use imagination freely. These factors are directly affected by the child's emotional state, and this in turn is often a reflection of the home life.

Sheila's home situation was chaotic because her father drank heavily and carried on until late at night. Since she dreaded going home after school, Sheila stayed at the playground as long as possible. Once home, she spent most of her time in arguments with her drunken father. Naturally, her grades suffered, but she didn't tell anyone at school why she was unprepared. Some of her teachers assumed that Sheila was incompetent. Others saw her potential but labeled her rebellious. At college, Sheila carried this unintellectual self-image with her, procrastinating rather than ever testing herself.

Many people still think of themselves in terms of the learning problems they had in school—trouble with reading or math, speech problems, or perceptual difficulties. Even though their skills may have improved over the years, they may never feel completely safe from the possibility that someone will discover their deficits. Procrastination can become a way of not revealing their weak areas.

Authority figures can also leave a lasting impact on a person's ability to get things done. There were probably teachers, coaches, principals, or counselors at school who helped you, as well as those who intimidated or humiliated you. Trying to please that teacher or coach who never seemed satisfied, no matter how hard you tried, can be such a discouraging experience that you procrastinate instead of continuing to make an effort.

Children will experiment with different strategies for coping with difficulties at home or school until they find one that suits them. They may respond by studying all the time, joining clubs and organizations, drinking or using drugs, or becoming the class clown. For several reasons, as a child you may have found that procrastination could be an appealing strategy for dealing with trouble. First, perhaps you could put things off and not suffer grave consequences because of it. Second, in a setting where teachers seem to have all the authority, procrastination is one way you, the student, could exert some control of your own by not following the rules or by turning work in late or not at all. Third, you could distract yourself from the things at school that might have made you nervous—tests, class discussions, or social activities: As long as you were busy doing something else, you didn't have to worry. Fourth, if you were bored with schoolwork because it was too easy, procrastination may have turned some of the dull material into a challenge—you could create a race to see how little time it would take you to do the work. Finally, procrastination may have given you special protection in the classroom. Your teacher could say to you, "I wish you'd try harder," but he or she could never say, "You just don't have what it takes," because the teacher never saw what you *had.*

Many people who were able to get away with procrastination during their school years are disappointed when that strategy doesn't continue to work as well later on. The demands and responsibilities of adult life are much greater, and procrastination begins to feel more like a prison than a game. Yet it can be very difficult to break free.

The Procrastinator's Code

One of the reasons that procrastinators have such a difficult time changing their ways is that they operate under unrealistic assumptions that only perpetuate their delaying. These notions are deeply cherished and tenaciously held, in spite of their creating repeated frustration. We have called them The Procrastinator's Code.

> I must be perfect.
> Everything I do should go easily and without effort.
> It's safer to do nothing than to take a risk and fail.
> I should have no limitations.
> If it's not done right, it's not worth doing at all.
> I must avoid being challenged.
> If I succeed, someone will get hurt.
> If I do well this time, I must *always* do well.
> Following someone else's rules means I'm giving in and I'm not in control.
> I can't afford to let go of anything or anyone.
> If I expose my real self, people won't like me.
> There is a right answer, and I'll wait until I find it.

At first glance, these beliefs may make perfect sense to you. But they truly are illusions and procrastination may be helping you maintain them. If you think you should be perfect, it may seem better to procrastinate than to work hard and risk a judgment of failure. If you are convinced that success is dangerous, you can protect yourself and others by procrastinating and reducing your chances of doing well. If you equate cooperation with giving in, you can put things off and do them when *you're* ready, thus maintaining your sense of control. Or, if you believe that people won't like the real you, you can use procrastination to withhold your ideas and to keep people at a safe distance.

The beliefs that make up the Procrastinator's Code reflect a way of thinking that keeps procrastinators from making progress. Self-critical, catastrophic, and apprehensive thoughts can make it impossible to move beyond the inevitable obstacles of daily living—they keep you stuck. Realizing that you are thinking unrealistically is a necessary step toward overcoming procrastination, but it is not sufficient. Procrastination has complex emotional roots.

We think that people who procrastinate do so because they are afraid. They fear that if they act, their actions could get them into trouble. In the following three chapters, we will look at how procrastination is used as a strategy to protect people from these basic fears: fear of failure, fear of success, fear of losing a battle, fear of separation, and fear of attachment. As you read through this section, we hope you will begin to understand the emotional roots of your own personal struggle with procrastination.

2

The Procrastinator on Trial: Fear of Failure and Fear of Success

Many people who procrastinate are apprehensive about being judged by others or by the self-critic who dwells within them. They fear that they will be found lacking, that their best efforts won't be good enough, that they won't meet the mark. This concern reflects a fear of failure. Other people are more worried that they might be judged as being too good or as doing too well, and they would therefore have to face some unpleasant consequences for being outstanding. They are fearful of success. Because these fears are so widespread in our success-conscious society, we will begin our understanding of how procrastination works by taking a closer look at how procrastination functions as a strategy for coping with these fears of failure and success.

FEAR OF FAILING: THE SEARCH FOR PERFECTION

David is a lawyer with a large corporate firm. He was an academic star in college and was accepted into a competitive law school. He struggled often with procrastination, sometimes staying up all night to write his briefs or study for exams. But he always managed to do well. With great pride he joined a prestigious law firm, hoping eventually to be named a partner in the firm.

Although he thought a lot about his cases, David soon began to postpone doing the necessary background research, making appointments with his clients, and writing his briefs. He wanted his defenses to be unassailable, but he felt overwhelmed by all the possible arguments, and sooner or later he'd get stuck. Although he managed to look busy, David knew he wasn't accomplishing much, and so was plagued by feeling he was a fraud. As the court date drew near, he would begin to panic because he hadn't allowed enough time to write an adequate brief, much less a brilliant one. "Being a great lawyer means everything to me," said David. "But I seem to spend all my time worrying about being great and very little time actually working at it."

If David is so concerned about being an outstanding lawyer, why is he, by procrastinating, avoiding the work that is necessary to help him achieve what he wants so badly? David's procrastination helps him avoid facing an important issue: Can he in fact be as outstanding a lawyer as his student record promised? By waiting too long to begin writing up his research, David avoids testing his potential. His work will not be a reflection of his true ability; it merely demonstrates how well he is able to produce under last-minute pressure. If his performance doesn't live up to his (and others') expectations, he can always say, "I could have done a lot better if I'd just had another week." In other words, the verdict of failure so frightens David that he is willing to slow himself down, even occasionally to the point of disaster, to avoid letting his best work be judged. He is terrified that his best would be judged inadequate.

Why would anyone go to such self-defeating lengths to prevent a judgment of failure on a task, whether it be writing a legal brief, selecting gifts for friends and relatives, playing bridge, or going to school? People who have inhibited themselves because of their fears of failing tend to define "failure" in a very broad way. When they are disappointed by their performance on a task, they not only think they have failed on that task, they think they have failed as people.

Richard Beery, a psychologist at the University of California at Berkeley Counseling Center, has been interested in the prevalence of fear of failure among students on campus. His observations suggest that people who fear failure may be living with a set of assumptions that turn striving for accomplishment into a frightening risk. These assumptions are: 1) What I produce is a direct reflection of how much ability I have, and 2) My level of ability determines how worthwhile I am as a person—i.e., the higher my ability, the higher my sense of self-worth. Thus, 3) What I produce reflects my worth as a person. Dr. Beery has formulated these assumptions into the following equation:

Self-worth = Ability = Performance

In essence, this equation translates into a statement of the following sort: "If I perform well, that means I have a lot of ability, so I like myself and feel good about myself." It's not simply how well you did at a particular time on a particular day under particular circumstances. Your performance is a direct measure of how able, and worthwhile you are.

For many people, *ability* refers to intellectual competence, so they want everything they do to reflect how smart they are—writing a brilliant legal brief, doing well on a test, saying something witty and eloquent in a conversation. Other people define ability more in terms of whether or not they can do something challenging—build a shelf, select a good car, prepare a gourmet meal for dinner guests—in just the right way. Still another way to define "ability" is in terms of a particular skill or talent, such as how well one plays the piano, learns a language, or serves a tennis ball. Less obviously, some people constantly assess how able they are to be attractive (by thinking about their figures, the clothes they wear), or to be entertaining (can they make people laugh, be the center of attention, or tell a good story).

However ability may be defined, a problem occurs when it is the sole determinant of one's self-worth. The performance becomes the *only* measure of the person; nothing else is taken into account. An outstanding performance means an outstanding person; a mediocre performance means a mediocre person.

For David, writing a legal brief for a case is the performance that measures not only his ability to be a good lawyer but also his value as a human being. If he works hard to prepare the brief and it isn't brilliant, he will be devastated—it means he is a *terrible* person who can't do *anything*. "I don't think I could stand it if I went all out and the brief still wasn't good enough," says David.

As Dr. Beery has pointed out, procrastination breaks the equation between Ability and Performance:

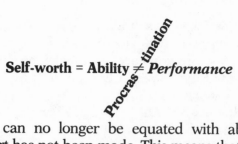

Self-worth = Ability ≠ *Performance*

Performance can no longer be equated with ability because complete effort has not been made. This means that regardless of how the performance eventually turns out, the connection between Self-worth and Ability can still be preserved. For example, if David is disappointed or criticized for his brief, he can reassure himself with the thought, "Well, I could have done better if I'd started sooner and given myself more time to do it." Or, if he manages to do well in spite of procrastinating, he can feel even more pleased with himself, thinking, "Look at how I pulled this one out of the fire. Just imagine how well I could do if I *really* worked at it!"

Procrastination allows people to take comfort in believing that their ability is greater than their performance indicates, perhaps even maintaining the belief that they are brilliant or unlimited in their potential to do well. As long as you procrastinate, you never have to confront the real limits of your ability, whatever those limits are.

The fear of being judged as lacking ability is so powerful for some people that they would rather suffer the consequences of procrastination than the humiliation of trying and not doing as well as they had hoped. It is more tolerable to blame themselves for being disorganized, lazy, or uncooperative, than to view themselves as being inadequate and unworthy—the failure which they fear so deeply. And it is the fear of *this* failure that is eased by procrastination.

People who worry about being judged inadequate or unworthy usually are afraid that inadequate is exactly what they are. They are afraid to take a realistic look at themselves and find out whether they're as good as they hope or as bad as they suspect. When such persons worry that they can't measure up, there is often another fear at work: They fear they are unlovable. As one procrastinator put it, "If I don't do well, who would want me? Who could love me if I have nothing to offer?" This procrastinator thinks that her ability, reflected by her performance on tasks, will determine whether or not she deserves to be loved. If she is unable to do well, she feels that she is a person of little worth, and people will reject her. Therefore, the consequences of not measuring up may appear to be much greater than simply "failing" in terms of your ability—it means failing as a person.

The World of a Perfectionist

Often without realizing it, people who procrastinate are perfectionists. In an attempt to prove that they are good enough, they strive to do the impossible, thinking that they should have no problem at all reaching their lofty goals. They usually put unrealistic demands on themselves and then feel overwhelmed when they are unable to meet them. Discouraged, they then retreat from the demands by procrastinating.

Most procrastinators don't even understand how they could possibly be considered perfectionists when everywhere they turn they find evidence of how they have messed up. Said Gary, a self-employed gardener, "I always do things in a half-baked way. I do a rushed job at the last minute and sometimes I don't even see projects through to completion. How in the world can I be a perfectionist?"

Perfectionism resides not so much in top-notch, perfect behavior, as it does in unrealistic attitudes. As psychologist David Burns has pointed out, people who are high achievers generally are *not* intractable perfectionists. The champion athlete, the extremely successful business person, and the Nobel prize-winning scientist usually know that there will be times when they will make mistakes or when they will have a bad day and their performance will suffer a temporary setback. Although they strive for high goals, they are also able to tolerate the frustrations and disappointments of sometimes failing to meet those goals. They know that they can improve their efforts, and they work hard to do so.

In contrast, the perfectionistic procrastinator usually expects more of him- or herself than is realistic. The woman who hasn't exercised in years wants to be in top physical condition in two weeks. The first-time novelist wants the first draft of his writing to be of publishable quality. A young man wants every phone call to land a date, a salesman expects to turn every customer into a sale. As a result, the high standards that are intended to motivate these people toward accomplishment often become impossible standards which hinder their efforts. An important question to ask yourself is: Are you setting standards for yourself that enable you to make progress, or are your standards so high that you become discouraged, frustrated, and get stuck? It's not how high your standards are that make you a perfectionist, it's how unrealistic and inhibiting they are *for you.*

There are several beliefs cherished by perfectionists who procrastinate; and, although these beliefs may seem noble, and even reasonable, they can make a person's life extremely unsatisfying and pave the way for procrastination rather than progress.

Mediocrity Breeds Contempt. For some procrastinators the thought of being ordinary can be so intolerable that they want everything they do to be outstanding. They wish not only for ideal careers and relationships, but also to make a masterpiece of the letter they write or the garden they plant. If you expect your everyday performance to be up to the level of your ideal picture of yourself, then whatever you do is bound to seem mediocre in comparison.

Since mistakes and flaws are an inevitable part of the human condition, people who believe that "mediocrity breeds contempt" can find comfort in procrastination. As we suggested earlier, when a mediocre or ordinary performance can be attributed to the last-minute rush, a person can continue to believe that he or she still has a great deal of "potential" to be tapped. This allows a perfectionist with little self-esteem to maintain some self-respect in spite of an average performance. Procrastination provides an excuse for mediocrity. It makes mediocrity seem temporary, an artifact of a half-hearted effort. As such, procrastination preserves the hope that if you ever did make an all-out effort, you wouldn't be mediocre at all.

Excellence Without Effort. The perfectionist believes that if one is truly outstanding, even difficult things should be easy. Creative ideas should flow ceaselessly! Studying should be pure intellectual joy! Decisions should be made quickly, and with total certainty! Using such impossible standards for comparison, the person who must work hard, or even exert a moderate amount of effort to get something done, is likely to feel inferior.

Suppose a student is faced with some homework problems. If he or she cannot tolerate the process of groping for the answers to the problems, the student will have trouble with the work. Said a physics major, "If I can't solve the problem instantly, I feel stupid. I understand the concepts and I'm pretty smart, so I *should* be able to see the answer right away—I get so mad at myself that I can't stand sitting there. I go out and play video games."

The expectation that one should be able to catch on instantly, no matter how complex the material, brings many procrastinators to a grinding halt. Their disappointment at having to work hard prevents them from making the effort required to grapple with the material and master it. Instead, they avoid it by delaying. In the long run, their need to be smart keeps them ignorant. After all, if you can't stand not knowing, you can't learn.

Going It Alone.   Perfectionists feel that they must do everything by themselves, believing that it's a sign of weakness to relieve themselves of any responsibilities by delegating or by getting assistance. There is no flexibility to consider what might be best for the situation, no room to admit that sometimes you just don't have the answer or that you can't do it all by yourself. Even when it would be more efficient to get help, many perfectionists are bound and determined to work, and suffer, in isolation. Then, when the burden becomes too heavy, procrastination becomes their one source of relief. Unable to do everything all by themselves, they resort to delay.

There Is a Right Way.   This is one of the most cherished notions held by perfectionists. They believe that there is one correct solution to a problem and that it is their responsibility to find it. Until they've discovered the right solution, they are reluctant to take *any* course of action or commit themselves to anything. So, rather than take the risk of making the wrong choice, they do nothing.

Consider the case of Charles and Brenda. When they married, they talked about moving from their small town in Ohio to a larger community, but they couldn't decide on the best place to live. Brenda felt the decision would change the course of their lives forever. She wanted to be absolutely sure they were doing the right thing before they moved, so she made long lists of pros and cons for each of the towns they were considering. No matter how many factors they considered, however, Brenda couldn't feel certain that any location would be the perfect place to live, work, and raise children, so they ended up not moving anywhere.

Brenda thought that if she could just find the one right answer, there would be no drawbacks, no cons to consider along with the pros. But is there one right answer, one risk-free solution for Brenda and Charles? They'll have to uproot and readjust wherever they go. They'll like some things and not others about any city they choose. But Brenda fears that if she makes a wrong decision, she will be judged badly for it. She believes that people will think less of her, because her ability to know what's right will clearly be doubtful.

Holding back from making a commitment serves another purpose for Brenda and Charles: It keeps all of their options open. As long as they don't actually decide where to live, any part of the country represents an ideal possibility. They can imagine a better life watching the leaves turn in the New England autumn, hiking along the California coast, enjoying gracious Southern living, or skiing in Colorado. As long as they keep on dreaming, they don't have to face unpleasant, imperfect realities.

I Can't Stand to Lose (Or: What, Me Competitive?) On the surface, it appears that many procrastinators are not competitive. Their constant delaying takes them out of the running, so they don't really compete—or do they? Randy, a contractor who often delays submitting bids until it is too late, made a typical comment: "I'm not interested in competing for jobs with millions of other people. I'll find a job without going through that conventional rigamarole—I like to run on my own track."

The truth is that many perfectionists hate losing so much that they avoid any activity that would bring them into direct competition with others. If Randy, for instance, stopped delaying and actively bid, he risks finding out where his company really stands in relation to the competition. If he didn't come out on top, he would feel inadequate and foolish, because to him not being perfect is failing.

A variation of this competition theme is played by people who "choose to lose." They procrastinate to such an extent that they guarantee failure, yet still imagine that they could have won if they had tried—like the bachelor who brags about all the hot romances he could have if only he had the courage to make phone calls. Underlying the idea "I can't stand to lose" is the more basic perfectionistic notion, "I should never lose." People who believe this can protect themselves from facing the reality of their imperfection by procrastinating. They can't lose because they never really enter the race.

All or Nothing. The all-or-nothing view of life is common among perfectionists who procrastinate. A person who believes that he or she must do everything usually has difficulty appreciating any progress made toward a goal: As long as the project is incomplete, it seems that nothing at all has been accomplished. No wonder it's so tempting to give up in despair before reaching the end!

The all-or-nothing notion can affect a person's initial formulation of goals, leading him or her to attempt to do everything at once because anything less seems insufficient. For instance, we asked Steve to select a goal that he wanted to accomplish during a two-week period of time. Initially, he planned to work out at his health club every day for the two-week period. Although he had joined the club more than a year earlier, he had never once used his membership. It took some work, but we finally convinced Steve that the goal of going to the club every day was pretty unrealistic. Reluctantly, Steve modified his goal, deciding that he would be doing well if he went to the club six times over the two-week period. Two weeks later, Steve was very discouraged because he had *only* used the gym three times. Even though Steve worked out three times more in two weeks than he had during the entire previous year, he felt as if he'd accomplished nothing.

With an all-or-nothing attitude, you can become discouraged for any of the following reasons:

You don't accomplish *everything* you set out to do.
You don't do things *exactly* as you had planned.
You do something well, but not perfectly.
You don't get as much recognition as you feel you deserve.

In situations like these, you can feel as though you have nothing because what you do have isn't exactly what you had expected or hoped for. If you can only be satisfied with perfection, you are doomed to be disappointed. As one perfectionist put it, "It's either gold or it's garbage."

Perfection is an ideal that is relinquished very, very gradually. Even if you can agree intellectually that perfectionistic standards are unrealistic and counterproductive, you may still find it hard to accept the fact that you aren't now, and never will be perfect.

One reason the goal of perfection is so hard to give up is that the foundations for unrealistic expectations are set early in life. In Chapter 5, we will explore the influence of family experiences in more depth, but for now, let's consider how you might have developed the idea that you must be perfect.

For most perfectionists, accomplishment represents much more than simply achieving goals or being remarkable. In many of their families, being outstanding seemed to be the most reliable strategy for earning recognition, acceptance, and love—accomplishments were valued above all else, and being second best seemed of no value at all. Other perfectionists never enjoyed the satisfaction of winning approval. Although accomplishments were highly valued, their ability to achieve was doubted, criticized, or undermined. In this situation, they may try to dispel doubts by striving to be perfect, believing that if they're ever going to earn respect and love, perfection is their last hope.

The Fate of the Imperfect: Consequences Real and Imagined

Perfectionists tend to think in absolute terms about what they do. In addition, they often think catastrophically; that is, they take one small event, such as a mistake, and exaggerate the consequences until the repercussions are staggering. They seem to react to one incident as if it were the beginning of the end, certain that devastation is just around the corner.

These catastrophic expectations are even more intimidating when they are nameless and vague, as they are in most people's minds. "My life would be miserable if I weren't perfect," they moan. But in what *specific* ways would their lives be miserable? It is often both interesting and helpful for procrastinators to articulate the nameless fantasies of dread that haunt them. Ask yourself the question, "What would happen if I weren't perfect?" In addition to the general sense of doom you might feel at the thought of being less than exceptional, what specifics do you foresee? How bad would things get? What chain of events would lead up to the final catastrophe?

Here is an example from a man whose expectations careened from perfection to mediocrity to disaster. Ted, a middle-level manager in banking, was, in outward appearance, very successful. He had a secure job, a devoted wife, and a comfortable home. Yet he always felt in jeopardy of losing everything. Ted feared that he would be fired if he didn't maintain exceptional job performance in every area—making decisions, managing his subordinates, projecting the budget, running meetings, etc.

This demand to be in top form all the time grew into a pressure greater than Ted could bear and he began to procrastinate, putting off paperwork and phone calls, delaying personnel decisions, and postponing preparation for meetings. He feared that his procrastination would be discovered and that it would lead to his being fired.

From one incident of imperfection, Ted anticipated total disaster: "If I don't have my agenda ready for Thursday's conference, I'll run a lousy meeting, and everyone will see that I'm not as competent as I pretend to be. I'll be fired from my job, and blackballed from the rest of the banking community—who would want to hire a lazy, no-good procrastinator? If I can't get another job making as much money, my wife will be furious and she'll leave me for someone else. I'll be alone with no family and no future. I'll have nothing to live for. I might even do myself in. Now I feel too depressed to work on my agenda. I need a drink."

Although you can probably see that Ted's picture of the cataclysmic consequences of one meeting is blown far out of proportion, to him the danger seems real. Disaster feels so imminent that Ted becomes paralyzed and unable to do any work.

This kind of catastrophic thinking is extremely undermining, especially if you don't realize that you're doing it. If you can learn to step back and take a hard look at what you are anticipating, you will have a chance to challenge the "inevitability" of your "fate." Ted, for example, began to contest his conclusion that running a so-so meeting would lead directly to his being fired. He eventually saw that there was a big difference between running a mediocre meeting and losing his wife, his job, and his hope for the future.

The next time you find yourself slipping into a paralysis of perfectionism, consider playing out your worst-case scenario for that situation. Perhaps as you do so, you can remind yourself that although these fantasies are your fears, they are almost certainly exaggerated.

FEAR OF SUCCEEDING: HELLO PROCRASTINATION, GOOD-BYE SUCCESS

Do you sometimes slow down on a project that's going well? Do you panic when you receive a lot of recognition? When your boss suggests a promotion, do you become uncomfortable and want to retreat? Do compliments embarrass you or leave you feeling apprehensive and wary? If you are successful in one area of your life, do you mess up in another? When things are going just fine, do you wait for the other shoe to drop? These are just a few of the situations that can spell danger to those who fear success.

Chances are, even people who fear success *want* to do well. But if it were as simple as that, why are they unable to continue when they are ahead, or on the very brink of accomplishment? What gets in their way and sends them into a tailspin of retreat? Why is it so hard for them to take pleasure in what they have achieved?

For many of us, success represents the fulfillment of a goal and brings with it an almost idyllic sense of satisfaction and completion. Wanting "success" as badly as they do, procrastinators feel thwarted by their habitual delay. Even if they've managed to achieve "success" by society's definition, some procrastinators don't *feel* successful when they recall the close calls, the many all-nighters, that required Herculean efforts to carry off. Though no one else knows they've pulled their success out of the fire, *they* do—and for them that means they still haven't made it.

These people criticize themselves for their lack of success and wish that they could be free of the chains of procrastination that block their rise to the top. But in their self-deprecation, they often miss an important issue: Perhaps they are afraid of being *too* successful.

Rick is an architect whose lifelong dream has been to have his own architectural firm. He is a creative thinker and has won several awards for his innovative designs, but he often delays putting his ideas down on paper. As a result, he tends to be disorganized and behind schedule, giving the impression that he can't juggle all of the responsibilities of his position. Other designers in his office ask him for advice informally, but no one wants to work with him on a project because he has lost out on accounts and fees. They are impressed with his talent, but when it comes to getting the ball rolling, he's not the man for the job.

Rick is anguished by his inhibition. "I hate myself when I don't commit my ideas to paper," he said. "I know exactly what to do to convey and implement my ideas, but I don't do it. It makes me sick. I'll never be able to start my own firm if I keep this up."

Rick's attention is focused on his bad habits and his self-disgust. But this preoccupation may be a distraction. Although Rick spends a lot of energy feeling badly about what he isn't doing, he rarely thinks about what awaits him on the other side of his goal. What if he *could* consistently draw out his designs and *did* ultimately have his own architectural firm?

If Rick were to express a fear that other people might not like his ideas, or that his plans won't look as interesting on paper as they seem in the privacy of his mind, we would explore his fear of failure. If his fear of committing his ideas to paper centered on his search for the elusive *right* idea and his fear that he might make a mistake, we would want to know more about his perfectionism.

But, in fact, these issues aren't of much concern to Rick. "I know people like most of my ideas," he reflected. "They think I create designs that are aesthetically intriguing as well as practical. And I think so, too. But, you know, it scares me to know that they think well of me. For some reason, it makes me nervous, almost as if I don't know what to do once I'm in the spotlight."

Exploring further, Rick begins to clarify his apprehensions. "If I had my own firm, I'd be competing with other architects for business. Assuming my work is good, I'd get good contracts, and earn a lot of money. I know it sounds strange, but I worry that this might irritate people who are my friends now—I'd be taking potential clients away from them and they might resent me for it. Also, after you've done one really fine design, some people expect everything you do to be innovative. To do that, I'd really have to work non-stop. I might never have any free time just to have fun and be lazy."

Rather than worrying about a judgment of failure, Rick is concerned that he will be judged too successful by his friends. In order to live up to continually rising expectations, he might have to change from working haltingly to working incessantly. By diminishing his possibilities for success, procrastination provides Rick with a buffer from the possibility of becoming exposed and trapped by success, forced to live a life he doesn't want.

It's natural to feel apprehensive when you're venturing into unknown territory or making a change in your life, even when it's for the better. Achieving your idea of success, whether it be going back to school, exercising and losing weight, becoming a Fortune 500 company, or writing a top-notch report, will inevitably involve facing both change and the unknown.

A writer we know learned that an article she finally submitted to a national magazine (after three years of agonizing delay) had not only been accepted, but was to be featured as the cover story. On hearing the news, her face immediately flushed and she felt nauseated. "That does it," she exclaimed. "I'm moving back home to take care of my mother!" Instead of pride, which eventually did surface, her initial reaction was panic. She wanted to crawl into a small, safe space and disappear. Although she had sought it, her success terrified her.

The important question for all of us is whether our apprehension about success gets in our way. Does it stop us from moving forward and taking risks that could enrich our lives? Does it lead us to restrict ourselves to such an extent that we lose our spontaneity, our curiosity, and our desire to master new challenges?

Take It or Leave It: Retreating from Competition and Commitment

By delaying, procrastinators appear to be disinterested in competitive struggles, and indifferent to the rewards of victory. It gives the impression that they can "take it or leave it," because they don't make an all-out effort.

When people are afraid of failure, they don't compete because they are afraid of losing. People who are afraid of success, however, don't compete because they are afraid of winning. In fact, these procrastinators are even afraid to reveal the fact that they have an interest in trying. Instead of making a competitive effort, they use procrastination to hide their ambition because they think there's something wrong with being competitive in the first place. So, they put off sending in an application until it's too late to be considered for a position; they delay preparing for a marathon run and can't be a serious competitor in the race; they postpone studying, saying "grades aren't all that important," and take themselves out of the running for a scholarship. Procrastination is a method of curtailing aspirations they feel they may be punished for, keeping them hidden from others, and sometimes even from themselves.

Another method procrastinators use to avoid success is to delay making commitments. If you don't commit, you can't move forward in any one direction and you can't rush headlong into success. Instead you spread yourself over numerous interests and activities and end up frozen, unable to progress toward a specific goal. Some people give the impression that they've made a commitment in one area—a job or a relationship perhaps—and seem to be seriously involved, but they know their efforts are only half-hearted. Procrastination distances them from what they're doing, it prevents them from becoming too absorbed in something that makes them a little uneasy.

Procrastinators who fear failure have trouble making commitments because they worry that they will commit to the wrong thing. Those who fear success worry that making a commitment will sweep them into the competitive process and move them toward success before they're ready for it.

Cultural Risks:
The Gender Factor

Some theorists offer a cultural explanation for fear of success, especially in relation to women and their careers. They cite the differences between the ways that men and women are reared to view success. From infancy, these theorists suggest, women have been culturally trained to be supportive of successful men, but not to be accomplished in their own right. Some of the earlier research studies have shown that when women imagine themselves being successful in a "man's world," they anticipate social rejection because they expect to be seen as unfeminine. They may achieve success, but it would be at the expense of crossing the sex-role barrier. Therefore, even after attaining highly successful positions in their careers, some women continue to feel inadequate.

Despite some shifts in contemporary attitudes, many women are still influenced by traditional prohibitions against their success. For a woman who feels conflict about crossing beyond the threshold of tradition, procrastination may offer some relief. As long as she continues to delay, she never fully achieves success, and thus never really challenges the tradition.

Men have had to live with another type of cultural training—pressure to provide for their families, to be responsible for other people, and to achieve success in a highly competitive society. Some men fear success because they are afraid they can't live up to these traditional expectations. Others avoid achieving success along traditionally male lines because, to them, it means being trapped in a role that contradicts their broader values in life. They fear they may have to give up other, more traditionally "feminine" sides of themselves—their ability to play, to enjoy leisure, to be tender, to have doubts and insecurities, to be in need of comfort. Or, like women, some men have to cross a gender gap in order to achieve their idea of success, as in the case of a man who wants a career that is traditionally reserved for women, such as nursing or homemaking. Rather than lose themselves to the cultural demand, men such as these steer clear of its pull by procrastinating. Procrastination allows them to remain suspended in limbo between what they want to do and what they think they ought to do.

Personal Risks:
Why I Shouldn't Succeed

Cultural norms, social status, and economic opportunities have influenced all of us, creating advantages for some and limiting others. But these factors do not tell the whole story. There are many women who are very successful and who enjoy their success, just as there are many men who, in spite of the prevailing cultural pressures, are able to take advantage of opportunities to create new challenges for themselves. There are also both men and women who are not particularly "successful" by society's standards, yet are happy and satisfied with their lives.

Thus, in addition to considering cultural influences, we must consider the more personal concerns that both men and women have that lead them to see success as something to be avoided, and procrastination as a way to avoid it. Let's look at some of these personal fears, which can be powerful forces of inhibition.

I'll Turn into a Workaholic. One of the most common fears we've heard expressed by procrastinators who fear success is the worry that if they stop fooling around and get down to work, they will work all the time and never fool around again. Against their wills, they will somehow be transformed into workaholics whose lives are a succession of productive days and nights; they will spend endless hours toiling away in desolation.

To explain how procrastination saves them from this dismal fate, some people have said, "If I start three weeks ahead of time, I'll be working solidly for three entire weeks. I might as well wait until I have only three days, so I only kill myself for three days. That way I can at least have a life for two and a half weeks." These people accept the axiom that work expands to fill the time available to it. It's as if the work, of its own accord, will take over and turn them into automatons, whether they like it or not. As one procrastinator described it, "Once I get into working, there'll be no stopping me. I'll think of people as 'interferences' that get in the way of productivity, so I won't want anything to do with them. I'll become a cold machine, instead of the caring person I want to be."

What we find so intriguing about this perspective is the implication that success invariably leads to a loss of control and a loss of choice in one's life. Procrastinators often assume that because their delaying seems to operate outside of their control, their working would become just as unmanageable. Without compulsive procrastination, they fear, they will be doomed to compulsive work.

If you are someone who fears turning into a workaholic, ask yourself: Why would you have no choice in the matter? Why couldn't you set limits on the amount of time you spend working, so that you also have some time to relax and play?

I Don't Deserve Success. Many people don't feel entitled to success because they think they've been too bad to deserve it. Lamenting things they've done or said, regretting evil thoughts they've had, or believing that they've harmed someone, they believe success must be denied to them to make up for all the suffering they've caused.

Some procrastinators feel guilty for unethical or hurtful things they actually have done, such as lying, cheating, manipulating, or defrauding someone. People also often feel guilty for actions which are really not very serious, or for situations which aren't truly their responsibility. In their guilt, however, they do not differentiate between crimes real and imagined.

One hard-core procrastinator felt guilty about the unhappiness he once inflicted on his family. "I was a big bully," he said. "My nickname was Vesuvius. Especially after my parents were divorced, I used to have tantrums that made my mother cry and my little sister hide in fear. Someone as mean as I have been doesn't deserve to live in peace. So, now it's my turn to be unhappy."

As an extreme example of an "imaginary crime," Mitchell stopped progressing in his job with the telephone company ever since his wife died in an auto accident three years earlier. Although he had also been injured in the crash, Mitchell survived and made a full recovery after six months. In addition to feeling a tremendous sense of grief, Mitchell felt responsible for his wife's death, even though the accident had clearly been caused by another driver. He thought that somehow he should have been able to prevent the accident, or that he should have been the one to die. Three years later he was still torturing himself for being an irresponsible, indeed, an evil person.

Mitchell suffered from "survivor guilt." As the one who had been allowed to live, he felt he did not deserve to have anything more, including a happy or fulfilling life. Procrastinating was one way to keep himself deprived. Although the stagnation of his life was painful to him, he felt a subtle sense of satisfaction when he punished himself, as if each time he procrastinated and denied himself progress, justice was being done.

Some people experience survival guilt in less extreme situations, as when they escape from a chronically bad situation, leaving others behind. They feel guilty because their lives are improving while others continue to suffer. For example, many college students who have moved away from difficult family situations feel guilty for abandoning younger siblings who are still living at home, coping with parents who may be volatile, abusive, alcoholic, or negligent. These students find themselves procrastinating in school, unable to allow themselves academic success. They feel they don't deserve to be free while the rest of the family remains imprisoned.

Similarly, some procrastinators inhibit their own progress because they feel guilty for competing with others and winning. Attaining more career, financial, or personal success than their relatives, friends, or colleagues can elicit so much guilt about bettering their situation that they use procrastination to put the breaks on their success. It's as if they feel they should punish themselves for being among the "haves" instead of the "have-nots." In come cases, the very wish to move ahead may evoke a feeling of guilt.

Sadly, the guilt most procrastinators feel is far out of proportion to their "crimes." Often, there is not even any "crime" to speak of, other than wanting to extend oneself and have a life of one's own.

If I'm Successful I Will Hurt Someone Else. Have there been times when you have belittled or hidden something good that's happened to you because you didn't want to offend someone else? Maybe you didn't tell your best friend who hasn't a had a date in six months that you just met the love of your life. Or you kept the A you got for your last-minute paper a secret from your friends who got B's and C's, even after working hard. Or you didn't tell your father about your latest salary increase because then he'd know you're not only earning more than he did at your age, but that you're already ahead of where he ended up.

You may be concerned that your good news will be bad news to someone else. In some cases, of course, keeping your success to yourself is simply courteous. But many procrastinators have taken more extreme measures than simply downplaying their success to protect someone's feelings. Here are two examples.

Marilyn decided to go back to work to augment the family income after her two children were both in school. Her husband, Ralph, was a building contractor whose business had hit hard times. Marilyn found a job selling new cars, and discovered, somewhat to her surprise, that she was a very good saleswoman and the income from her commissions was higher than she'd anticipated. But instead of maintaining or improving her sales record, Marilyn began to delay with her paperwork to such an extent that her job was threatened.

"Even though I liked my job, it would almost have been a relief to lose it," said Marilyn as she looked back over what had happened. "It got harder and harder for me to bring home news of my latest commission when Ralph wasn't getting any work. I knew we needed the money, but I couldn't stand the look in his eyes when I was doing well and he wasn't. It wasn't his fault business was bad." Without realizing it at the time, Marilyn hoped that her problems at work would help to protect Ralph's pride in himself.

At age 47, Donald had just lost his seventh small business because of his procrastination. Among other things, Donald delayed orders to customers, was late with his payroll, put off filing necessary forms, and was delinquent paying fees—all of which added up to bad business practice.

Donald's father had been a "dreamer" who had never held a job for long, but who was always optimistic that he'd come up with a scheme "worth a million bucks." In spite of the fact that these schemes never came to fruition, Donald's father was the eternal penniless optimist, always believing that his next idea would make him rich. Filled with his own grand plans, he was quick to criticize Donald for his business failures, chastising him for his poor judgment and his lack of success.

It took a while for Donald to realize that his problems were helping to maintain his father's morale. "It gives the old man some stature to criticize me for my failings," he mused. "It keeps him from having to look at the pretense of his own life. If I were the one who made a million bucks, or even if I earned a comfortable living, and I did it not by grandiose schemes but by hard work, he'd be stripped of the only thing that keeps him going—his fantasies. He'd be pathetic. Somehow I just can't do that to him."

Sometimes people are even willing to hurt themselves to sustain their own *image* of the troubled person in their lives. Donald didn't see his father as he really was from the start— ineffectual and self-deluded. Instead, he kept alive a notion of his father as a powerful man whose limited success was nevertheless greater than Donald's. By procrastinating, Donald in effect handed over to his father the club of his own failure, which his father used to strike him down.

Often we worry that our success will hurt other people, when actually they are stronger and more generous than we give them credit for. It may be a distortion in our own thinking and not the reality around us, that prepares us to be criticized for our success. Believe it or not, some people can truly enjoy the success of others they are close to, without feeling deprived, wounded, or left behind.

Unfortunately, there may also be people who will indeed react as if your success has been used as a weapon against them, and they will punish you for it by trying to undermine your achievement. We were struck by the story of a young couple who struggled financially until the wife, a social worker, finally left her part-time job in a community agency and began a private counseling practice. After a few weeks, she proudly brought her husband in to see the office she had rented. As he looked around at the furnishings, the view from her window, and the waiting room outside her office, his only comment was, "You should have more current magazines for people to read while they wait." Her husband was apparently threatened by the woman's success, so he assumed a critical stance, instead of sharing in her pride.

I Could Get Hurt Myself. One danger many people foresee in achieving success is that they would get what they want—and will then be punished for it. They fear that success will put them into the spotlight where, once noticed, they will be vulnerable to abuse. Someone, somewhere, will challenge or criticize them—and they don't feel strong enough to fight back.

Andre, whose procrastination keeps him in a job far below his capabilities, is an example of how this fear of retaliation works. When he was hired by a large manufacturing company, Andre and his first boss expected that he would rise through the ranks into management. Instead, he put in minimal effort and delayed on projects that might have gained him some special recognition. He was never given a promotion. "If I got into a supervisory job," Andre explained, "I'd have to make decisions and stand behind them. People could fight those decisions and criticize me for them. There are a lot of aggressive people in this company; I'd just as soon stay out of their way."

If Andre were content with his position he would have no problem—he'd have found a comfortable niche for himself. After all, not everyone has to want to zoom up the ladder of success. But Andre wasn't satisfied. "I'd really like to have a chance to run things in this department. I've complained enough, and I have some ideas for improvements around here. But management probably doesn't want someone like me challenging their policies. They could really make life difficult if they saw me as a troublemaker."

Andre lives with a view that it's a dog-eat-dog world, and as the dogs get bigger, the bites get worse. Since he does not expect to be encouraged by his superiors, but instead anticipates a heavy attack, Andre feels he must protect himself from them. So he delays, he doesn't get promoted, and he never has to fight.

As children, many of us have learned that our successes can indeed trigger punishments: if the drive to master our own goals interfered with an angry or preoccupied parent; if our accomplishments were consistently mocked or ignored; if we feared being punished for having unacceptable thoughts or wishes. Recurrent experiences like these can create a world view in which success seems a set-up for punishment.

Success Isn't in the Cards for Me.   Some people have such a low opinion of themselves that they can't incorporate success into the picture of themselves and their lives. Feeling inadequate, unskilled, or unappealing, they don't expect to succeed at anything, so they simply don't try in the first place.

Holly, for example, is a shy person who remains in the background most of the time. Although she often fantasizes about having a close, loving marriage, Holly makes no effort to take advantage of situations that would give her the opportunity to develop friendships with men. "Happy marriages are for other people, not for me, so why should I even bother trying?" sighed Holly. "Besides, I know that no man would be interested in me, so why should I knock myself out reaching for something I'll never get?" In both manner and appearance, Holly conveys a sense of chronic despair. She makes her lack of success a self-fulfilling prophecy.

Even if people like Holly do manage to attain some kind of success, they usually are not able to enjoy it. Since they feel that success has no place in their lives to begin with, their accomplishment seems a stroke of luck. As easily as it arrived, success may vanish at any moment.

People like Holly fear that if they allow themselves to feel successful, they may start to have hope—and begin to believe in themselves. They may start to have dreams for their lives. Such hope can seem dangerous because once they've allowed themselves to count on their good fortune, the disappointment of fleeting success would be crushing. It is far safer to detach themselves from any remote possibility of such disillusionment and assume that success is just not in the cards for them. Such a position of hopelessness is difficult to counter because the lethargy and apathy inherent in it are often extremely powerful.

What if I'm Too Perfect?   Strange as it may seem, there are people who worry that if they let themselves loose on the road to success, it will come to them too easily. They will have "everything" and have it with so little effort that they will no longer be in the mainstream of the human race.

When fear of failure is the primary issue for a procrastinator, he or she tends to assume, "I *should* be perfect, but I'm afraid I might not be good enough to make it." In some cases of fear of success, the assumption is, "I am perfect, but I shouldn't be. I have to hide it." These are opposite sides of the same coin, and while some people remain faithfully on one side or the other, there are others who move back and forth, sometimes feeling not good enough and other times worrying they are too good.

Claudia, a vivacious, attractive woman with an adoring husband and two delightful children, expressed her dilemma in this way: "People seem to think I have everything—a great marriage and family, lots of friends, economic comfort, and community interests and involvements. The one thing I don't have, though, is a college degree, and although I would like to get a degree in Art History, I just can't seem to let myself go back to school. Then I would really feel as if I had it all."

Like Claudia, people who worry that they are too perfect often feel they need a tragic flaw, one that proves beyond the shadow of a doubt that they are human, just like everyone else. In a rather curious way, it reassures these people that they are not really so different from others. But why do they feel they have to prove they're no different to begin with? After all, even though they may *feel* perfect, nobody *is* perfect. The question is: Why is it important for them to maintain such an illusion about themselves?

The sense of superiority that goes along with feeling "too perfect" is a cover for a deeper sense of inferiority that quietly haunts people like Claudia. Even though they may procrastinate to hold themselves back and be "like" everybody else, such people nevertheless depend on feeling "special" to feel adequate. For as long as these people believe that they are flawed *by their own choice*, they can maintain the belief that they still *are* perfect.

So, perhaps you have been using procrastination to avoid success because you harbor one or more of these fears: you might turn into a work machine; you might gain something you don't deserve; you could hurt someone or be hurt yourself; you might begin to hope when it's safer to give up; you might feel too perfect. The theme that is common to all of these fears is the belief that you must choose between having success and having love. If you were an uncaring workaholic, who would be your friend? If you achieved an undeserved success, wouldn't you be shunned for being presumptuous? If you are too perfect, who would accept you as one of the gang? If you expect your success to be evaluated in a negative light, you may not want to risk the possibility of alienating the people around you.

How did you come to conclude that your success will push people away? Chances are that your accomplishments had an unsettling impact on your family. For example, you may have sensed that when you accomplished something, a sibling may have felt jealous or left out; the family may have seemed out of balance; your parents may have even seemed threatened. Eventually, you may have concluded that all would be better off, and you would be most accepted, if you accomplished less rather than more.

As you consider the relationship between your procrastination and your fear of success, try to stand back and take a more objective look at your situation. It may help to remind yourself that just because you fear something doesn't mean it's true. If you can challenge the assumption that at the first sign of success everyone will leave you, then you may be surprised to notice that there are some people who will not use your success to decide whether to stay or go. However, some people may resent your success—perhaps even some of the most important people in your life. If so, the question you must confront is: Can you make progress for yourself *in spite of* their resentment or their retreat from you? Are you strong enough to survive without their total support?

We understand that success might have its dangers for you. We know these dangers are powerful. But we also think that you may be in a better position than you realize to tolerate the risks. You are not totally defenseless. You *can* change and adapt to new circumstances, even to success.

3

The Procrastinator in Combat: Fear of Losing the Battle

You're building up a new business and you need more clients, but when you get a message from someone you don't know asking you to call back between 1–2 p.m., you feel indignant. The caller isn't giving you much leeway, it seems. You delay returning the call, finally doing so at 3 p.m., even though you were free at your desk between 1–2 p.m.

Last month's utility bill arrives and, as always, it's higher than you'd like. You resent the rising costs of fuel and you think about recent media reports of big profits by the oil companies. Though your checking account balance is more than adequate to cover the payment, you hold on to your check for so long that you have to deliver it in person to prevent the company from shutting off your electricity. When you finally do it, you have a feeling of satisfaction for having made the company wait for its money and causing it additional inconvenience.

Your wife asks you for the twentieth time to finish the favor to her that you've been putting off. You promise you will do it, but you never actually get around to it. The more she nags, the more you feel pushed into a corner. Eventually she becomes frustrated and angry about the delay, which she feels is an act of hostility.

In situations like these, procrastination has little to do with preventing you from making your best effort. It's unlikely that you delay paying your utility bill because you are concerned about not doing it well enough or doing it too well. Another, quite different, fear is at work here.

THE BATTLE FOR CONTROL

Many people procrastinate because they want to feel they are in control of things. Proud of your independence and determined not to compromise yourself, you may procrastinate to prove that no one can force you to act against your will. Your procrastination serves as a way of saying, "No! You can't make me do this!" That caller was presumptuous for assuming that you would obediently jump through the hoop, and so you return the call at *your* convenience. Utility companies may be very powerful, but they can't make you pay the bill on time. You'll do the favor for your spouse when you're good and ready, not when he or she tells you to. Procrastination becomes your strategy for fighting a battle with someone—a battle for control, a battle for power, a battle for respect, a battle for independence and autonomy. But always hovering in the background is the possibility, and the fear, that you might lose.

Fighting a battle via procrastination can be such an automatic and reflexive way to defend yourself that you may not even be aware you're doing it. You may think of yourself as someone who simply can't "get it together," perplexed by the constant chaos of your life, and worried about your difficulties in getting things done. If that is the case, take a moment to consider what impact your procrastination has on the people around you. Are there people who are inconvenienced by your delays? Do you ask others to make special arrangements for you because of your lack of organization and preparation? Is anyone thwarted by your procrastination, unable to carry out a plan of action because you didn't get your part done? Does anyone else have to do more work because you didn't do yours?

Consider, too, how other people respond to your procrastinating. Do they become irritated by your slowness? Frustrated with your excuses? Angry because you didn't do what you said you would do? Do they give up trying to influence you and eventually let you do things your own way? Without realizing it, you may be using your procrastination to assert your independence from other people. You may be more of a fighter than you think and your procrastination may give you a much greater sense of control than you had realized.

Let's look at some of the themes that come up when people do battle-by-procrastination. There is an interpersonal struggle going on, but subtle variations give each battle a particular quality of its own.

Rules Are Made to Be Broken. There are probably times when obeying rules becomes tedious for you, and you feel an urge to break free of them. For some people, this occurs only in specific situations; other people experience themselves as constantly subjected to rules that they feel compelled to rebel against. Whether you fight against rules occasionally or constantly, you probably feel restrained by directives that seem to be too confining for your lifestyle.

A travel agent recalled his experience in high school and junior college. "When the class was given an assignment that was open-ended, like writing a short story about anything we wanted, I didn't have any trouble doing it. But when the teacher *told* us what to write about, I felt there was no room for me to express my own individuality or to be creative. I would end up asking for an extension, and then writing about something different from what was assigned anyway. Somehow, this helped me feel that I wasn't just a cow in a herd of cattle."

This man needed a lot of leeway to put his own personalized stamp on what he did and when that leeway was narrowed by the imposition of rules, he rebelled. This is a common experience for many of us and procrastination is one way to get around it.

Rules come in the form of restrictions or expectations imposed on us by external forces—the time we're supposed to be at work in the morning, the law saying that we must pay our taxes by April 15, the policy on borrowing library books. If you feel that following a rule somehow makes you indistinguishable from others, then you may feel compelled to break it. As one procrastinator said, "The rules of mortal men do not apply to me."

Rules can also be "policies" that you have internalized from important people in your life. Although you may have adopted these policies as "rules to live by," there are occasions when you feel constrained, rather than helped, by them.

Adrienne describes her experience. "Sometimes I feel like I *should* sit down and write out thank you notes or wax the kitchen floor, and then I instantly have this feeling of not wanting to do it. I don't want my whole life to be spent doing chores like these. My mother always made me write thank you notes the minute I had opened a present, and I had to wax the kitchen floor every Saturday morning for years. Those are two things I invariably put off now, and when I do I feel wonderful, like I've given myself room to breathe." Even though Adrienne now lives 1000 miles away from her mother, the pressure of these rules is as strong as if she were still a teenager living at home. Procrastination increases her sense of freedom and reassures her that she is not an involuntary prisoner of these injunctions.

Power to the Underdog.   Battle-by-procrastination also occurs in situations where there is a formal hierarchy of power—and you aren't on top. The very fact that there is someone in a position of authority over you may leave you feeling small and helpless. This reaction to authority is common in corporate and academic settings where, to enhance their own sense of power, subordinates delay doing work for their superiors.

Perhaps you delay turning in papers or memos, or put off preparing presentations for your teacher or your boss, even though you may be on time doing things for friends or for your family. If, as you delay, you worry about whether your report or presentation will be good enough, or about how it will compare to others, your procrastination probably has more to do with fear of judgment than with fear of losing the battle. If, instead, you find yourself thinking, "This is a ridiculous assignment. I shouldn't have to do this!" or "Why should I do it *her* way?" then you are probably struggling for a greater sense of control. In this kind of situation, procrastination can act as a power equalizer. You feel you have more control because you've done things on *your* terms—late. Your superior seems less powerful, because she or he wasn't able to force you to be on time.

Suppose on Monday your boss asks you to take on an extra project that he needs by Thursday. You agree to do it, only to find yourself putting it off. Every time you think about it, you feel a slow burn inside. He's the boss, and he has the power to tell you what to do, but you don't like it. Because your job is at stake, you eventually get the project done, but you wait until the last possible moment and you finish it Friday afternoon instead of Thursday. It's not late enough to get you fired, but it is late enough to get the message across to your boss that you're not a puppet who will dance when *he* pulls the strings. You'll deliver the goods, but at your own pace.

Get off My Back. There are times when a person feels restricted not so much by rules or someone else's power but by a sense of intrusion. Procrastination becomes a way to resist that intrusion. You might feel that someone has invaded your personal territory, as did a woman who resented her neighbor's insistent request for a secret family recipe. "She had no business asking for it! She knows it's a secret." Rather than say "No" to the request, the woman told the neighbor that she could have the recipe—and then kept "forgetting" to write it down. "Eventually, after I'd procrastinated for over three months, my neighbor gave up and stopped asking. I was so relieved to finally have her out of my hair!"

Sometimes people feel intruded upon by a task they see as an unnecessary imposition on their time and energy. Think of how you feel when, in early January, those inevitable tax forms arrive in the mail. Said one procrastinator, "As soon as those forms arrive, they seem to take up all the space in the house. So I put the forms in a drawer and forget about them. That way I can still enjoy the rest of my life—at least for a while."

A simple request can feel like an intrusion if you don't believe you can refuse it, or if it comes from someone who already demands a lot from you. Sometimes even things *you* have asked for feel like intrusions. After putting it off for months, a young man finally advertised to sell his car. Receiving thirty messages on his machine the first day the ad ran, he didn't return one call. "It was just too much! All those people were after me, wanting something. I felt like telling them to go away and leave me alone. Of course, that was ridiculous because I put the ad in the paper so that people would call. But when they did, I felt as though I'd been invaded."

Procrastinating to resist intrusion usually has the effect of increasing the procrastinator's feeling of protection and safety. By putting someone off and making them wait, you can feel more in control of things, and, therefore, less vulnerable to invasion.

Beat the Clock. In contrast to the safety procrastination can provide from intrusion, there are times when it *increases* a person's sense of danger and risk. Many procrastinators describe the thrill of being on the brink of disaster. They feel elated when, by delaying, they take a situation to its limits and emerge victorious. As one procrastinator described, "It's like walking along a very narrow cliff and trying to see how close you can get to the edge before falling off. You never know whether you're going to make it this time or not." Some people get this thrill from driving race cars, playing the stock market, or risking their lives in the line of duty, as in police work. The excitement comes from flirting with danger and surviving by your own wits and skill. Your senses must be totally alert since you risk your job, your security, or your life at every turn.

Some procrastinators feel a similar sense of risk when they delay until the last possible moment. They take things so far that their lives and well-being are jeopardized. How much lateness will the boss put up with before firing you? How long can you delay work for a client before being sued or dismissed from your profession? How much will your spouse tolerate before becoming infuriated with you? Finally, when there seems to be no chance for escape, these procrastinators act. And, if they are lucky, they survive, elated and triumphant.

Tony, a college undergraduate, lives for this feeling of excitement. "I almost want to see how little time I can give myself to study for an exam and still get an A on it. The more important the course, the more I feel I have to do this. I won't do any work all semester, then I'll cram everything into the last two days. My best record so far is eighteen hours straight for one of the toughest political science courses offered at the university." When Tony dares to defy the odds, he feels "an incredible rush of adrenalin." He considers himself special because he is able to overcome the obstacle of time in a way most students can't. By increasing the risk of doing poorly, procrastination makes Tony's victory sweeter.

The Taste of Revenge. Procrastination can also sweeten the victory of revenge. If you have felt hurt, angered, slighted, or betrayed by someone, you can use procrastination as a way to retaliate against them. Perhaps your boss said something critical about your last report; perhaps your spouse doesn't pay as much attention to you as you would like; perhaps your supervisor changed the rules without warning or said something against you in a meeting. Procrastination becomes your means of inflicting some pain or discomfort on those who hurt you.

For example, your boss needs your report so that he can prepare for his meeting with the company president. When you delay, your boss looks bad to his boss and, inwardly, you are delighted. Or, suppose you haven't studied much for a class because you felt the teacher wasn't putting enough time into planning the lectures. You convince your teacher to give you a make-up exam. He or she now has to create a new exam just for you and must schedule time to be with you while you take it.

You can also retaliate against people by procrastinating on things they have come to expect from you and which you normally provide. "When I'm mad at my husband," said Lorraine, "I stop doing things for him and go on a slow-down strike. Dinner is late and disorganized. I put off the errands I normally do for him. All sorts of things can set it off—if he doesn't bring me flowers on special occasions, if he hasn't said something nice to me in a while, if he criticizes something I say or whatever I've cooked for dinner. I feel so hurt that I don't want to give him anything!" Lorraine achieves her revenge by depriving her husband of the things he takes for granted.

In each of these scenarios, the procrastinator is in a struggle against some other person. It seems important to emerge from the battle victorious, whether that means breaking the rules, defying an authority figure, resisting intrusion, barely escaping destruction, or achieving revenge. This feeling of victory may be based on the belief that you have been strong enough or clever enough to repel the other person's control over you. By procrastinating, you were able to fight back—and feel you have won.

THE ISSUE OF AUTONOMY

Procrastination is often a proclamation of one's independence, a way of saying, "I am a person in my own right. I can act in the way I choose for myself. I do not have to go along with your rules and your demands." By using procrastination to resist domination, you may be preserving your sense of individuality and reassuring yourself that you are living your own life.

Like procrastinators who measure their worth by their

experience of success or failure, people who use procrastination to resist the control of others tend to rely on the extent of their autonomy as a measure of their personal worth. Procrastination becomes the evidence which indisputably demonstrates that you are *not* under someone else's control. When you capitulate, or even cooperate, you may feel deferential and weak, and your estimation of yourself may dwindle, or even disappear.

The self-worth equation that we described in the previous chapter applies here too, though with some modification. The procrastinator again defines self-worth in terms of performance, but in this case, it is by *not* performing, i.e., by procrastinating, that self-worth is enhanced. *Not doing* is a *demonstration* of the procrastinator's ability rather than a way to avoid testing it. The difference here is in the definition of "ability." For the person who fears judgment, "ability" refers to how well he or she is able to do on a given task. For the person who fears losing the battle, "ability" refers to how well he or she is able to resist control or the restriction of his or her autonomy. Thus:

**Self-worth = Ability (to be autonomous, = Performance (on *my* terms,
defy control)   via procrastination)**

The importance of winning the battle becomes clearer when we recognize that it is being fought for more than just control. It is a battle for self-worth and self-respect. Unfortunately, if your entire sense of self-worth is based on your ability to defy domination, every encounter can take on exaggerated importance. A single, small defeat can leave you feeling as though you have compromised yourself, that your ability to live autonomously is in doubt. This is why losing the battle is such an intense and powerful fear—and why these procrastinators are so stubbornly resistant to change.

For some of you, the fear of losing a sense of autonomy is secondary to worries about failure or success. In the heat of the moment, you may temporarily rely on procrastination to prove your independence or power, or to express your irritation. Your personal integrity may seem to hinge on your winning the battle and coming out on top, so you do what you can to bring about victory. There may be other times when you *do* follow rules or tolerate intrusions, times when you express your anger or hurt directly, times when you assert your power and independence in ways other than by procrastinating. It might be interesting to ask yourself what it is about certain circumstances that leads you to fight with procrastination.

There are others of you who will find that your concern with the issues of autonomy, control, and power is a pervasive part of your existence. Your life may be a constant battleground on which you fight every rule, argue about anything, ask for special consideration in large and small ways, and generally make trouble wherever you go. In the back of your mind, you may be always assessing who is stronger, who is in control, who has the upper hand. You are ready, at the least provocation, to rebel against authority and assert your own influence in the situation.

Henry, the accountant we described in Chapter 1, is a case in point. His major concern in life is making sure that he is not controlled by anyone. "I am my own man," he asserts. "I know I'm supposed to be at work at 8 a.m. or have an audit report prepared for a client by a certain date. That's just it—I'm *supposed* to. I hate that word. If I go ahead and do it, I feel awful, so I don't do it or I do it late. That way, I can show them who's in charge—*me!*" Henry not only delays fulfilling work responsibilities, he also resists the smallest request or expectation from anyone. If Henry's wife, Eileen, asks him to do an errand on the way home, he invariably "forgets." If some friends suggest getting together for dinner, he will find something wrong with the day, time, or place, and offer a counterproposal of his own. Henry regards taxes, monthly bills, and late notices as nuisances. Saying that he won't let his life be governed by such trivialities, he pays his bills only when he feels so inclined—usually once every six months. Henry even fights when no one is involved but himself. He has run out of gas on the freeway because driving out of his way to look for gas while the indicator reads "empty" makes Henry feel as though he's giving in to the petty requirements of everyday life. So he doesn't do it.

Henry is a procrastinator whose battleground is everywhere. In the form of pervasive procrastination, Henry's defiance of authority allows him to feel as though he's acting on his own terms and playing the game of life his own way. When Henry procrastinates, he experiences himself as a person who deserves respect and esteem. When he acquiesces to the authority of his employer, his wife, or an empty gas tank, Henry sees himself as a weak and impotent person.

Whether your tendency to do battle by procrastinating is pervasive, like Henry's, or limited to certain circumstances, the consequences of your delaying can range from a mild disturbance to a major setback in your life. It's not such a big deal to pay late library fines, to send thank you notes two or three weeks late, or even to be late to work now and then. But some procrastinators are so determined not to lose the battle that they are willing to pay a very high price to win. Procrastination may lead to their being passed over for a job promotion, or even losing a job. As a result of putting things off, some procrastinators suffer financial disaster, jeopardize their health, forfeit their homes, or lose an important relationship. Yet, sacrificing something of great personal significance may seem a necessary price to pay for the feeling of leading a life of one's own.

Does this sound far-fetched to you? Before you conclude that all this talk of battle and extreme consequences is not relevant to your own situation, consider the story of another procrastinator. Maureen didn't realize she was caught in a struggle for independence, and in the process, diminished her own life.

Maureen is an intelligent, 34-year-old woman who presently works as a department store sales clerk. As a child, she was able to do well in school with little effort. Though her parents valued intellectual and academic achievement, Maureen's accomplishments never seemed to satisfy them. Whenever Maureen did do well, her mother took credit for the accomplishment and bragged about Maureen's successes as if they were her own. Maureen's father, a prominent attorney, viewed her good grades as enabling her to attend law school and join his law firm. He took her grades for granted, just as he unquestioningly assumed that Maureen would work for him after finishing school.

When Maureen went away to college, she did a lot of socializing and very little studying. At the end of her first year, her grades were so poor that she was dismissed from school. Maureen then attended the local community college, where she started each semester well, worked hard through the first mid-term exam, and invariably earned her A. At that point, Maureen would simply stop studying, and instead would go out with friends, read novels, or go to movies. To avoid failing her courses, Maureen withdrew on the last possible day, feeling demoralized and angry with herself. "I couldn't figure it out then. I actually enjoyed most of the classes, especially the sciences. I even thought about going to medical school to become a pediatrician. I know I had the ability to make it. But there seemed to be another part of me that wanted to destroy that possibility."

It wasn't until years later that Maureen realized her procrastination in school had something to do with her parents' control over her. Growing up, she felt that she had no life of her own, with her mother directing her current life activities and her father deciding what her future would be. "I refused to give either of them the satisfaction of making me into what they wanted. They each had their reasons for wanting me to be successful, but none of it was for me. I couldn't let them have that. The sad part is that I really *wanted* to do well in school and to make something of my life. I guess at the time I didn't think it was possible for me to do well and maintain my self-respect and independence at the same time. And I *had* to keep my independence. It was the only choice I thought I could make."

By procrastinating, Maureen gave up the possibility of a professional career in order to prove that she could resist her parents' attempts to direct her life. But Maureen's behavior was not truly independent because it was so closely tied to her parents' actions. Although she did not do what her parents wanted, she also did *not* do what *she* wanted. Years later, with more distance from the situation, Maureen regretted the compelling forcefulness of her desire to prove her autonomy. "If I had felt more secure about my independence, I wouldn't have had to work so hard to prove it. I wish I could have believed then that doing well in school didn't have to mean that may parents were controlling me. Then I could have done what I really wanted to do, no matter how they felt about it."

The Secret Battle

When a need for autonomy is the overriding theme in a person's life, the process of making decisions and committing oneself to a person or to a course of action can be very difficult. Committing yourself to a relationship, putting words down on paper, or carrying out a business decision, may mean that you are making your interests known, exposing your preferences for all the world to see. But once you've done that, you are no longer completely in the driver's seat. For procrastinators who fear losing the battle, exposing what they want, think, or feel, leaves them vulnerable to attack and control by others. They are not so concerned that, once exposed, they will be judged as lacking ability or as being too successful. Instead, they expect that they will be humiliated, their weaknesses probed ruthlessly.

The Procrastinator in Combat: Fear of Losing the Battle

Jerome, who puts off everything from establishing personal relationships to deciding on a career path, described his experience this way: "I think of life as a poker game. I want to find out what cards the other person has before I make a play. Does he have aces, a full house, a flush, or just peanuts? Until I find out, I keep my cards close to my chest and try not to reveal a thing. So, I won't ask a woman out until she's let me know she's really interested in me. I refused to request a promotion at work because I didn't want people to know which departments I was really interested in. I figured someone would try to block my transfer. I hold off making any decision because once I do choose, I've given away my position, and someone could take advantage of that. Usually what happens is that things end up getting decided for me because I put off choosing for such a long time."

Procrastinating on decisions and commitments can help you feel you are less vulnerable to someone else's power. No one can pin you down or get a clear idea of where you stand, so they can't interfere in things that really matter to you. As long as you remain uncommitted, you can shift around in any direction you wish. You feel that your freedom is unlimited because you haven't closed off even one possibility for yourself.

As soon as you make a decision or commitment, however, you may begin to feel trapped. Your sense of safety, which came from being uncommitted and elusive, evaporates. The only protection, then, seems to reside in avoiding any commitment, big or small. That way, you can shift to something else at the slightest intimation that someone might try to control or take advantage of you. Escape is always at hand.

Procrastinators who are concerned with losing the battle often avoid open competition. But in truth, they are competing all the time. They simply keep their competition secret. They don't want to let anyone else know that they are vying for power because if they do, they risk losing, exposing their weakness and vulnerability.

Jerome told a story which conveyed this idea well. In high school, his favorite class was physical education, because there he had more freedom to be active and to do what he wanted than he had in regular classrooms. One day, the class went out for a ten-mile run with the instructor. Jerome secretly decided to compete with the instructor and was the only student in the class even close to finishing with the teacher. Said Jerome, "When I achieved that, I felt great. For a moment, I considered trying out for the track team, but then I immediately thought about how humiliated I would be if somebody ever beat me. People watching would say, 'Who does he think he is, going out for track? It's ridiculous to even think of it! What an idiot he is!' From then on everyone would sneer at me and look down on me, and I just couldn't take that." The threat that he might demonstrate his interest and then lose a competition he'd entered made Jerome feel so vulnerable that he avoided the possibility altogether.

Some procrastinators rationalize opting out of the competition by convincing themselves that if they did compete, they would completely overpower the opposition. So they magnanimously bow out. In other words, they can withdraw by implying that this particular competition is beneath them somehow. This strategy helps them feel stronger: if they never play the game, they can continue to believe they are invincible.

What makes it hard to fight battles openly? Perhaps for you, the prospect of a confrontation inevitably means a disagreement— and disagreements might mean that someone has to lose. You may never even think about the possibility of negotiating to reach a *mutual* agreement. When you fight secretly, your opponent doesn't *know* that a battle is on and so has less chance to mobilize his or her efforts against you. Your chance of winning the battle thus improves.

Additionally, fighting secretly allows you to *appear* to be co-operating with others and thereby keep up a "Nice Guy" image. You can actually be extremely frustrating to others, but when you are indirect about it, they can't always pin it on you. Take Tom, for example: whether it be ordering the supplies needed at work, or doing an errand for his girlfriend, Tom is consistently behind schedule. Because he's also very busy and overcommitted, he usually has a convincing rationale for his lateness. His schedule was so incredibly tight that he just *couldn't* have done it any sooner. Tom is genuinely sorry for his delay, and he then is so generous in offering to make it up somehow, that most people swallow their irritation and try to be friendly in spite of the inconvenience they've suffered. Conflict boils beneath the surface, but Tom manages to keep it sugar-coated enough so that other people don't challenge him. In the end, Tom is doubly frustrating— he's constantly thwarting other people, and he won't admit to it.

Further, if you fight indirectly, even if someone *does* confront you about your behavior by saying that you're making things difficult or that you're being hostile, you can deny it. After all, you haven't actually done anything overtly hostile or competitive. You even may have maintained a pleasant, friendly demeanor towards other people. And you can fall back on your old friend, procrastination, claiming that you're just so disorganized and unable to keep track of time that you couldn't do all that you wanted. This way, not only can you hide your actual feelings, you can also claim that your behavior is beyond your control. If you *could* be on time, you *would,* but procrastination always seems to get the better of you. It's not your fault! It's because of procrastination!!

If you're very practiced, you may even be able to turn the situation around enough to make it seem that you, not the other person, are the one who deserves an apology. You can play up how horrible it is to be afflicted by a condition like procrastination, especially when there's nothing you can do about it. When you are such a helpless victim, how could anyone hurt you? It would be like punching someone who is wearing a thick pair of glasses.

The indirectness of procrastination can also protect you from admitting the power of your own anger. Expressing your anger indirectly may be a way for you to keep your emotions under control. Perhaps you've come to believe that all of your feelings should be kept under wraps. Any expression of irritation or anger might show that you can be gotten to, that someone can push your buttons. Your opponent would then know how to get to you the next time.

A Philosophy of Defense

Whether procrastination is used to fight minor skirmishes or to wage open war, people whose main concern is winning or losing the battle seem to make several basic assumptions about the world and their power to influence it.

The World Is an Unpredictable Place. For the embattled procrastinator, uncertainty lurks everywhere. Relationships with other people are not to be trusted. You never know whether someone will encourage and support you, or attempt to control and manipulate you. Rather than allow yourself to be lured into believing the best, you feel safer if you simply assume the worst.

Such procrastinators are convinced that people will indeed take advantage of them if given the opportunity. They are constantly on the lookout for people or institutions that will strip them of their power, leave them vulnerable and exposed. Since they can't predict whether they'll be helped or hurt, the world not only seems unpredictable, it seems dangerous. They feel they must conceal their weaknesses and never reveal their neediness or dependency.

Your procrastination not only protects you by preventing you from being hurt by others; it also serves as a way of hurting the opposition so that they can't hurt you. In a sense, the safest rule is: control the opposition before it controls you. In an unpredictable, dangerous world, as the saying goes, the best defense is a good offense.

If Someone Is Strong, then I Must Be Weak. The person who fights by procrastinating usually feels powerless in the face of someone or something they perceive as being stronger. This is common between employees and employers and between children and their parents. The other person is viewed as having control over your life, telling you what to do, and when to do it. Decisions are made without your input; rules are laid down arbitrarily and your opinions don't seem to count much one way or another. Because you see the system as one in which there is a fundamental inequality between your position and the position of the powerholder, a direct confrontation seems destined to result in your defeat. Your opponent is too big, too strong, and too smart to yield to you. So you have to defeat the power-holder by disempowering him or her. Through procrastination, you render the person impotent. He or she controls you only to the extent that you actively perform your duties and tasks. If you stop doing them, you take back some of the control. Because of this change in the balance of power, you can feel assured that you won't be obliterated by the other person. You can stand your ground.

Cooperation Is the Same As Capitulation. Someone like Henry feels that he is capitulating whenever he goes along with someone else's rules or is asked to do something for another person. For some of you, the mere *idea* of cooperation evokes a fear that you might be diminishing your own power and giving up your independence. The idea of *choosing* to comply because you *want* to, or because it's *necessary* in order to obtain a goal that you seek, may not even occur to you. Instead, you may feel as though you have been forced against your will to compromise yourself. Given the nature of the world (i.e., that it is an uncertain and dangerous place), such a state of weakness would be a precarious position to be in.

To Thwart My Opponent Is More Important Than to Get What I Want. As in the case of Maureen, thwarting your opponent can become such a primary concern that it outweighs all other considerations, including getting what you want for yourself. It's as if you're saying, "If you want me to do it, I won't do it, even if I might actually want to do it." You get more satisfaction from frustrating or defying someone else than you would if you accomplished what is important for your own life. Some procrastinators, in fact, are so focused on defeating the other person that they don't even *know* what they want. They only know that they don't want what other people want for them! The irony in all of this is, of course, that if you are procrastinating to say, "Screw you!" to someone, the person who is really getting screwed is you.

The Roots of the Struggle

Have you been wondering how you might have come to view the world as a battleground in the first place? How have you come to regard people and situations as opponents who have the potential to hurt you? We've talked in depth with procrastinators whose concerns center on the issues of power, control, and autonomy, and found that most of them grew up in situations that did not encourage a sense of mastery and control over their own lives.

All children have a natural drive for independence and take great pleasure in discovering and exercising their own wills. But, unfortunately, many parents are not able to enjoy their child's attempt to gradually reach an autonomous state and, instead of encouraging the child's moves toward self-determination, they try to bring the child back into line. Children may experience these parental efforts at control in many different forms—strict discipline, intense interest that begins to feel intrusive, constant criticism that undermines confidence and therefore inhibits moves toward independence. It is important to remember that children may experience the feeling of being controlled even if the parent is not intentionally trying to achieve domination over the child.

To some extent, every parent feels a sense of loss as his or her child grows up and needs the parent less and less. Just as it is a major task of childhood to develop the capacity for autonomy, one of the tasks of parenthood is to let go, to allow and even to help the child to have an independent life. Parents who have trouble tolerating the feeling of loss inherent in the natural process of separation may try to hold on by squelching any move the child makes toward independence. Spontaneity may be frowned upon. Excessive rules and structure may be imposed. The child may be restricted beyond what is necessary or helpful. Open rebellion may not be permitted.

Often the result is that the child experiences thousands of small encounters with the parent, in which the child's autonomy is discouraged or even made fun of. When such tiny encounters occur repeatedly over the years they have tremendous impact. The child begins to feel that there is something wrong with wanting to be independent. He or she comes to expect that his or her attempts to be autonomous will be met, not with encouragement and support, but with restrictiveness. For such a child, one way to survive is to do battle.

A child of such restrictive parents may resolve never again to suffer under such control. By building a psychological fortress, a child defends against attack by the outside world and also prevents him- or herself from feeling vulnerable or hurt. Procrastination is one of many mechanisms that a person can use to maintain this sense of strength and impenetrability.

Whether or not you can expect a lifetime of sensitivity to being controlled depends in part on how pervasive and how strong your resistance to control is. If being controlled is a highly charged issue for you, as it is for Henry, then yes, you will probably always feel some wariness whenever you are faced with a deadline, a request, or an expectation. You may rebel instinctively, turning left as soon as you have the least indication that someone wants you to turn right. Your immediate response will be to say no. But since you are also wary about exposing yourself to a possible opponent, your impulse is to say no indirectly, by slowing down and doing nothing.

How might you use your automatic resistance to your advantage? Once you know that you are sensitive to being controlled, you can use your resistance as a warning signal.

Thus, when you find yourself "on alert," feeling the pull to resist, one of the first questions you may want to ask is, "What am I reacting to?" There will be times when your resistance will alert you that someone is trying to control you, restrict your individual effort, or take advantage of you. Also, there will be times when your alarm will sound in reaction to your own apprehension and fear, instead of to the realities of the situation. Your choice of action will depend upon what actually is at stake—your autonomy and integrity, or your apprehension and fear.

You may always choose procrastination as your response to the situation. Or, after thinking things over, you may try a different way of resisting control or asserting your individuality and independence. You might, for example, decide to say no directly in words. You might decide to tell someone that something they've done has irritated you. You might choose simply to thank the other person for his or her suggestions and then proceed to do exactly what you wanted to do in the first place. But you might also decide that of all the options available, procrastination is the best way for you to express yourself.

The question to consider is: Is procrastinating in your best interests? What are the advantages and the disadvantages of delaying? What's at stake? There are times when another person does have real power over you. Two classic examples occur in the settings of work and school. In college, you have to take required courses and earn a minimum grade point average in order to graduate and obtain a degree. At work, you have to fulfill certain responsibilities in order to receive your paycheck. In situations like these, playing the game by other people's rules ultimately may be to your advantage.

Some battles will be more important than others for you to fight. You must decide which battles are most important. When you fight every battle that comes along, you don't have much energy for anything else.

Consider the story of the Japanese samurai. This samurai was a master swordsman, one of the greatest and most renowned in all the land. He was so fast and so accurate with his sword that he never needed an umbrella.

Why no umbrella, you ask?

The master swordsman didn't need an umbrella because when it rained, he would pull out his sword and flick away the raindrops before they could land on him. He used his tremendous skill to keep dry. Although this meant that the swordsman was very busy during a rainstorm, it never occurred to him to use an umbrella, to seek shelter, or even to have fun getting wet in the rain.

Like the master swordsman, you may be expending much effort to protect yourself from the rain. Is that truly how you want to use your energy?

4

The Comfort Zone:
Fear of Separation and
Fear of Attachment

Procrastination can do more than protect a person from judgment or provide a covert way to engage in battle. Delay and postponement can also regulate the degree of closeness that a person maintains with other people, preserving whatever interpersonal distance seems safest and most comfortable.

How deeply involved with others should we be? We all have to make choices about how many relationships to maintain, the degree of our commitment to each, how much time we spend with others, and how much time we need to be alone. Just as some people's lives are dominated by their need for approval or the desire to win, others' are dominated by their need to find a "comfort zone" that determines the degree of closeness they have with those around them. Moving out of that comfort zone—being too close or too far away—can be so distressing that these people go to great lengths to stay within it. Procrastination is a device they use to regain their equilibrium.

Kaye was a 22-year-old senior in college who was living with her boyfriend, Jerry. After work, Jerry often liked to invite friends over or go out for the evening. Kaye liked to spend as much time as possible with Jerry. When she was with him, she had lots of energy and motivation, but she had little interest for independent projects. So they did everything together—shopping, cooking, laundry, exercises, reading, watching TV, seeing friends. Although she often had schoolwork to do, Kaye didn't like to study when Jerry was at home, because it kept her apart from him. On rare occasions she studied at the college library, but she was always sure to come home early to spend the evening with Jerry.

Shocked when she was put on academic probation at the end of the semester, Kaye reflected on how she'd spent her time. "Studying was never my first priority, I guess. I always put it off in favor of being with Jerry. I get kind of nervous when I'm away from him, but I calm down as soon as I'm with him again. We're just like two peas in a pod."

Kaye's need to be close to Jerry was the greatest concern in her life. She could not generate on her own the feeling of stability and reassurance that being with him provided. School was an independent activity that made her feel too separate from Jerry for her own comfort—so she put it off.

Other people value their separateness above all else and feel threatened when they become too closely involved with others. These people may use procrastination to avoid doing things that would nudge them closer to entanglement and personal commitment.

For example, Cliff worked as a troubleshooter, repairing computers in businesses that leased the machines from his company. One of the things he liked about his job was that he didn't have to interact with many people. He was relieved not to be in an office where people worked together every day. His boss was impressed with his work, and discussed plans to make Cliff a supervisor. At that point, Cliff's work deteriorated. He arrived late to his appointments and delayed turning in the reports on his service calls.

Cliff was not afraid of success itself. He believed in his competence and enjoyed it. Rather, Cliff's procrastination was a signal that he didn't want to be in a new situation that would demand the increased involvement of supervising people. "Just leave me alone and I'll do my job," he said. "I don't want a bunch of people hanging around, making small talk. They'd just be a drain on me."

Both Cliff and Kaye function in the world with a special sensitivity to the amount of involvement they have with others. Kaye needs to be close to Jerry, while Cliff feels most comfortable by himself. For each of them, the threat of moving too far in the other direction presents a danger. Procrastination helps them stay within their respective "comfort zones."

FEAR OF SEPARATION: I'LL NEVER WALK ALONE

When we talk about feeling more secure by being connected to someone else, we are not speaking only of the preference most people share to have close relationships, to get companionship, support, and love from others. Rather, we are talking about a need that comes close to being a requirement for self-preservation. We're suggesting a state that might have led you to say about someone, "It's as though we're two halves of the same person." It's not only that you want someone else around, but that you don't feel truly complete unless you're part of someone else and they're part of you. When people have an empty inner experience, it can be very difficult to make efforts that require independent functioning. Left to their own devices, they feel lost. Let's look at some ways people rely on procrastination when they're not sure how solidly they can stand on their own two feet.

Help Wanted. If you feel unsure of yourself, of the validity of your own ideas, or even of creating ideas of your own, then you may feel that you can't act without looking to other people for help—not simply in terms of feedback or brainstorming, but help that will provide a viewpoint or a structure that you can adopt as your own.

For example, some procrastinators put great effort into compiling advice and information from outside sources, but postpone synthesizing what they've heard to form their own conclusions and express their own views clearly. Many college students, for instance, devote weeks to gathering research for a term paper, but never actually write it because they have to sort through so many contradictory opinions to offer a perspective of their own. They know how to consult outside resources, but when they try to look inside themselves, they come up empty-handed.

You may have noticed yourself asking a lot of people for advice on some matters of consequence, such as whether to invest in stocks or bonds, how to treat your lower back pain, or which microwave oven to buy. But when it comes down to deciding on the best step to take, you don't actually *do* anything. If your outside sources offer conflicting opinions, you will at some point have to make your own decision and take the consequences. But if you don't *know* what your own preferences are, how could you possibly *choose* between different ideas offered by different people? You can't—so you do nothing.

There may be times when you can on decide the best course of action but feel you need the presence of another to make it happen. Without a partnership you are afraid you'll sink into lethargy. "When I'm working on a team project, I'm really hot, but when I have to prepare something alone, I'm not," said Terry, a financial analyst. "The difference is astounding! In a group, I'm full of ideas, I have a lot of motivation, and I get things done. But when I'm alone at my desk trying to do financial projections, I feel as if my brain has died. Apathy takes over and I can sit there doing nothing for hours. I need someone to come along and provide that spark, because if I'm left on my own, I'll just sit."

Trying Harder to Be Number Two. You may feel very comfortable in a secondary position under someone else's wing. You play an important supportive part, but someone else makes all the big decisions and takes on the tough responsibilities. The buck stops with *them.* If you don't would rather have someone else take both the pain and the glory that comes with the spotlight, then you may postpone doing things that would force you up to the top and into the open.

Gloria, for example, was an extremely efficient and organized person, both at home and at work. On the home front, Gloria was the one to ask if you needed to know how to remove a wine stain from your grandmother's lace tablecloth, or whether to plant your seedlings in April or in May. But Gloria did not transfer this self-sufficiency into her job as assistant to a product manager in a cosmetic company. At work, she devoted much of her time to revising and updating the filing system and keeping track of office projects. But, much to her supervisor's disappointment, she delayed on assignments that required her to contribute to new product ideas or new marketing strategies.

If both Gloria and her boss had agreed on her job requirements to begin with, there would have been less of a problem for everyone. But Gloria's supervisor could see right away how clever and creative Gloria was at organizing things and wanted her to show some initiative. Unfortunately, that wasn't what Gloria wanted. "I like doing what she tells me to do and making things run smoothly in the office. My ideal work situation is one in which I can maintain a low profile. I don't want to be in the spotlight." Gloria's boss wanted a more independent assistant who needed less direction. To Gloria's great amazement, when she was unable to shift gears and contribute more of her own ideas, she was fired.

Gloria doesn't hold herself back because she is afraid of making a mistake or being too successful. She keeps herself in second place because if she were in charge, she would feel too separate and alone. Gloria doesn't want to be an innovator. She can follow procedures, but she can't create them. She needs someone else to tell her what to do, whether it be her supervisor or Dear Abby.

Wishing Will Make It So. Sometimes people procrastinate in order to maintain a dependent relationship with someone they hope will take care of them—even if it isn't in fact actually happening. They yearn to be attached to a protector or mentor, even if only symbolically. For example, many graduate students postpone taking their oral exams or have difficulty finishing their dissertations because they don't want to give up the protection of the university or leave their faculty advisors. They equate graduate school with their final opportunity for the guidance and tutelage that they feel they need in order to maneuver successfully in the grown-up world.

In other areas, people may procrastinate because they feel some hesitation about leaving their first boss who taught them about the business, or the first person who took them seriously in a personal relationship. They may believe that if they move on, they may never get that kind of attention again. Even if they suspect that it's time for a more challenging job, or that they've outgrown a relationship, they convince themselves that this may be as good as it gets. This can be a particularly sad situation when a relationship actually offers little in the way of protection, support, guidance, or nurturance. Rather than recognizing the limitations of the rela-tionship, or perhaps the destructiveness of it, some people cling to an idealized image of what they wish to see. Although they may actually be diminishing their lives by remaining in the relationship, it seems preferable to be with *someone* than to be alone in the world, with no one at their side. Their fear of separation prevents them taking an action which might ultimately be in their own best interests.

S.O.S. Some procrastinators dig themselves into a deep hole in the hope that someone else will come along and dig them out. Procrastination is their way of making themselves so miserable, so pitiful, so desperate, that someone is *bound* to try to rescue them. Sadly, these procrastinators believe that unless they are in dire straits, no one will be interested enough to look after them. They may even get involved with people who actually *do* like them better when they're in a jam.

As an example, some people take on so many projects that they inevitably fall behind. They're so exhausted and haggard-looking that other people can't fail to notice and usually take pity on them. Perhaps people observe their weakened condition and ask what's wrong or how they could be of help. They may even offer solicitous advice about how to limit their commitments and suggest spending a week at a health spa. The harried procrastinator may receive the reassurance of people's interest and concern for them, but they had to put themselves through agony to get it.

Some people use a procrastination emergency to create a special relationship with someone whom they fear might not notice them otherwise. There are students, for example, who hesitate to talk in class or to meet with a professor during office hours, but when they fall behind in a course, they approach the professor to ask for an extension or an "Incomplete." In this way, they create a relationship where none existed before. They have found a way to stand out, to receive special acknowledgment, even if they've had to procrastinate in order to get it.

The ultimate rescue you can receive as a procrastinator is to have someone else do your work for you. How many times have you hoped that if you just wait long enough, or if you're in deep enough trouble, someone else would magically appear to do the horrid thing for you?

A divorced woman we know procrastinates on all financial matters, from paying bills to saving money to preparing her taxes. She finally realized that she'd always expected the man in her life to handle the finances. Doing it for herself meant that she was really on her own, that no one was taking care of her, and this triggered her fear that maybe no one would ever take care of her again. If she didn't do the work, surely somehow someone somewhere would appear, calculator in hand, to rescue her from the dreadful fate of being alone.

Occasionally, you may succeed in relinquishing responsibility for yourself and finding someone who will rescue you, but there is often a high price to pay. A college student majoring in engineering delayed so long on doing his homework problems that he fell dangerously behind. In the eleventh hour, he would go to his friends in the class to get answers from them, or he would call his father who worked as an engineer. His dad, who had always enjoyed helping his son with schoolwork, was pleased that he could still be of assistance. Although this student enjoyed the gratification of being helped, he never learned whether he could master the material on his own. He created a crisis so that he would be rescued, but this prevented him from learning what he could do for himself.

Most people who hope to be or arrange to be rescued are operating with the belief that they will get more response from others if they are in some kind of difficulty than if they are independent and competent. They worry that if they demonstrate that they can take care of themselves, they will be left alone. Procrastination may be their way to insure the involvement of others and soothe their fears about being separate.

Keeping the Past Alive. A rather subtle way to use procrastination to maintain connections is to continue old relationships through the repetition of familiar patterns. If, for example, you used to struggle with your parents or teachers over doing what they told you to do, you may find yourself in a similar struggle with your spouse over completing chores or requests. Your spouse has become a substitute who is provoked by your procrastination into the role of the badger. There you are again, back on familiar ground, feeling defiant or chastised, expecting to be punished. Usually, neither you nor your new taskmaster realizes fully what is going on, but you're both caught up in a cycle which keeps you procrastinating in a familiar way.

One of the purposes of replaying old scenes may be to keep alive the connection you had with the original cast. Jack, an appliance repairman, frequently gets into tangles with Marty, his supervisor. Marty complains that Jack doesn't arrive at appointments on time, he doesn't submit requisitions for replacement parts until he's run out of his supply, and he turns in his weekly time sheets months late, disrupting the accounting and payroll departments. Although Marty is unaware that he is being cast in a familiar role, Jack is very much at home when someone puts him in the doghouse. His mother used to get after him constantly for things like coming home late to dinner and keeping the whole family waiting, or leaving his laundry unwashed until he discovered that he hadn't a single pair of clean underwear left. When Jack hears his supervisor roar, "This whole business doesn't revolve around you, you know!" it plays a familiar tune for Jack, whose mother used to say, "You're not the only one in this family!"

As long as people currently in your life seem to echo people from your past, you don't really ever separate from those early figures. Procrastination is the price you pay for maintaining this connection, but it may seem a lesser price than feeling that you've lost your old ties and have to navigate through life on your own.

A Constant Companion.   When you're in the throes of delaying, facing unfinished projects, unresolved decisions, or unpaid bills, you probably carry the burden of procrastination with you wherever you go. If you do have some emancipated moments, the memory of your obligations can return to spoil your freedom in an instant.

Yet, while procrastination can be a constant burden, it can also be a constant companion in your life, a "person" reminding you of all you have to do. In this way, it may keep you from feeling lonely or abandoned, since you are always accompanied by mental lists and half-completed projects. Your projects proliferate, and you don't complete them or let them go. When you procrastinate, you never say "good-bye" to anything.

Even though you may feel more plagued by these accumulations than "accompanied," your procrastination still provides a constant presence in your life. It serves as a continual reminder of things that must be done, and there can be something reassuring about its constancy. You may carry it around like heavy baggage, but at least it is always with you!

Of course, there are better ways to be accompanied. Get a dog. Make a friend. Keep a journal. Procrastination is a lousy companion: faithful, but as you know, quite a troublemaker.

All of the strategies we have mentioned so far are ways of using procrastination as a means of staying close—to be aided, to be rescued, to be taken care of by a protector, to keep connected to someone or something. How does one come to feel that it's safer to be connected and protected than to be on one's own? Perhaps there were times in your life when you were left alone in a situation that you weren't ready to handle. A little child lost in a crowd or accidentally left behind when everyone else has gone may be terrified that he or she will be lost forever. If someone who was very important to you went away suddenly, even for a short time, you may have felt abandoned or betrayed. Such experiences, particularly if they occur repeatedly, can lead a child to cling to people, as if in the hope that they will never be separated again.

Another way you might have come to be fearful of being on your own is by having had very little experience developing your own opinions, attending to your own needs, and living according to your own preferences. Perhaps some of your early efforts at becoming a more independent person have been thwarted. How were such attempts handled, for example, within your family? Were you encouraged to explore the outside world, or were efforts made—subtly or overtly—to keep you close to the hearth? Was there support for you to make friends at school or in your neighborhood, or was there always something wrong with the friends you brought home? Your parents may have taken pleasure in and encouraged your newly acquired skills, or they may have warned you of the dangers of being too adventurous and taking too many risks.

Some families encourage independence or dependence as part of their ethnic or cultural tradition. In other families, parents may struggle with their own private anxieties and conflicts and have difficulty encouraging their children to explore and enter the outside world. Yet, most parents try to do their best at the very difficult job of raising children. How can they know when well-meaning support evolves into overprotectiveness, or when providing security shifts into undermining a child's independence? Unless they were fortunate enough to have had parents who knew the difference, they probably don't know where to draw the line. Whatever the reasons, people who don't develop a comfortable sense of themselves as separate individuals are left with the feeling that they just can't make it alone out in the big world.

If you have had any of these experiences, you may be left with a trail of questions about whether your sense of self is developed enough for you to stop procrastinating and function more independently. Ask yourself: Would you really be unable to take care of yourself if you put a little distance between you and other people? Would you be as incapable of making your own decisions and motivating yourself as you fear? Can you work on being more independent, so that you are less needy and more comfortable as an autonomous person?

If these are important issues for you, it is probably better to work on them directly than to keep using procrastination to maneuver into a protected position. If you can learn to rely more on yourself, you can slowly start to build up your internal confidence and will need other people less intensely. There are people who can be interested in you, and even love you, without the provocation of desperate dependence.

FEAR OF ATTACHMENT: TOO CLOSE FOR COMFORT

People who fear separation derive great security from being close, close, close. In contrast, people who fear attachment are more comfortable keeping a "respectable distance" from everyone.

Those who prefer distance may be highly attentive to the possibility that someone might be moving in on them, crowding them, tugging at them, demanding of them. Some go through life with their own built-in radar system, constantly scanning their surroundings for signals that someone has entered their territory, and might soon be closing in. Their anxiety is activated as soon as someone appears on the edge of the radar screen, and they rapidly mobilize to retreat. The retreat can be physical: leaving a job or moving to a new town because they feel the pressure of intimacy with colleagues or neighbors. Sometimes the retreat is more emotional: holding back or withdrawing in a relationship that seems too demanding. Sometimes the retreat occurs mentally: changing the topic of conversation when the talk becomes "too personal."

Procrastination can play an important role in keeping people at a safe distance. If you're ambivalent about whether you really want to make the effort to be with people, you can postpone calling to arrange a get-together for Saturday night until everyone already has plans. It may look as if you've tried to be sociable, but you've delayed so long that you end up going to a movie by yourself, more relieved than sorry to be alone.

One computer programmer used his procrastination to protect himself from women. His life was a total mess: He was so far behind at work that he was about to be fired; creditors were after him to pay old debts; his car was deteriorating because he didn't make repairs. As soon as he began to date a woman, he would tell her all about the disarray in his life. As you might imagine, most women responded cautiously to becoming intimately involved with a man who was always on the brink of disaster. They invariably backed away after a few dates, but actually this was a relief to him. Deep down, he was afraid of becoming emotionally attached to a woman, so he hid behind the shield of his extreme procrastination.

When you use procrastination to keep people at bay, perhaps you are worried about what would happen to you, or to them, if you did allow them to get too close. In previous chapters, we've considered several dangers that procrastinators fear in relationships: When someone is important to you, they could judge you to be a disappointment; they might be envious of your success; they might try to conquer you. We've just described how people can seem to be so indispensable that you think you couldn't exist on your own.

Now we want to look at procrastination from the perspective of those for whom closeness itself may seem so confining, so entrapping, that their own identity could be lost. Their fear is that too much contact would change them, but not for the better. Procrastination is one strategy they can use to insure that a wide margin of distance is maintained at all times, thereby providing self-protection.

In talking with procrastinators whose delay is a strategy for creating distance from others, we have heard several themes which delineate some of their fears about allowing people to get close to them.

Give 'Em an Inch, They'll Take a Mile.   Some people believe that relationships will drain them. They fear that others will never be satisfied, and will demand more and more until they eventually deplete everything a person can offer.

Wally was an auto mechanic who realized that he was in the wrong job. Although repairs had long been his hobby and he'd spent many hours working on his own cars, he hadn't really wanted to do it as a lifetime career. When a job had come along in the shop where he'd hung around a lot, he had taken it, and five

The Comfort Zone: Fear of Separation and Fear of Attachment

years later he was still at it. As much as he had thought he had wanted to make a career change, Wally never tried to find a new job. He never even considered what other careers he might prefer.

While discussing his inability to look for another job, Wally began to expound on his theories about working with people: "If you're in a job where you work with a lot of people, they start to expect things from you. They want to get to know you, find out about your life, go out after work. Then they want to meet your family, see how you live. Next thing you know, they'll be asking to borrow money, telling you all about their troubles with their wives, or wanting you to help paint their houses. If I worked in a place like that, I'd be aggravated all the time and I'd probably get blasted every night. At least in this shop, they're not always coming to me with their problems. Sometimes they go out together for a few beers after work. They used to ask me to come along, but I'd never go, so now they pretty much leave me alone and that's fine with me."

Part of Wally's difficulty in searching for another job was his fear of leaving the safe work setting he had created. He let his co-workers know that he didn't want to be part of a gang, and they respected his preference, although they didn't understand it. "You could almost say I've trained these people not to get too personal with me," explained Wally. "When they ask questions I don't want to answer, I make a joke or something. Sooner or later, they've all gotten the message." Of course, there were times when Wally was lonely, and wished he were in a job that he really liked; but the thought of having to "train" new people to keep their distance was so unappealing that Wally stayed in his familiar, if lonely, territory. Procrastination protected Wally from a world in which he thought people would take a mile if he gave them an inch.

Procrastinators like Wally give the appearance of living in splendid isolation: they don't need anybody, and nobody needs them. They are usually well aware of their view that people are too demanding, too instrusive. What they are sometimes less aware of is their own inability to resist intrusions. They can't count on themselves to be able to draw the line once they start to feel drained. "If I invite somebody over for dinner," said Wally, "he'll stay all night. I'd never get him to leave, and then I wouldn't have any time for myself."

Wally uses all kinds of indirect means to retreat from people— he jokes, changes the subject, becomes quiet and moody, is sarcastic, and of course, he uses procrastination. What Wally doesn't do is say "No" directly. Once he's involved with someone, he feels unable to state his limits, and feels resentful when the other person oversteps these unspoken boundaries. No wonder he feels drained by the other person.

What's Mine Is Yours—So What's Left for Me? If you stopped procrastinating and actually finished something, you'd then have the pleasure of taking the credit for your accomplishment, right? Well, not necessarily. Some procrastinators expect that at the culmination of all their hard work and effort, someone else will be standing by to take the credit away from them. They worry that if their recognition is stolen, they will fade into the background, robbed of their identity. In response, they sometimes conclude, "If I'm not going to get the credit, why bother to make the effort at all?"

We all know people who like to take credit for someone else's work. At a party, you may hear someone else telling *your* joke as if it's an original. You may work for a boss who gets ideas from his employees but submits them to his supervisors as if they were his own. But for some people, being robbed of their deserved credit is so painful and upsetting that they would rather procrastinate than give someone else the opportunity to steal what rightfully belongs to them.

For example, Don is a chemist in a pharmaceutical company who works on independent research projects. He rarely gets his lab reports in on schedule, and he puts off updating his progress to his colleagues. Don avoids talking to the other researchers about his findings because he is concerned that someone will copy his ideas, taking the credit for work he has done. It's hard for Don to get very far on his experiments because he resents the fact that, in the end, his work will belong to the company.

Don's sense of self is intimately tied to his accomplishments, so if someone steals them away from him, Don is shaken at his core. "If somebody takes credit for my work, it's as if they've robbed me of myself." In order to keep people from stealing his thunder, Don doesn't make any noise at all.

Don could be more productive if he understood that there is a difference between sharing his ideas and losing himself. Then he wouldn't have to use procrastination to keep himself from gaining ground for fear that someone else might overtake it.

Similarly, some people don't let themselves progress because they don't want anyone else to share the pleasure of their accomplishments. John learned his trade while he was apprenticed to a master electrician. Although he realized that his mentor had taught him a lot, John couldn't tolerate giving his boss any of the credit for these skills. So John didn't utilize his skills to the utmost. He took manuals home but didn't study them; he left necessary tools in the shop and had to go back for them; he arrived late for some appointments. John said, "I know my boss taught me the trade, but I can't stand it when he says that I'm top-notch. He taught me everything I know, but it's *my* hands that do the work, not his."

John is threatened by his boss's pride in him. He gets confused about who actually does deserve the credit—mentor or apprentice. When someone else takes any credit at all, even if it's deserved, John feels that he's left with none for himself.

Procrastinators like Don and John may unfortunately end up being so protective of their skills and accomplishments that they lose sight of what it actually is they want for themselves. If you are afraid that your true interests, once made known to a predatory world, will be appropriated, you may go through life in the shadow of your true desires. Sometimes even you will believe this false picture of yourself.

Some procrastinators we've talked to learned to hide themselves because their true interests were often met with dismissal, criticism, or scorn. But for others, the need to hide seemed the only way to keep their interests from being taken over. One woman, who never had been able to choose a career, described how she had become hesitant to reveal, even to herself, what she really wanted. Anne remembered that as a child she had once announced to her family that she wanted to take piano lessons because her best friend was doing it. Suddenly, she found herself not only enrolled in piano lessons, but also in sight-reading and music composition classes. She was flooded with books on music, classical records, and posters of famous pianists. Everyone Anne knew was invited to her first piano recital, although she had hardly practiced for it. "I was mortified that it had become such a big deal. All I wanted was to learn to play the piano like my friends, and the next thing I knew I was caught up in a whirlwind of music that had nothing to do with me. Somehow the idea had captured my mother's imagination and she jumped in and took over. I'm sure there are a lot of kids who would have loved all the attention, but it didn't really feel like attention to me. It taught me a lesson, though.

When I wanted something, I had to keep it completely to myself, because as soon as I said anything, *zoom*—we were off and running. I got so practiced at keeping things to myself that I acted as if nothing ever mattered to me, and after awhile, nothing did. School was the same way: I never did my homework, so that it would look as if I didn't really care about anything. If I'd let myself even notice that I was interested in biology, I think my parents would have built a laboratory in the basement!"

Adaptations from childhood often extend into adult life and continue to hold people back. Without realizing the origins of her confusion, Anne's inability to choose an occupation was reminiscent of the old days when she couldn't afford to let anyone know what mattered to her.

The Second Time Around. Some people postpone getting involved with other people because they've witnessed first-hand the kind of trouble that it can bring. Perhaps they've seen some destructive relationships and have decided that they're not going to risk repeating those harmful patterns. Or maybe they themselves have been badly hurt and have vowed never to get into such a vulnerable position again. Procrastination can prevent them from getting into relationships that may result in that kind of pain.

A familiar example is the person who hesitates to get into a committed relationship because of problems previously experienced within the family. If you once had to stand by helplessly as your parents criticized, abandoned, ignored, or otherwise hurt each other, you may have concluded that settling down with someone is just asking for trouble. So, you delay asking for dates, improving your appearance, going to parties, or participating in other activities that might lead from meeting people to a more intimate involvement. Perhaps you maintain several superficial relationships, none of which ever evolve into the kind of dangerous coupling you're trying to avoid. It's as if you've looked ahead and decided that this romantic road can lead only to disaster, so you've decided not to embark on the journey at all.

Procrastination may also be protecting you from reliving some bad experiences in close relationships you've had yourself. For example, Dorothy's procrastination was most severe whenever she had to do anything that involved her new mother-in-law. Although the woman seemed nice enough and made numerous friendly overtures toward her, Dorothy put off returning her phone calls, delayed accepting invitations to dinner, and was always late sending gifts or cards for special occasions. "I'd like to feel closer to her," said Dorothy, "and I know my husband would like that, too. But I get so apprehensive at the thought of her becoming a part of my life that I freeze up."

Dorothy had a pretty good idea about why she was so frightened of getting closer to her mother-in-law. Her relationship with her own mother had been riddled with conflict and hostility. They fought about everything, from the way Dorothy dressed, to the boys she dated, to the right way to scramble eggs and make hot chocolate. "I was devastated by all her criticism," reflected Dorothy. "No matter what I did, she attacked me for it and used it as evidence of what a degenerate person I was." Further, her mother's relationship with *her* mother-in-law (Dorothy's grandmother) was competitive and antagonistic. "They were always arguing about the right way to raise children and to run the household. They couldn't seem to say anything decent to one another, and each of them wanted the rest of the family to take her side in the battle. People were pitted against each other all the time, and I think that's what eventually led to my parents' divorce. It was a real mess!"

For Dorothy, a close involvement with her mother-in-law seemed to threaten the harmony of her marriage. She feared that she would once again find herself in the kind of relationship she had had with her own mother, and that would lead to the replaying of her unhappy family experience. Her procrastination arose from the belief that letting her mother-in-law get too close was like handing over a loaded gun.

The Werewolf Within. If one reason for using procrastination to keep people away is the fear of what people could do to you if you became attached, another is the fear of what you could do to the people you became attached to. If procrastination is in some way holding you back from people, ask yourself what it is that you think would happen if you were to become more involved with others. Would you reveal a dark side of your nature that most people don't get close enough to observe? Might you be as demanding and judgmental with people as you are with yourself, making life miserable for everyone? Or perhaps you would discover a side of yourself that even you haven't yet seen but fear that the pressure of prolonged intimacy might bring to light.

We know many people, for example, who have postponed the decision to have children for fear that once they become parents, they will abruptly become replicas of their own mothers or fathers, adopting both the qualities they admire and the characteristics they deplore. One woman who came from a large family watched her mother's mental health deteriorate further with the arrival of each new child and concluded that there was a connection between staying childless and staying sane. Although she was lonely, she feared becoming more socially active—which, in her mind, would lead to meeting a man, which would lead to marriage, which would lead to having children, which would drive her to insanity and precipitate her own demise. She was a social procrastinator, but because she was convinced that parenthood would reveal the same dark side in her that she had seen in her mother, she paid the price of loneliness to keep her sanity.

The fear that behind your Dr. Jekyll persona there lurks a Mr. Hyde who, under certain circumstances, will leap out and take over keeps many procrastinators from working hard. They may have seen some hard worker be impatient or even cruel to people close by and assumed that there is a cause-and-effect relationship between being busy and being mean. Or they may have undergone a similar change of character themselves at a time when they became preoccupied with work. To prevent the werewolf within themselves from emerging, they may work hard in a social vacuum or avoid hard work and remain friendly. Sometimes they even double lock the werewolf's cage by being both remote *and* unproductive.

If you're worried about what kind of person you might turn into under the pressure of a close attachment, or what trouble you could unleash on others, you may also wonder how people would react to seeing the uglier sides of yourself. Could anyone know what you're really like on a long-term, day by day basis, and still like you? If you stopped procrastinating and became more intimate, could someone accept your quirks, your ill temper, your worst moments? In all likelihood, you are not as hurtful to the well-being of others as you might fear, and there are probably friends and lovers who will always accept you, even at your worst. But you'll never know if you persist in keeping yourself locked away, using procrastination as the key to safety.

It's Better Not to Love Than Lose. Most people who experience the fears we've just described are aware of not wanting to get close to others. Ironically, what they don't often realize is how much they long for the very closeness they so carefully avoid.

Some people want closeness so much that they feel frightened or overwhelmed by the intensity of their longing. One way of coping with these intense feelings is to block them out completely. In this way, a person may convince him or herself that relationships are a waste of time, that there are better or more important things to do in life besides developing personal bonds with others.

Underneath it all, however, these people are probably fearful of what might happen if they *allow* themselves to be close to another person. They are afraid that an intimate relationship might unleash not the werewolf within, but the side of them that needs people, that longs to be loved and comforted, and that wants to depend on someone for support, nurturance, and care.

Why is it so frightening to recognize a side of one's self that is as natural as the desire to become independent and autonomous? We've heard several themes repeated often by procrastinators who put off establishing intimate relationships. One is the apprehension: "If I want someone else, will he or she want me?" It is the fear that if they acknowledge their desire for closeness, first to themselves and then to another person, they might be rejected, or worse, their desire might drive the other person away.

"I would much rather wait for people to come to me," explained Tony, a cautious 26-year-old truck driver. "I don't like going after people, especially women, because when they turn me down I feel terrible. It's as if I had a big hole right in the middle of my body, like nothing's there anymore." When Tony is rejected, he feels more than just the disappointment and wounded pride that most experience in such a situation. By reaching out toward another person, he is extending *himself*, and if he is refused, he feels that he has lost a vital part of who he is.

Another fear some procrastinators have expressed is that if they let themselves develop a close relationship, they might discover how emotionally needy they really are. It's as if they worry that they might open up their own Pandora's box and in it they would find a deep and powerful longing for emotional intimacy. Once opened, the box could not be closed, and they fear they would never be free of that longing again.

One of the reasons that these people are so frightened by their longing is that, deep down, they are hoping for the perfect relationship with a mate who will unconditionally accept *every* facet of their behavior. Yet they realize that such complete and total acceptance is impossible in any human relationship. So, rather than face the reality of imperfect relationships, they avoid them altogether. It may seem best to keep the box closed right from the start, and procrastination may be their strategy for doing that.

For some procrastinators a related fear is the worry that once established, a close relationship would become so important, so essential, that they could no longer live without it. "What if I got close to a man and then we had a big fight? Or got divorced? Or, worst of all, what if he died?" said an apprehensive Marguerite. "I don't know if I could stand being separate from him after he had become a part of me and I had become a part of him. I would need him the way I need oxygen to breathe." The possibility of losing a person who had become important to her was so painful to contemplate that Marguerite decided long ago that she would never let anyone matter that much.

You may have learned the hard way that it's no use depending upon someone else. Your isolated self-sufficiency may be a survival tactic developed out of necessity, if your own needs for others were discouraged, ignored, or rejected.

If you were fortunate enough as a child to be able to take your needs and disappointments to a person who would comfort you or listen to you with compassion, then consider yourself lucky. Many weren't so fortunate. We've learned from many procrastinators who keep their distance from people that when they were feeling upset, unhappy, or needy, they found they were unwelcome in the family circle. Their dependence was met with such responses as, "If you're going to cry, go to your room," or "You're too sensitive— grow up."

The message that was conveyed implied that they weren't supposed to reveal their vulnerabilities to anyone: Strong people keep their troubles to themselves and only weak people ask for help. In a sense, they were taught to distrust their own dependent feelings and to assume that other people also would find that side of them unappealing. It's easy to understand how these beliefs could induce a person to keep to him- or herself.

Another common scenario in the early life of procrastinators who keep their distance is the child who is used for someone else's purposes and is not allowed to grow up for his or her own sake. This experience of being used can contribute to the fear that people will be a drain or will deplete you if you allow them to get too close.

For example, if you took primary care of your siblings in the place of a parent who was working, socially preoccupied, ill, alcoholic, or in some other way indisposed, you may have missed out on the carefree pleasures of childhood by having to grow up too soon. There may be some beneficial remnants of this early role of responsibility: a flair for leadership, an interest in helping others, an acceptance of obligations. But you may also feel that you are *expected* to accomplish things that are well beyond your capabilities, and so you exhaust yourself trying to do the impossible.

The experience of having given too much of yourself takes many forms: perhaps you were the family counselor or mediator who was always trying to make peace, or you tried to make an unhappy person happy, or you tried to take the place of an absent or incapacitated parent. All of these efforts, while they may have been the most appropriate role for you to play at the time, may also have been teaching you that getting involved can be at your own expense. These roles may have cost you your childhood, your hopes for nurturance, and your ability to be intimate. In retrospect, it seems a high price.

Procrastinating to keep yourself safe from the dangers of closeness may also cost you the opportunity to experiment with intimacy and commitment. You can't learn what your limits are or how to establish those limits with other people. You can't develop satisfying ways to moderate the demands of others. You can't experience the relief of being accepted and loved just as you are, or the confidence that you can tolerate intimacy without losing yourself.

Whether your primary fear is of separation or of attachment, procrastination may be your way of taking care of yourself, of maintaining the limits of your comfort zone. But relying on postponement and delay for your comfort does not address the more fundamental issue of your personal vulnerability. Procrastination may keep other people at the distance you feel you need, but it can't help you develop a more secure sense of yourself. It can't help you grow.

If you choose to become more involved with people, you will probably see that not everyone you meet will be eager to lean on you, depriving you of your own life. Nor will everyone reject you, unable to tolerate your desires for closeness. Yet, conflicts and disappointments will inevitably arise, as they do in all human relationships. Sometimes, a person who fears attachment gets hooked up with someone who fears separation, so that as one feels pursued and retreats, the other feels abandoned and pursues, and they both end up feeling that their worst fears have been realized.

It's important to face the issue of vulnerability directly, so that you can learn how to work out differences, overcome hurts and disappointments, and still have a satisfying relationship.

You may find that it is possible to be both dependent and independent in a relationship—in fact, it is *important* to be both. What makes a good relationship reassuring is that it provides a reliable, safe place to obtain comfort. What makes it fulfilling is that it permits, indeed encourages, each person to develop and grow as a separate individual. A good relationships needs a balance.

5

How You Came To Be a Procrastinator

In the last three chapters we've described how procrastination may be protecting a fragile sense of self-worth that is shaken by threats of judgment, control, closeness, or distance. All of us have to cope with times when our work or our characters are evaluated, times when we are subjected to someone else's power, and times when we are more alone or more intimate than we would like. And, as we have suggested, it is often the fear of such situations that sets the stage for procrastination.

But these fears are not random events that occur in a vacuum. They are triggered by certain kinds of circumstances, or by particular people, or by certain ideas. Some of your fears are probably based on situations that probably occurred for the first time long ago. Since then, they have influenced your perceptions and reactions to more recent events that continue to fan the fires of your procrastination. Now let's explore questions such as: How did you learn to define your self-worth on the basis of how you are judged, or how well you defend yourself from being controlled, left alone, or taken over? How did you develop procrastination as a strategy for self-protection? Which situations have contributed to your difficulty in doing what is important to you?

MODELS OF
SUCCESS AND FAILURE

One way to begin looking for the answers to these questions is to think about the people who influenced you as you were growing up. Parents, teachers, neighbors, siblings, and people you've read or heard about all can have a lasting impact. Sometimes they represent models of the kind of person you would like to be, for example, the young boy who wants to be "just like my dad" or the student who decides she wants to grow up to be like her third grade teacher.

There are also people who may also be models of what you do *not* want to be. A parent may be highly disorganized or inefficient, leading a child to decide that he will never be as disorganized as *that*! Or a parent may be so extremely efficient, giving top priority to work over everything else—including the family—that the child vows never to put work ahead of people.

Take a few moments to think about some of the people who were important models for you. In particular, who were your models for "success"? What about them made you think of them as being successful? What kinds of people were they? How were they viewed by others? How did they treat you? How did they treat themselves?

Now, think of the people in your early years who may have been models of failure. Who were the ones that everyone knew would never "make it"? What was it about them that made you think they were failures?

Who were the procrastinators?

Consider how these various models have affected you. You may, for example, have tried hard to be just like the most successful of them, doing your best to live your life the way you saw them living theirs. Or, you may have assumed that you could never hope to be as successful as they, and felt doomed to be like your models of failure. Or, you may have decided that, at all costs, you must *not* emulate one of your models, and so you tried to be everything he or she wasn't. If it's helpful, you may want to list your models, writing down your ideas about them and how you think they've affected you and your procrastination.

Here are a few examples of models that some procrastinators have described to us. One man remembered being awed and intimidated by his successful father, a hard-driving man who had pulled himself out of poverty and become an award-winning scientist. He worked twenty-four hours a day, non-stop, even using his time on the toilet to read scientific journals. "If you aren't doing something important," the father would say, "you're wasting the space you're standing in!" To the young child, his father was the epitome of success. As the child grew older, he drove himself relentlessly to emulate his father. In fact, because he started off in life with far more advantages than his father had as a child, he felt that he should surpass even his father's accomplishments. Doing anything for the sheer pleasure of it seemed a waste of precious time. There was no room to make a mistake, ever. Not surprisingly, he was often inhibited and unable to produce.

Another procrastinator, a restaurant manager whose delaying kept her business in constant jeopardy, viewed the women in her family network—her mother, her grandmothers, and her aunts—as having made nothing of their lives. As she put it, they were all "just housewives," content to spend their years living for their husbands and children. To her, they were failures. She was determined to have a busy career. Yet she was afraid of losing her family's support as she developed in her profession and grew further apart from them. Her procrastination kept her from going too far in her work and becoming an outsider in her own family.

Then there was the insurance salesman who would work very hard for a day or two and do nothing for the rest of the week. His model for work had been his divorced mother, who'd needed three jobs to support herself and her four children. She was so busy she rarely saw them, and when she did she was harried, overworked, and exhausted. Finally, the pressure became too much, and she suffered a nervous collapse. Determined not to end up like his mother, the salesman always relaxed for several days "to recover" after putting forth any effort on the job.

A final example is of a procrastinator who was strongly influenced by two of her elementary school teachers. One teacher was the model of efficiency. Every day she told the class exactly what would be covered. And, invariably, she would do everything exactly as she had planned. The procrastinator experienced this efficient teacher as humorless and unavailable, and remembers her with little warmth or affection. The other teacher, in contrast, was constantly disorganized and running late, yet she was a woman who really enjoyed life and who was playful with her students. For that young child, disorganization and delay seemed a much more appealing model than did efficiency.

Obviously, our decisions to be like or unlike specific people we have known are not always in our best interests. If you valued having a sense of humor and the capacity to enjoy living, and the only person you knew who had those qualities was a procrastinator, then you may have assumed that you had to procrastinate in order to have a good time in life. Or you may have thought that the only way to be successful was to be *exactly* like your model of success, with no deviations. So you came to think that you, too, must work twenty-four hours a day, and read scientific journals while sitting on the toilet. As adults, it's easier to look back and see that there were both positive and negative aspects to each of our models, and that it is possible to choose the characteristics you want to incorporate into your own life.

FAMILY ATTITUDES: THE MAKING OF A PROCRASTINATOR

Like all families, the family of the procrastinator transmits a set of values, attitudes, and beliefs to its children from a very early age. You were probably taught some basic ideas or rules about how the world works, about how people treat each other, about what is right and what is unacceptable, about what is safe and what is dangerous, about how to handle conflict, negotiation, and decision making. You may have accepted these notions without question, assuming that they were true for everyone. Or, you may have rebelled fiercely against the rules or values that your family espoused, disregarding their approval or disdain.

For most of us, separating our own personal values from those of our parents is a lifelong process. Indeed, the influences of our families are deep and pervasive enough that, even as adults, we are often affected by them without being aware of it. It's as if we become so accustomed to looking at things from a particular point of view that we forget that it is *only* a point of view. One procrastinator was startled when his boss approached a co-worker and said, "Mary, you've made a mistake." "Oh good," said Mary. "Tell me about it." The procrastinator had expected Mary to react with either defensive self-justification or tearful hysterics, but she did neither. Later, after talking with her about it, he understood that Mary views her mistakes as learning opportunities. It had never occurred to him that a mistake could be anything but an invitation for criticism.

When the assumptions and rules we learned in our families *automatically* govern our thoughts, feelings, and behavior, we can be headed for trouble, particularly if the rule is a very rigid one that inhibits our development as competent, creative individuals. It's like eating everything that is put on your plate without ever considering whether you like it, whether it's good for you, or even whether you're hungry! You just open your mouth and swallow.

It's important that you look over the array of ideas, assumptions, rules and expectations that have been laid before you by the significant people in your life. Some of what you have learned from your parents and other family members has been and will continue to be invaluable to you. Some of it probably gets in your way. Remember, even rules that seem to be carved in stone are, ultimately, only points of view. You can change them to suit you.

Among the expectations and beliefs that we grew up with were many different messages about who we were, what we were capable of, and what was expected of us. Originally, these messages came from the people around us, but over time they may have become so familiar to us that we made them our own. Ultimately, some of these inner voices may have contributed to our procrastinating.

Consider some of the messages that your inner voices convey to you. Recall the messages you got from people in your family—parents, siblings, or other relatives. In particular, consider several types of messages: those which you experienced as *pressures* to succeed, those that seemed to communicate *doubts* that you would succeed, and, finally, those that came through as *basic support* for you, regardless of your degree of success or failure.

You might find it helpful to write down each message you can remember in these categories and to identify the person it originally came from. If the message was an indirect one, try to identify what was communicated between the lines. One person may have given you different messages which seem contradictory and so may appear in more than one category.

Below are a few examples of messages that procrastinators have heard.

Pressures to Succeed

Mother:	I *know* you'll be a success! You can do *anything!*
Father:	If it's not done *right*, it's not worth doing.
Father:	I've always wanted a son to follow in my footsteps.

How You Came To Be a Procrastinator

Grandfather:	Coming in first is all that counts.
Father:	A mistake is an indication of a disorganized mind.
Mother:	You should have no problem. You were born with talent.
Father:	With your pitching ability, you ought to make the major leagues.
Mother:	You're such a good kid. What would I do without you?
Sister:	You're so pretty, you'll never spend a Saturday night alone.

Doubts About Your Success

Father:	All you have to worry about is finding a good husband.
Mother:	You're just a good-for-nothing loafer!
Father:	What do you want to go to college for?
Mother:	If you'd listened to me in the first place, you wouldn't be in this mess.
Father:	I was expecting too much from you. I should have known better.
Mother:	Why can't you take care of yourself?
Father:	I'm your father. I know what's best for you.
Brother:	All you'll ever do is just slide by in life.
Mother:	Well, at least you're cute.

Basic Support

Grandfather:	Whatever happens, we're always behind you.
Grandmother:	I love you no matter what you do.
Father:	That's not what I would do, but I hope it works out for you.
Mother:	You should live your life the way you want to.
Father:	Don't worry, everybody makes mistakes. It's only human.
Mother:	You're old enough to make your own decisions.

Look at your own list of inner voices and think about how they presently affect your life. In particular, how do they contribute to your procrastination? For example, as you begin a difficult task, do you hear your father's voice within you saying, "If it's not done *right*, it's not worth doing?" Or, as you begin to approach something that's new and unfamiliar, do you hear your mother warning you, "Be careful. You're not ready to take care of yourself." Your response to these internalized voices may be to feel so demoralized and apprehensive about your capabilities, that you then put off the task.

Though they may have been expressed with positive intentions at the time, many of the messages conveyed to you by your family can be extremely inhibiting for you later on. How can you respond to these unhelpful messages? When that inner voice says, "If it's not done *right*, it's not worth doing!", you might respond, "That's not true. It's worth getting started." Or, if that inner voice says, "Be careful! You're not ready!", you might stand up for yourself by saying, "It's all right if I don't know exactly what I'm doing. I can give it a try anyway."

The critical issue here is that it's important to separate your own self-image from the one you may have adopted in response to others' views of you. You do not have to accept as truth every assumption about how you fit into a scheme of success or apply those assumptions to how you live today. The more you are aware of the original sources of these familiar messages, the easier it is to lessen their influence over you.

In talking with many procrastinators over the years, we have heard five primary themes concerning their families described over and over again: Pressuring, Doubting, Controlling, Clinging, and Distancing. All five themes exist to some degree in every family. But each separate family system develops its own combination of methods for encouraging its members toward achievement, acknowledging the limitations of each person, making rules and enforcing them, holding the family together, and letting each other go. In your particular family, one theme may stand out as primary. Some families, for example, hold all their members up against a standard of achievement, while others are primarily concerned with demonstrations of family loyalty. Sometimes one issue is the source of most of the major disagreements, while other issues cause less trouble. By contemplating the interplay of these five themes in your own family, you may see a fuller picture of the development of your self-esteem and of your tendency to procrastinate.

The Pressuring Theme

The Pressuring Theme is apparent in families that are extremely achievement-oriented. Anything short of being at the top is a disappointment, is viewed as evidence of mediocrity. The adults in the family may be extremely successful themselves; for example, the parent who has won recognition, made a lot of money, or is exceptionally attractive. The family may be well-regarded in the community and communicate the importance of upholding the family name. However, the parents may also be people who are not satisfied with the degree of success in their own lives and therefore place their hopes for great achievements onto their children.

Jerry told us of an incident that is common when pressure is prevalent in a family. At the age of ten or eleven, he remembers sitting down to dinner one evening after he had come in second at a swim meet. His father, a serious, perfectionistic man, began to scold him: "Coming in second is a disgrace! You are either first or you're nothing! Do you want to go through your entire life being just like everybody else?" This same father declared, when Jerry once brought home a report card with a C on it, "No son of mine gets a C. You'll have to do better than this!"

In pressuring families, high standards are so rigidly adhered to that the child is not rewarded for many of the things he or she does do well. You may have made one mistake during a music recital and heard the comment, "How come you goofed up?" Or perhaps you brought home a report card with all A's and one B, and heard, "What's this B doing here?" Even when they are couched as jokes, such comments can be terribly undermining for a child. When they occur repeatedly, it is not surprising that a child would begin to place exaggerated importance on trying to achieve perfect performance. Perfection seems to be the only thing that's appreciated.

Pressure can also appear in another, quite different form. Were you ever told, "I know you can do *anything* you want!" Did your parents ever brag to their friends, "This kid is a genius. He'll get into *any* college he applies to!" Some families exert pressure by being overconfident in the abilities of the child, lavishing extravagant praise on his or her every effort. If you've ever had your average performance responded to as if it were the major event of the century, you know how such distorted and indiscriminate praise can leave a child feeling embarrassed, confused, fraudulent, and ultimately inadequate. It's as if your true ability can't stand on its own, but must be falsely embellished to get noticed.

An average performance may also elicit a reaction such as, "That teacher is an idiot for trying to teach such difficult material to young kids" or "Those judges don't know what they're doing. Of course, *you* should have gotten first place!" Comments like these blame external factors for the child's unspectacular performance, thereby preserving the cherished belief that were it not for such factors, the child would achieve great things.

Whether you grew up in a family in which nothing you did was good enough or everything you did was remarkable, it was probably difficult for you to assess your strengths and limitations realistically. Strengths didn't matter unless they were perfect; limitations were treated as if they were unacceptable.

Sometimes children are caught between two pressures: Nothing was good enough for one parent, while anything they did was outstanding in the eyes of the other. Pulled in opposite directions, they may have stumbled onto procrastination as a solution that allowed them to escape the head-on collision of these contradictory views. By delaying, they didn't really have to take either side.

Your siblings may have added to the pressure. If you had a sibling who was "perfect"—smart, attractive, talented, well-behaved—you may have felt pressured to keep up. If you felt you couldn't, it may have seemed easier not to try.

Conversely, if your siblings failed to meet the standards that your parents were hoping for, the pressure on you to be outstanding might have increased. Being the family's last hope for success is a tremendous burden for a child to carry. A freshman in college who was in danger of flunking out tearfully insisted that he *couldn't* fail. He *had* to go to medical school because his father desperately wanted one of his sons to be a doctor, and his three older brothers had all chosen different careers. In spite of the fact that he hated chemistry and never did any homework, he wanted to make up for his father's disappointment, and the high expectations had paralyzed him.

Such pressures can extend well beyond the immediate family. A very intelligent Chicano man was the first person from his small farming community to graduate from college. Everyone in the town proudly followed his progress through college, and later, graduate school. When he was home for vacations, people would tell him that his accomplishment was a triumph, not only for their community, but for all Chicanos. The young man experienced this praise not only as an honor, but also as a responsibility—one that he was not sure he could live up to. He began to feel that he was the representative of an entire culture, and, doubting his capacity to carry the mantle successfully, he struggled for years with his doctoral s thesis, never sure when it was good enough.

However the pressure was conveyed in your family, the focus might have been, and may still be, on what you *did* rather than on who you *were.* You are left with high standards for accomplishment and tremendous fears of disappointment and rejection if you don't live up to these standards. If your acceptance in your family has been tied to your potential to achieve greatness, it may seem safer to procrastinate and never risk falling short—particularly if you assume that the rest of the world functions the same way, demanding the impossible and being unhappy with anything less. You may have lost sight of the fact that most people will accept your own human limitations more than you think.

The Doubting Theme

In contrast to pressures which prod a child toward success, the Doubting Theme communicates the family's uncertainty and perhaps even outright disbelief in the child's ability to achieve. Doubts may be conveyed directly or indirectly, with force or subtlety, but in every case they let you know that little, if anything, is expected from you.

There are, of course, a variety of ways in which doubts can be communicated. You can, for example, be compared to a sibling who performs well academically. "Your brother got the brains, and you got the looks" is a classic remark which suggests that you have no brains at all. It also implies that there is room for only one intelligent child in the family. One procrastinator recalls his father's surprise when he got the school's top score in a math competition. "Wouldn't it be funny," mused the father, "if *you* turned out to be the smart one!"

Doubts can also be conveyed through comments that overtly devalue, undermine, or make fun of what the child accomplishes. Did your parent ever say, "What are you so proud of"? It's only a baseball game." Or, "Your lab partner must be real smart for you to get an A in chemistry." Or, "Don't kill yourself trying. You should just learn how to type, get a job, get married, and forget about it." The child who repeatedly hears remarks like these is likely to doubt his or her capabilities and put off doing anything that feels like a test, whether it's batting practice or homework.

A parent's lack of interest in a child may also be experienced as doubt. If you were given the lead in the school play and your parents didn't come to one performance, or, if you came home with an A on a test that you studied hard for and your father didn't even look up from the evening newspaper, or, if your ideas were repeatedly ignored during the dinner table conversation—you may have assumed that you weren't worthy of recognition, that you just didn't have what it takes to get them to be interested and involved with you.

Sometimes a parent is interested in a child only when he or she does well in those certain areas that the parent values. You may have been rewarded when you did something that fulfilled your parent's interest but ignored when you pursued an interest of your own. For instance, if you loved to draw, but your mother had no interest in art, she may never have given your work more than a token glance. Or, your father may have been helpful and attentive when you joined him on one of his fishing expeditions, but looked bored when you needed to talk about your new best friend. Without your parents' support, you may have doubted your ability to pursue interests and activities that were outside the scope of their interests. Doubting yourself, you may have put off activities which trigger the fear that you couldn't really do it on your own.

Parents who had unsuccessful or chaotic lives themselves may convey the idea that their children should not expect their own lives to be any better. Often, this is because the parents feel threatened by their children's progress. For example, some parents who did not have the opportunity to go to college won't come to their child's graduation ceremony, or if they do come, they find a lot of things to criticize. Very bitter parents may become especially critical when the child is enthusiastic about possibilities for the future. "The more I try to pull my life together, the nastier my father gets," said a man who was in the process of changing careers. "He never had a job he liked, and he doesn't seem to think I'll like mine any better."

Doubts may be conveyed in the context of the role you were somehow assigned in the family. If you were the family jokester, you may have difficulty taking yourself seriously. If the boys in your family were respected more than the girls, as a woman you may doubt your value because of your gender. If you were said to be "just like Uncle Jack," who played the piano as you do, but who was also alcoholic and depressed, you may lack the confidence that you could escape his fate and turn out any better.

How You Came To Be a Procrastinator

In doubting families, children learn that their efforts are likely to be downplayed, ridiculed, or ignored. They sense that there is no one on their side, ready to congratulate them if they do well or to cushion the fall if they fail. Failure may in fact be met with a self-satisfied, "I told you so!" The message that these children get is: You don't have what it takes.

Procrastinators who received doubting messages tend to live out their lives in one of two ways. One is to believe the doubts and act in accordance with them, as when a person retreats from anything new, challenging, or important. His or her spontaneous reaction is to feel apprehensive and think, "I can't do this." Even when they do take the initiative, they may give up as soon as the least difficulty is encountered. By not doing, the procrastinator is fulfilling a prophecy, reinforcing those old doubts.

The other way that procrastinators tend to respond to their doubting families is to rebel against them, taking on an attitude of, "I'll show them how wrong they are!" So they push themselves hard, determined to demonstrate that they can succeed in spite of the doubts, and indeed, they may accomplish much more than their families would ever have predicted. But such procrastinators often get caught in the trap of perfectionism. Being perfect seems to be the only way to disprove those old doubts once and for all. And we've already seen how such pressure to be perfect inhibits, rather than helps, progress.

Whether you have retreated or taken a defiant stance, you may need to realize the problem is this: you have internalized the doubts to such a degree that, when faced with the prospect of doing something new, you begin to lose heart. Procrastination appears to be a safe course of action, because it protects you from ever finding out what you fear to be the awful truth: You can't do it.

Procrastinators who come from families that continually expressed doubt tend to assume that any failure, big or small, means that all those old doubts are true, and therefore there is no hope at all for them in the future. What they have lost sight of is that one failure, or two, or even a hundred for that matter, does not make a person incompetent for a lifetime.

The Controlling Theme

The Controlling Theme is evident when family members take over and direct the child's life. A parent may make all decisions for the child—what to do, what to wear, how to act, whom to befriend—and give "advice" that the child is expected to follow without question. The controlling parent has difficulty tolerating the child's moves toward autonomy and quickly acts to restrict the child as soon as too much independence is apparent.

Parents can have several different kinds of inner experience that may lead them to control a child beyond what is necessary or helpful. Some are frightened and perplexed by the demands of parenthood. They may not know how or where to seek help. Bewildered, they may adopt a stance with their child that hides their uncertainty by acting as though they know exactly what they're doing. But deep down, they feel insecure and are threatened by any challenge to their competence.

These parents often feel more adequate if they demonstrate control and authority over their children. In their need for reassurance, however, they often exert too much control, becoming inflexible. Such rigid demands can only conflict with the child's natural inclination toward autonomy and individuation.

Other parents are so invested in their children that they insist that a certain image or expectation be fulfilled. Perhaps the investment takes the form of an unrealized dream the parents had. Perhaps it is the determination to shape a perfect person, one to be proud of and to show off to others. In any case, the problem is that the child's wishes are completely ignored or dismissed. The parent works hard to make the child into someone the child is not.

Still other parents tend toward overcontrol because they long to keep their children dependent. They may have yearned to have someone to take care of, someone who needed them and made them feel important. A helpless baby is perfect for this, since an infant cannot survive without a caretaker. However, as the infant starts to crawl and walk, becoming independent, the parent may feel his or her power slipping. Often a struggle ensues, with the parent rejecting every new attempt the child makes, punishing every infringement of the rules, insisting on cooperation just when the young child is intent on exploring his or her new-found independence.

The battle for control often begins during the earliest years of life, when a young child is least able to defend itself. A parent may explode with misplaced anger, and the child has no choice but to absorb cruel, hurtful comments, rage and hostility, and sometimes even physical abuse. Such explosions tend to depend on factors in the parent's life that are totally unrelated to the child:

a bad day at work, stress in the marriage, financial difficulties, the parent's own feelings of anxiety or self-doubt. Attack can occur at any moment, regardless of whether the child has been good or bad, done well or poorly, succeeded or failed.

Other children are taken advantage of more subtly, being consistently misled by one or both parents. A child may be taken on an outing for "fun," only to discover that the parent wanted the child's presence for his or her own needs, perhaps for company, to show off to friends, or as a buffer in an uncomfortable situation. Or, a parent may assign a chore, promising a reward when it is completed. Then when the child has almost finished, the parent suddenly changes the rules without warning. The child may now have to do "a better job" in order to "complete" the task, or an additional chore must be done before the reward will be given. The reward might be withdrawn altogether. Having been led to believe one thing, the child feels deceived because the tables have been turned unexpectedly. Too frightened to protest directly, the child may in the future slow down and do chores at a snail's pace.

If you grew up in a controlling family, you probably had little encouragement for experimenting with your independence or for mastering new skills on your own. When someone else is always directing your life, there's not much you can do but go along with it, particularly when you're dependent on that person for survival. You may have had experiences of being restricted or deceived, or of being attacked and humiliated. In such an environment, it is dangerous to be weak, since weakness can be exploited and abused by others.

In an effort to feel some measure of control, the child in a controlling family may turn to procrastination as a form of passive resistance. By delaying and refusing to do things, you could exasperate an intrusive mother or a demanding father and weaken their hold. Although in the long run procrastination may not have been in your best interests, this passive resistance may have afforded you a relatively safe way to fight back at a time when direct, open rebellion was too dangerous.

Procrastinators from highly controlling families often have problems in other relationships. Some are unable to make decisions or act independently. Many of them are so used to taking a passive role within the family that they seek out friends and partners who will control them as their parents did. Their initial relief may eventually turn into resentment, however, as they begin to feel constricted by the other person's directiveness. The very control that they had sought now infuriates them, but they are unable to express that anger directly. Procrastination may again become the chosen strategy for thwarting the other person and gaining a sense of control.

In contrast, those procrastinators who have fought against being controlled may be so wary of other people that they strive to remain completely independent. Developing intimate relationships is extremely difficult for these procrastinators, since the only kind of relationship they can imagine is one in which the other person will try, whenever possible, to control them. These people feel they must therefore be constantly ready to push back, to define themselves by the defiance of their procrastination. In pushing back, they push other people away.

The Clinging Theme

Clinging families encourage dependency even when it is no longer necessary or helpful. Family members aren't encouraged to grow up and leave home, to create lives and families of their own. Instead, the importance of holding the family together is stressed, perhaps by alluding to dangers waiting in the outside world, by implying that harm may come to those left behind if any family member should stray too far. From this perspective, it can seem cruel or foolish to leave home.

In some families, parents assume that children need to be helped, protected, and taken care of not only when they are young and needy, but even beyond adolescence and into adulthood. These parents become not just a source of support and encour-agement for their children, but a *lifeline* without which it is assumed the child cannot survive. For example, a high-school student delays writing his papers until the last possible moment, so his mother helps him. She not only discusses the papers with him, but she also comes up with suitable topics, writes detailed outlines for him to follow, and then checks and types his work before he hands it in. In her attempt to be helpful, this mother is depriving her child of the important experience of learning what he can do on his own. Instead, he has learned to turn to her rather than to rely on his own efforts to pull through.

Another example is a teenage girl who played hooky from school and went joyriding with a group of friends. They were all caught and referred to the vice-principal for disciplinary action.

Although the other students were punished, this girl was not, because her father spoke with the vice-principal on her behalf. She never knew how he got her off the hook—he just told her not to worry about it, he'd taken care of it. This was one example from a pattern of being rescued and suffering no consequences. As an adult, this woman puts things off until she's dangerously close to getting caught—her phone is about to be disconnected before she pays the bills; her cold is almost pneumonia before she sees a doctor; her husband is on the verge of leaving her before she will sit down to discuss a problem. Because she received so much help at home, she still expects to be rescued with no consequences.

Too much help makes the child feel supported but fundamentally incapable. Instead of becoming a separate person, the child feels he or she can only exist as part of this larger family organism. The feelings of inadequacy persist into adulthood, long after the person is able to live independently.

Another form of clinging is manifested in the expectation that the child take care of other family members. Explicitly or implicitly, a parent may convey the message, "I need you, don't leave me." The parent may be ill, in low spirits, or emotionally distraught; perhaps there is tension in the marriage and one or both parents turn to the child for support and reassurance. Or the parent may look to the child for assistance with one of the other children who always seems to be in trouble. This child may become a "parentified child," meaning that he or she takes over as the competent adult in a role reversal with the parent. Needy parents who, as children, did not get nurturance themselves, often expect their offspring to provide it.

The child who experiences such clinging pressures may believe that it is indeed his or her responsibility to look after parents or siblings. He or she may try to mediate disagreements, attempting to prevent any rupture in the family bonds. He or she may listen alertly for signals of discord, attuned to the moods and nuances of conversation and gesture, ready to step in and smooth things over whenever necessary. Or the child may feel so responsible that his or her own interests are sacrificed. The child may not go on dates or join in after-school activities; he or she may postpone doing homework in order to attend to family matters—playing cards with a bedridden mother, sitting up with a lonely father, or keeping an errant brother off the streets. In the end, children from clinging families may feel too needed to be able to leave the family. Or, if they do manage to leave, they do so with lingering feelings of guilt and apprehension. Indeed, it is with the family's tacit approval that these people may put off doing things that would take them away from home.

The ties that bind people to one another sometimes pull family members together against the rest of the world. In some families, there is a notion that *"We* are special" and corresponding ideas that *"They* don't understand us"; "don't share our values", "are out to hurt us." Thus, no one from the outside is invited in, and family members are not encouraged to mix with people beyond the family relationships. Outsiders are seen as being "too uppity" or "not our kind"; boyfriends and girlfriends are barely acknowledged. The sabotaging of friendships reflects the fear that outside relationships will destroy the cherished family ties.

A woman who postpones many social activities, such as calling people, accepting dinner invitations, and taking classes to pursue hobbies she enjoys, recalled that her family rarely had visitors. Bringing friends into the house had been considered an imposition on the family routine, and the idea of having guests always seemed to put a damper on things, since the family seemed to have more fun by itself. Weekends and vacations were always spent together, and family members rarely did anything from shopping to dentist appointments, alone. In effect, her family didn't seem to want her to meet other people, for that might eventually lead her to shift her loyalties outside the family. She learned her lesson all too well.

Members of a family in which the clinging theme is very strong usually don't realize that they represent an extreme of ordinary involvement and interdependence. They believe that this is how the whole world operates, and they expect other people will want to hold onto them just as tightly.

Like children of the doubting families, people from highly clinging households often react to this overinvolvement in one of two ways. Some continue to cling together, not having enough confidence or experience to dare living on their own. These people put off things that would make them more separate, such as getting a driver's license, leaving a job or a relationship, experimenting with some new activity that is not of interest to others in the family, perhaps even voicing a differing opinion.

The other common response is to struggle for some autonomy, to create some distance between themselves and other people. If the experience of being close has meant being smothered, leaned on, or isolated from the rest of the world, a person may decide that such entanglements are too unappealing to repeat. In later life, being so sensitized to feeling smothered, they may put off anything that might bring people closer to them. Such people live with a powerful fear of attachment, because their experience of attachment has been so stifling.

The Distancing Theme

The Distancing Theme is evident in families in which the members are unable to develop emotional closeness, physical affection, attentive interest, or protective comfort. One of the more apparent examples of distancing can be seen in parents who behave almost as if they have no children. They send out the message, "Go away, don't bother me," sometimes in words, sometimes in their behavior. Think of the father who comes home and plops in front of the television set for the whole night, ignoring everyone else in the house.

A parent may show disinterest in his or her child by being too busy or by preferring his or her own friends, work, or hobbies to joining in at the child's level. For example, a mother who loves to shop for clothes takes her 7-year-old daughter with her from store to store and does not understand why the child becomes restless after five hours in fitting rooms. Or, while parents are going through a divorce, they sometimes get so caught up in thinking about how the separation will affect their own lives that they don't give enough thought to the effects on their child, or pay enough attention to the child's distress.

More subtly, there are families in which people live very comfortably together, giving the appearance of being a "close" family, yet they really do not know each other. Each person lives within his or her own separate world, never sharing inner thoughts, memories or experiences with other family members. The household is like a well-oiled machine—it is smooth-running but impersonal. Work demands may consistently take precedence over family time; feelings are rarely expressed or even alluded to; upsets are played down, if acknowledged at all. In such a family, it seems impossible to connect with each other in an intimate way. Other families that manage to remain close when things are going well, become distant from one another when things are bad. When stress hits, each person withdraws and shuts out the others. In a distancing family like this one, everybody suffers alone.

One consequence of distancing is that children begin to wonder why no one is close, interested, or involved with them. In an attempt to account for the distance, they may conclude that there is something about them that keeps people away. Children in distancing families often come to feel that they are a burden, an intrusion, and that their needs are unwanted or intolerable. Rarely do they realize that they are in a situation that exists apart from them. Just as children often blame themselves for any distress, misfortune, or unpleasantness in the family, they also may feel responsible for the emotional distance that exists.

Following in the family footsteps, such children are often cautious about closeness, and may even pass these attitudes along to the next generation, by creating their own distancing families. The lesson they learn is that when they are in trouble, they are expected to keep their frustrations and disappointments to themselves. Sometimes this training lays the groundwork for procrastination, as when a person struggles alone with a problem, dragging it out and falling behind, rather than seeking help.

Because he couldn't stand feeling helpless and refused to ask for assistance, one man who grew up in a distancing family stayed home from work whenever he got behind on his job. As a child, he had learned to withdraw when he was unhappy, waiting until he felt better to rejoin the family. A characteristic incident occurred when he was five and fell from a tree. Although he had badly hurt his shoulder, he didn't cry. He didn't even tell anyone that he'd fallen. He suffered the pain in silence until someone noticed several days later that he could not carry a package he'd been handed. By the age of five, this little boy already knew that he was supposed to take care of problems on his own.

When children are afraid of their parents they may also withdraw. "Whenever my father came home from work," recalled one procrastinator, "I made sure I was in my room. As soon as I heard his car pull into the driveway, I headed down the hall. I always tried to have my door closed by the time I heard his footsteps inside the house. If I crossed his path, he was as likely to hit me as to say hello." Years later, as an adult, this man was still wanting to hide, and his procrastination afforded a way of keeping his ideas and opinions to himself. Like many other children who were kept at a distance by unpredictable or violent parents, this man had difficulty being in the spotlight or standing out in even the slightest way.

In an attempt to spark a connection with a distant parent, some children may try to make themselves so delightful, interesting, and appealing that people can't resist being drawn to them. In other words, the child tries to be perfect, thinking, "If I just make myself *better*, then they're bound to be interested in me." "Better" can be anything: more intelligent, more attractive, more self-reliant, more athletic, more dignified. "Better" is defined by the child's understanding of what the family values.

Under such pressure, the temptation to delay may be irresistible. We've seen the relationship between perfectionism and procrastination: the more you expect of yourself, the more frightening it may be to discover whether you can actually reach the sights you've set. When the purpose of having such high standards is to make yourself appealing enough to be worth someone's interest in you, the gamble may seem especially risky.

Some people from distancing families react by searching for relationships in which they can count on being close. Detachment has been so painful that their goal is to be as connected as possible, even to the point of not letting go.

The Family's Influence on Self-Esteem

There is no *direct* connection between family themes and fears. Coming from a pressuring family does not necessarily lead to a fear of failure, nor does a controlling family automatically instill a fear of losing the battle. People who have experienced a lot of pressure to achieve may be as afraid of success as they are of failure. They may be afraid of closeness because of the pressures they expect intimacy will bring, or they may be afraid of independence because they're not sure how much they could accomplish without the motivation of pressure behind them. In every family, there exists a combination of the themes we've mentioned, and the particular experience of one individual is influenced by the messages, the personalities, and the circumstances that occurred in his or her unique family life.

However, a family atmosphere of pressuring, doubting, controlling, clinging, or distancing, in any combination, can have important effects on the experience of an individual later on in life and, specifically, can play a key role in the shaping of a procrastinator. Perhaps the most tragic of these repercussions, and the one that is most directly linked to the fears we've discussed, is the inhibition of the development of a child's self-esteem.

A fundamental lack of support is common to all five family themes. The child may be overly or insufficiently praised for achievements, but little attention is paid to the child as a multi-dimensional person. The overly praised child is left with an unrealistic sense of omnipotence—"I can do anything!"—because the parent did not help the child tolerate failure and accept realistic limits. On the other hand, the child who received too little praise may continue to believe that he or she can never be anything but a disappointment—"I am nothing!". When aspects other than achievement are ignored, the child cannot develop a broadly-based image of him- or herself. A sense of humor, the capacity to make and keep friends, the development of hobbies or creative talents, the ability to empathize—these are only a few of the human qualities that are ignored or undervalued in many procrastinators' families.

This lack of reinforcement weakens a child's sense of self-confidence, leaving him or her more vulnerable to anxiety and fear. Difficulty within the family may contribute to the belief that the outside world is a dangerous place. Instead of feeling that life is a delightful experience that can bring fulfillment, the child is afraid that it's simply too difficult and that he or she is not up to the task.

All family experiences leave children with certain ideas about how to be loved. In some families, for example, one must take care of other people in order to be appreciated and shown affection. In other families, that same behavior would be considered intrusive or insulting; love is given instead to those who take care of themselves and leave others alone.

The child may come to believe that it is possible to be loved only when certain special conditions are fulfilled. In the child's mind is the assumption that I will be loved only if:

I am the perfect child
I don't threaten you with my success
I am always strong
I take care of you
I don't demand too much from you.

But these conditions for love provide a person with a very narrow foundation on which to build self-esteem. The child with such a precarious foundation becomes an adult who experiences a sense of well-being only when a similar set of conditions is met. Such an adult may say to him- or herself: I can only feel good about myself if:

I can be perfect
I don't stand out too much
I don't let anyone push me around
I'm attached to someone else
I'm separate from everyone.

In reality, though, no one can actually be perfect, protect everyone else from harm, be strong in every situation, or maintain optimal distance from other people at all times. Procrastination only helps to maintain the illusion that these conditions *can* be met and that once they are, love and self-confidence won't be far behind. But self-esteem does not develop from meeting limited conditions. It requires acceptance of a broad view of oneself as a complex human being. It requires self-love.

Remembering your own family experience can shed some valuable light on the reasons you've come to rely on procrastination. Even if you didn't actually start to put things off until you were an adult, the seeds of delay were planted early in life, when confidence and self-esteem were most vulnerable to family attitudes. If procrastination is a strategy you've developed for coping with some of the fears we've discussed, then looking back at the evolution of your life can be an important first step to understanding what you are afraid of and why.

6

Looking Ahead To Success

So, procrastination isn't so simple, is it? We've come a long way from attributing it to mere laziness, lack of discipline, and disorganization. And yet, your procrastination is understandable—it is not a phenomenon that just happens to you by chance. It is a behavior that you engage in for particular reasons, many of which we've discussed in the last four chapters.

In a sense, procrastination has served you well. It has protected you from what may be some unpleasant realizations about yourself and the way you live. It has helped you tolerate some uncomfortable and perhaps frightening feelings. It has provided you with a convenient excuse for not taking action. But, regardless of the reasons for your procrastination, and in spite of whatever "comfort" it has given you, you have also paid a price for it.

Look at the costs. You've inhibited your efforts both at work and at school; you've held yourself back from taking risks or exploring new possibilities; you've put a lid on the natural and spontaneous expression of your ideas and emotions; you've kept yourself acting in accord with a limited view of who you think you must be. Not to mention the price of impaired work performance, lost relationships, diminished self-confidence, feelings of anxiety, resentment, fraudulence, or despair. If you did let go of procrastination and faced your fears head on, what would happen? So what if you're not perfect? What's so dangerous about being successful or realizing your limits? Would you really be trapped if you made a commitment? If you stated your own opinion? Who says you can't be an individual if you did things according to someone else's timetable? You can begin to do something about your procrastination in spite of the fact that you are afraid. In the next section of this book, we're going to offer a number of specific techniques that can help you get started.

THE DANGERS OF IMPROVEMENT*

For people who have felt frustrated and thwarted by procrastination, the prospect of delaying less and accomplishing more may seem very appealing. In fact, you might think life would improve 100 percent. Many people believe they'll have the time to do whatever they want and the sense of relief and freedom that has eluded them for so long. They foresee new opportunities opening up as they accomplish things and become more successful. Many people also hope that after conquering procrastination they'll like themselves more, feel less stressed, have better relationships with people, and feel happier about their lives.

But people often don't realize that making progress can also be an uncomfortable process. For, when they finally do get rid of procrastination, the fears and apprehensions that they've managed to keep hidden will almost certainly rise up to meet them.

For example, if you become noticeably more productive at work, you could be promoted to a new position with even more demands and greater responsibilities. You might anticipate that you'd be in over your head, or you could feel awkward about supervising your old cohort. Or, if you finally make the decision to buy a house, you and your spouse might begin to argue about issues you've been avoiding, such as how much money you have

*We would like to acknowledge the members of the Brief Therapy Center of the Mental Research Institute in Palo Alto, California, who developed the term "Dangers of Improvement," in particular, Richard Fisch, Paul Watzlawick, John Weakland, and Lynn Segal.

to spend, or whose job location would determine where you both will live.

We are asking you to consider the "Dangers of Improvement," the troublesome consequences that might result if you were to give up procrastination. The potential dangers people foresee are not necessarily reasonable or logical. We're all so used to thinking about the wonderful aspects of ending procrastination that it often takes a great deal of effort to think about the potential problems.

Consider this: If you stopped procrastinating, what new problems or situations would you have to face that you don't have to contend with now?

Take a few minutes to think over this question. Try to come up with at least five Dangers that you might face if you stopped putting things off. Let your imagination go. Nothing is too far-fetched to be considered.

Below are some of the Dangers of Improvement identified by procrastinators we've known. They are listed according to several themes.

My illusions could be shattered...
> I'd have a concrete measure of my limits, talents, and failings.
> I couldn't feel superior if I found I was in the same boat as others.
> What if I finally do my best, but still am mediocre?
> I might not be able to achieve some things I'd like to.

There's always more work to do...
> I'll become a workaholic.
> I'll take on more responsibilities and put my own needs last.
> I'll become cold and unfeeling toward others.

It's lonely at the top...
> People will try to cut me down and find my flaws.
> If I discover I'm very smart, I'll no longer be an acceptable female.
> Other people might avoid me because of my success. I'd lose friends.

I'd lose control over my life...
> I'd have to accept a lot of other people's routines and expectations. I would lose my independence.
> I'd have to learn new things and be a novice again. I'd rather be the expert.

My relationships with people would change...
>   I'd start to feel competitive with everyone else.
>   I'd say "No" to others and they'd resent me.
>   People would stop comforting me.

Life would seem boring...
>   I would miss the excitement of "cutting it close."
>   I wouldn't be inspired—I might become predictable.
>   Things done early will seem too easy—nothing will be challenging anymore.

I'd be completely responsible for myself...
>   I couldn't blame other people or circumstances—I'd be fully responsible for what I do or don't do.
>   What would it be like to be completely on my own?
>   I'd have to make a lot of difficult decisions about how to spend my time.
>   If I stop, I might find out that I'm just covering up deeper problems.

I wouldn't be a nice person anymore...
>   If I'm successful, I might turn into a pompous ass.
>   I'd become self-righteous and disdainful of others who still procrastinate.
>   I might be dull, less fun, no longer a unique person.

Maybe I don't deserve this...
>   I'd have to admit I'm worth something.
>   I haven't punished myself enough for procrastinating.

I'd be even more disappointed in myself if I started to procrastinate again.

These Dangers of Improvement provide some clues as to why the cycle of procrastination is so hard to break. If you stop procrastinating, things will change. They may change for the better, or you may feel that you're on dangerous and unfamiliar ground. Until now, procrastination has seemed the lesser of many evils, by offering refuge in spite of its costs and restrictions. Your new, unprocrastinating self is unknown, and therefore represents a risk. One of the greatest Dangers of Improvement may be having to discover a new way to define yourself.

PROCRASTINATION AS AN IDENTITY

People vary greatly with respect to how much of their identity is wrapped up in being a procrastinator. Before you make a move to reduce the extent of procrastination in your life, we'd like you to consider some of the ways that delaying may give you a particular kind of personality or image that may be difficult relinquish.

The Lovable Clown

One way that people deal with procrastination is to treat it as a joke—and then build an identity around it. They may use their experiences with procrastination as comic material: entertaining friends with tales of their latest close call, making jokes as they arrive hours late for dinner, or laughing all the way to the post office at midnight on April 15. These comedians have made procrastination such an important part of their repertoire that giving it up could severely cramp their style.

Eddie regaled people with his procrastination stories. He told everyone he knew about the time he had to tape the unfinished hem of his pants cuffs in a department store bathroom because he bought a new suit thirty minutes before meeting the executive director of his company. At his office, Eddie was teased about taking the same work home with him weekend after weekend. In his college fraternity, he'd been voted "Most Likely To Rush." Eddie's procrastination gave him a role to play and a way to entertain people. It was hard to imagine what Eddie would be like if he weren't always late, and always joking about his last-minute crises. If he gave up the comic role, he wasn't sure exactly who would emerge, or whether people would still find him appealing.

The Saint

Some people add purpose and direction to their lives by taking care of others' needs while procrastinating on their own. This connection makes them feel needed and special and distracts them from the fact that they're stuck themselves. You may be so available to others, in fact, that you never have time to attend to your own duties. Even if you've planned to spend the evening on work you've brought home, if a friend calls in tears, you're on the phone for two hours. When the PTA asks you to be chairperson of the spring festival, you agree, even though it means you won't get your inventory figures in on time. All because you are *needed.*

You may be pleased that you are the one people call on when they want advice, comfort, or assistance. Doing for others has some very obvious rewards: people like you, feel grateful to you, are dependent on you. It's possible to offer them so much of yourself that you both begin to believe that you are indispensable.

Because it seems so justified, being available to other people is a deceptive kind of procrastination. At each moment when you choose to do for someone else instead of doing for yourself, you seem to be making an unselfish, generous, praiseworthy decision. Under these conditions, it's very difficult to develop a sense of yourself and what's best for you. Your own identity and your own goals never have a chance to emerge as long as you're playing a role that is designed to take care of someone else.

We're not advocating that you lead a completely selfish life, intent only on pursuing your own goals. But if taking care of others has become one of the main ways in which you delay, then in order to stop procrastinating you will have to learn to take care of yourself as well.

The Renaissance Man

Some procrastinators create an identity based on knowing something about everything. They want their lives to encompass every dimension of human interest, from politics, art, and philosophy to jogging and basketweaving. They refuse to be limited to one field of study, one special interest, one predictable career.

Often, these people are unable to use their considerable talents to their own benefit. The need to be well-versed in *everything* often prevents them from pursuing *anything*. Believing they can embody the Renaissance ideal, they end up spreading themselves in so many directions that they can't move forward.

The Miracle Worker

Another kind of identity is that of the troubleshooter who is admired for resolving last-minute crises. With heroic effort, these people are able to prevent disaster and save the day—they meet a deadline by working frantically for thirty-six straight hours or come up with a brilliant solution to buy more time. They are seen as miracle workers.

Often, the crises these people are heralded for resolving are of their own making. Disaster is imminent only because they've procrastinated themselves into a corner. Without their delay, they would have no problem to solve, no miracle to work in the first place.

The Blank Slate

Procrastination can camouflage the fact that you may not be very clear about who you are and what you want for yourself. It may look as if you haven't achieved your goals because of your problem with procrastination, but perhaps in fact you haven't come to grips with what your priorities are in the first place: What *are* your interests, preferences, values, needs, and goals? Without such self-knowledge, even if you were to stop procrastinating, you might not know what to do with your new-found ability to make progress.

If you haven't asked yourself questions about what you really want out of life, or if you've asked and not been able to find any answers, you may be left with a sense that your life hasn't much direction or purpose. This lack of direction may set the stage for procrastination. People who can't clearly discern what really matters to them may be equally interested in each new opportunity that comes along. Incomplete work may pile up as they abandon one activity after the other. If you are up to your eyeballs with half-finished projects, lists of things to do, anxiety about deadlines upcoming and deadlines missed, you may be filling yourself up with worries because you need to fill up with *something*.

The Person Beneath the Procrastinator

There is a big difference between the outward appearance of being on time and the internal experience of eleventh-hour anxiety and pressure. The greater the discrepancy between how you appear and how you feel, the greater the likelihood that you will feel like a fraud.

Whether delay has been a limited or pervasive part of your identity, in order to change your patterns of procrastination you will have to take a clearer look at who you are without it. The first step in moving ahead is getting to know yourself apart from your procrastination: recognizing your values and interests, your strengths and weaknesses. Then you can begin to accept yourself as you are, not as you wish you were or think you should be.

Identifying your values and priorities may require you to separate yourself from some of the ideas and roles that you have incorporated over the course of your lifetime. You'll need to recognize what's important for you, independent from what's important to your parents, your siblings, your spouse, your children, your boss or mentor, your friends, and other significant people in your life. Sometimes delaying behavior reflects the discrepancy between what you think is expected of you and what you really want to do.

Similarly, procrastination may be a warning that you are trying to pursue a course that raises some moral or ethical questions for you. For example, a carpenter berated himself for being repeatedly late to his new job. When he analyzed the situation, he realized that he questioned his boss's business practices. The contractor who hired him was involved in several shady business deals, including using illicit monies to build houses. The carpenter's tardiness was a sign of his reservations about working for a man he didn't respect. In another case, a young woman lamented her delay in making an investment decision until she realized that she didn't want to be a stockholder in the company that her brother was promoting so enthusiastically. The company had been accused of unfair labor practices and discrimination in the hiring of new employees, and the woman felt that she could not, in good conscience, support it.

At times, you may find that your values and priorities are actually congruent with those that other people have transmitted to you. You may want for yourself exactly what someone else wants for you. If this is the case, then it is important that you be able to retain these priorities even though they also match someone else's expectations. As we have seen, many people procrastinate as a way of resisting the influence and control of others, giving up what they want in the process. If this is relevant for you, consider: Is it really more important to rebel by denying your values than to pursue what matters to you?

It is sometimes hard for procrastinators to trust their own priorities because they tend to judge their values and actions so harshly. They constantly compare themselves with some standard that seems to reflect the *right* way of being a person and the *right* way of doing things—as if there were in reality one right way. Procrastinators are very hard on themselves. In fact, for some, their own "internal judge" is often so critical, so biased, and so impossible to please, that it is more appropriately called a prosecutor than a judge. A judge hears evidence from all sides and tries to make a fair decision. A prosecutor wants to prove guilt and only produces evidence that will help fix blame. And an inner prosecutor has free reign to make vicious personal attacks whenever it likes. It acts as no friend would, hitting in the aftermath of disappointment, offering no consolation or encouragement for the future.

The inner prosecutor's specific criticisms will vary, depending on the issues most sensitive to the procrastinator. Rick, the architect who wanted his own firm but was afraid of being too successful, heard his inner prosecutor saying, "Who do you think you are, anyway? What makes you think you can take the pressure of having your own company? Who are you to take business away from people who have been your friends?" Henry, the accountant who resists feeling controlled, heard from his inner prosecutor, "Only a weakling would go along with that order. Next thing you know they'll be walking all over you." Unfortunately, for many people, the critical voice of the inner prosecutor dominates their lives and goes unchallenged.

To counter the allegations of their inner prosecutor, procrastinators can develop another inner voice, that of a "defense attorney," to speak on their behalf when the prosecutor starts in. David, the lawyer who wanted to prepare every case brilliantly, wrote down a conversation between his inner prosecutor and his newly-hired defense attorney. You could try the same exercise, mentally or in writing.

Prosecutor: You stupid idiot! You screwed up again. You're not smart enough to be working for this firm, and sooner or later they'll find you out.

Defense: I think I could have gotten the jury on our side if I'd found a more convincing argument.

P: A law school student could have been more convincing than you were! You didn't think of the really important points until it was too late, and what good does that do?

D: Now, wait a minute. I wasn't *that* bad. Our firm knew that case was a risk when we took it on. No one thought it would be the open-and-shut kind.

P: Then you were stupid to take it on. You should have kept your nose out of it if you couldn't deliver. That's a real sign of incompetence.

D: Losing one case doesn't make me incompetent. I did a reasonable job on it, even though it wasn't perfect. Nothing ever satisfies you.

P: I'm only demanding for your own good. Without me, you'd have no drive, no motivation.

D: That's not true. I could do more if you didn't constantly attack me.

The challenge, then, is learning how to come to your own defense, to allow your own values and actions to emerge as much as possible, judgment-free. There is no absolute right or wrong answer to the question: What do I want for *myself?* This means that you have to separate yourself not only from the influence of others, but also from your own well-practiced critical perspective. You have to get out of your own way.

By diminishing the power of the prosecutor, you can gradually develop a more realistic perspective of yourself. With this broader view, you can acknowledge your limits, realize you won't win every battle, and let people come and go in your life—without worrying about your ability to survive. You can then get on with living—discovering what you want and feeling sure you'll take the necessary steps, working toward it, and deriving pleasure in the process.

In the next part of this book, we're going to describe some steps you can take if you're ready to give up the protection of procrastination. If you're ready to know yourself better by experimenting with goals, limits, accommodations, and relationships, we have specific suggestions for taking action. It's up to you. What do you want in your life—progress, or more procrastination?

Part II:

Overcoming Procrastination

7

Taking Stock: A Procrastination Inventory

In Part I, we focused on the emotional factors involved in procrastination. Now we want to look at behavior: what you've done and what you're doing when you delay.

A step toward managing procrastination is to familiarize yourself with your own personal way of postponing. Although most procrastinators are used to living with delay, they usually don't think much about it except to wish it would go away! It helps to look at your procrastination as if you were an objective observer. If you can, put aside any tendency to criticize and condemn yourself. For now, you're just taking inventory, trying to become more aware of your own experience with procrastination. We'll ask you to consider your procrastination on three different levels: what you do, how you think, and how you feel.

EXAMINE YOUR WAR STORIES

Think back over some of the occasions when you put something off. People often remember one or two particular incidents that stand out for them. The incidents may have happened two hours ago or two years ago; they may have been catastrophic, or perhaps they wouldn't even seem significant to someone else. Sometimes a situation that looks very innocuous on the surface can have a great emotional impact.

Write down two or three of the experiences that you remember best. What happened? Who was involved in the incident? What led up to your procrastinating? How did you feel? What was the eventual outcome? Who else was hurt or inconvenienced?

An example: A man in his mid-thirties described an incident of procrastination that really upset him. As he was leaving his house one morning, he remembered that he had forgotten to make an important phone call. He was already late, had been busy doing a number of last-minute things, and was feeling rushed and irritable. Still, he went back in, dialed the number, and to his annoyance got a recorded message informing him that the person was unavailable. In a burst of frustration, he slammed the receiver down and it broke in two. Appalled by what he had done, he began to worry about what the phone company would do when they found out what happened. In his mind, they would be horrified and would think that he must be a bizarre person to break a phone in anger. Feeling embarrassed and afraid, he avoided calling the phone company, even though it meant he was without telephone service. As the days passed, he rehearsed several plausible stories that he could use to explain the broken receiver to the phone company personnel. Finally, after ten agonizing days, he summoned up enough courage to make the dreaded call.

You can probably guess the outcome. He told the company representative that his receiver was broken, and before he could launch into his carefully prepared fabrications, the representative said, "Oh, don't worry. It happens all the time. When can you stop by to get a new phone?"

Review the incidents you've described and ask yourself if there are any common themes or patterns among them. Were you afraid of something each time? Did you try to accomplish too much? Was there something you were angry about or dissatisfied with? Were you asserting your independence? Did you begin a project and give up just before you completed it? Or did you have trouble just getting started? Was someone looking over your shoulder, or were you all on your own?

Procrastination, like all behavior, has consequences. The repercussions vary. Sometimes the consequences are obvious to you and to everyone else: the car that ran out of gas in the middle of the freeway, the woman who is fired because of chronic tardiness and lack of preparation, the garage that is filled with half-completed projects and boxes still unpacked from the move ten years ago. These are some examples of *external* consequences. They are apparent and observable.

As we noted in the first section of this book, many procrastinators experience *internal* consequences as well. These can include feelings of inadequacy, sadness, guilt, fraudulence, panic, and a sense of never really being free to enjoy the pleasures of living. Although a person may appear to be successful, competent, talented, intelligent, and generous, the internal consequences of procrastination place a tremendous strain on any life and prevent a feeling of confidence and satisfaction.

Consider the following list of the possible consequences. Which ones apply to you? Are there others?

Consequences

External	Internal
monetary loss	self-criticism and deprecation
loss of friendship	embarrassment
lowered grades	anxiety
incomplete academic program	lack of concentration
conflict with boss	inability to enjoy other activities
conflict with co-workers	guilt
decreased job responsibility	sense of fraudulence
lowered credit rating	tension
tension with parents	panic
tension with spouse or partner	depression
tension with other friend or	sense of excitement or thrill
family member	physical exhaustion
job loss	physical illness
marital separation or divorce	
governmental penalties (e.g., tax	
fines, arrest warrants for park-	
ing tickets)	
accidents or physical injury	

Now that you have reviewed your procrastinating behavior and its consequences, how do you feel? Sad? Angry? Relieved? Sobered? If you are caught up in berating yourself for your stupidity, your moral weakness, or your unchangeable character, try to step back for a moment and quiet your internal critic. Remember, taking stock of where you have been is a very important first step.

YOUR PROCRASTINATION TODAY

Your Areas of Procrastination

There are many different ways in which procrastination can appear in people's lives. Some people procrastinate only in one specific area and in every other area do just fine. A woman who was married, had two children, and a full-time job was very efficient at work and in organizing the household, but could never seem to keep up with correspondence and financial records. She had a room full of papers to be filed, letters to be answered, and receipts to organize. She would feel so overwhelmed whenever she went into the room that she simply kept the door closed and ignored it as much as possible. Except for that room, she felt that her life was going pretty smoothly.

In contrast, some people procrastinate in almost every aspect of their lives. An airline pilot in his forties didn't pay his taxes for years, put off necessary home and car repairs, didn't pay his parking tickets, never developed a lasting relationship with a woman, and planned for years to stop smoking.

It is rare indeed to find a procrastinator who puts things off in *every* area of his or her life. Even the pilot mentioned above was always on time for work, and, procrastination or not, he did make it through flight school. The important idea here is that there is no such thing as a "hopeless" procrastinator. Even if you think of yourself as completely lazy or undisciplined, it is unlikely that procrastination carries over into every facet of your behavior.

To help you distinguish between those areas in which you procrastinate and those where you don't, we've compiled a checklist of activities grouped into six categories: household, work, school, personal care, social relationships, and finances. You will probably find that no matter how pervasive you believe your procrastination to be, when you take a closer look you'll see that you procrastinate selectively.

Household

____ day-to-day chores (e.g., dishes)
____ minor home projects or repairs
____ gardening and yard maintenance
____ calling a repairman
____ returning defective or unwanted merchandise
____ large home or yard projects
____ car maintenance and repairs
____ paying household bills
____ grocery shopping
____ running errands for spouse or children

Work

____ being on time for work
____ being on time for meetings
____ making business phone calls
____ making decisions
____ doing paperwork
____ writing reports
____ confronting someone about a problem
____ complimenting someone
____ implementing creative ideas
____ billing clients
____ asking for a raise or promotion
____ arranging a meeting with your boss
____ keeping up with work-related reading
____ looking for a job, planning a career direction

School

____ attending classes
____ doing homework assignments
____ keeping up with reading for classes
____ studying for tests
____ writing papers
____ talking with a teacher or advisor
____ applying to college
____ doing bureaucratic tasks (paying fees, etc.)
____ completing degree requirements
____ returning library books
____ completing a graduate program (finishing a thesis, taking oral or comprehensive exams, etc.)

Taking Stock: A Procrastination Inventory

Personal Care

_____ getting physical exercise
_____ losing weight
_____ stopping smoking or use
of alcohol or drugs
_____ making medical or
dental appointments
_____ personal hygiene
(bathing, grooming)
_____ shopping for new clothes

_____ getting a haircut
_____ reading for personal
interest
_____ pursuing hobbies or
personal projects
_____ taking courses for
personal interest
_____ taking vacations
_____ making long-term life
decisions

Social Relationships

_____ calling friends
_____ asking someone for a
date
_____ personal correspondence
_____ inviting people to your
home
_____ visiting relatives
_____ calling or writing
relatives
_____ planning recreational
activities with other
people
_____ expressing appreciation

_____ giving gifts or sending
cards
_____ giving parties
_____ being on time for social
events
_____ asking for help or
support
_____ confronting someone
about a problem
_____ telling someone you're
angry or upset
_____ ending an unsatisfying
relationship

Finances

_____ filing income tax forms
by April 15
_____ paying quarterly taxes
_____ organizing receipts and
tax records
_____ finding an accountant
_____ budgeting your money
_____ making financial
investments
_____ calling the bank about a
problem
_____ paying credit card bills

_____ paying parking ticket
fines
_____ paying back institutional
loans
_____ paying back personal
loans
_____ collecting debts owed to
you
_____ paying insurance
premiums
_____ balancing your
checkbook

In each area, consider how much your delaying bothers you. The areas in which you procrastinate most extensively may or may not be causing you the most trouble. For instance, you may be in the habit of leaving dirty dishes for several days in a row, but a sinkful of dishes may not bother you. However, even though the problem arises only periodically, you may be very upset about your tendency to put off buying cards and gifts for friends and relatives.

Think about what differentiates the things you put off from the things you do on time. What themes or patterns do you observe? What do they tell you about your procrastination? Do you put off minor maintenance chores or do the most important things get postponed? Are the activities you put off areas in which you're expected to excel or areas in which you have little experience? Are you aware of any fears or anxieties about the things you postpone?

Your Style of Procrastinating

People procrastinate in very different ways. One person may spend a lot of time on the telephone and never get around to cleaning the house, while someone else may vacuum twice a day instead of returning phone calls. A woman goes sailing for the weekend, whereas a young man sits at his typewriter fantasizing about being a successful professional, a talented athlete, or a Don Juan. There are thousands of things people do when they procrastinate. Here are just a few samples of what we have heard:

I raid the refrigerator.
I read mystery novels and science fiction.
I start calling up my friends.
I work on something that's less important.
I become obsessed with cleaning my desk.
I go out jogging.
I sit and stare.
I keep doing research.
I watch TV.
I read the newspaper.
I go to sleep.
I go shopping.

What do you do when you procrastinate? Notice as many things as you can think of, including both your typical patterns and your most unusual delaying tactics.

At times it can be tricky to distinguish between procrastinating and not procrastinating. For example, when is reading the newspaper delaying and when is it doing something you enjoy? Or when is housecleaning a task that needs to be done and not procrastination? If you are someone who constantly gets angry at yourself for putting things off, it is important to learn the difference between goofing off and relaxing. Even procrastinators deserve to have fun.

Most people experience some clues that tell them that they are procrastinating. Often it's a nagging voice in the back of their minds that says, "You've got to get started sooner or later!" or "You know you shouldn't be doing this." They may have a visual image of what they are avoiding or of the consequences that might follow. One procrastinator said, "When I procrastinate, I see a vivid picture of my boss scowling and shaking his finger at me." Some people feel a physical cue, such as tightness in their stomachs, headaches, or tension in their shoulders, necks or backs. Or they may be unable to concentrate or to enjoy what they are doing. What are the specific clues that tell you that you are procrastinating?

Your Excuses for Procrastinating

Think about that moment in time when you could either get started on a project...or put it off. Here you are, faced with the possibility of making the phone call, writing the first sentence of the report, unpacking the first box, or whatever you might need to do. Now, what do you say to yourself at that moment that somehow justifies *not* doing it?

One excuse that we frequently hear is, "I'm too tired right now. I'll take a rest and then I'll feel more like doing it." Or, "I don't have enough time to do it all right now, so there's no point in starting." Some other common excuses are: "I've got plenty of time to do it later," "I've got to organize my desk first," or "It's too nice a day to spend on this."

What excuses do you use when you procrastinate? List your excuses and give yourself time to identify as many as you can.

Some people have trouble thinking of their excuses at first. These thoughts may occur so rapidly and so automatically that they don't seem to be thoughts at all. But these kinds of ideas do indeed occur and can be discovered if you give yourself time to think slowly through your temptation to delay. Here are some other common excuses for procrastinating:

I don't have the proper equipment.
I've been working so hard—I deserve a break!
It might not be good enough.
If I wait, I can do a really first-class job.
I'll wait until I'm inspired.
I need exercise first.
It's important to keep up with what's going on in the world, so
  I'd better read the newspaper.
It's too late in the week to start.
Why mail it Friday? No one will look at it until Monday anyway.
If I wait long enough, they'll forget about it.
I'll call later when the rates go down.
Why bother to ask? The answer will be "no" anyway.
I've done the worst part of it; the final step will be a breeze.
Two hundred years from now, will this really matter?

Try to keep track of your excuses over the period of a week. In particular, pay attention to the thoughts that occur at those very moments when you first put off something you want or need to do, the thoughts that provide you with a justification for waiting. It's a good way to become more aware of what goes on inside your mind and also to observe how your thoughts have an effect on your behavior.

There are a number of ways to monitor your excuses. We'll describe several methods, and you can choose those that seem best for you. First you might want to monitor the frequency of your excuses as they occur each day. If you rely on the same excuse more than once, notice how often you used it.

Another method of monitoring is to focus on the context of your excuses. See if you can identify what happened *just before* you came up with a reason to procrastinate. What were you thinking, feeling, or doing at that earlier moment? What were the circumstances? This is referred to as identifying the antecedents of your excuses—those events, feelings, or behaviors that precede a reason to delay.

For example, one man promised to build a table for his girlfriend. Instead of heading into his workroom, he found himself thinking, "It's too nice a day to be cooped up inside." What was the antecedent?

That morning she had called to discuss the table. "You're such a craftsman," his girlfriend had said, "everything you build is a work of art." He envisioned the look of disappointment on her face once she saw the finished product. He thought about how much he wanted to please her, and he started to brood about where the relationship was going. These worries were the antecedents to his excuse.

Remember, the goal in monitoring your excuses is to *observe* yourself. Don't try to change your actual behavior just yet. Being able to identify your excuses more rapidly doesn't necessarily mean that you'll suddenly be able to get started. In fact, we sometimes suggest to people that they deliberately continue to procrastinate for at least a couple of weeks in order to have time to observe their current behavior more fully.

As you become familiar with your excuses, it may seem to you that they are not excuses at all. You probably *do* need exercise, and you might truly be tired, bored, uninspired, hungry, or sick. The house probably could stand to be cleaner, and your desk could be a lot more organized. Each of these statements has a grain of truth in it, and probably seems compellingly true when you are faced with something you would rather avoid.

But even if a statement is in fact true, its *function* is to help you avoid doing something else. A statement of fact may become an excuse. You are using a true statement to conclude, "Therefore I don't have to do it now." For example, "It might not be good enough, so I don't even want to think about it now"; "I'm tired, so I can't do this now"; "There's an interesting program on TV. I want to watch it, so I'll do this later."

Everybody feels tired, bored, uninspired, or too busy from time to time. But some people still manage to get something done under these adverse conditions, at least some of the time. Why do procrastinators find it more than just a little harder?

Some procrastinators experience difficult conditions and feel discouraged, thinking that nothing can be accomplished, so they give up. Other procrastinators resent difficulty and feel thwarted, thinking that they shouldn't have to be bothered. In either case, they are ready to believe their excuses—and stop.

Non-procrastinators experience difficulty, too, but they probably think about it differently and are able to come to different conclusions. They do not always allow a difficulty to become an excuse. They consider what they *can* do and get started. Below are some examples of how a non-procrastinator might think:

"It might not be good enough, but I'll give it a try anyway."

"I'm tired. I'll just work for a half hour and then I'll go to bed."

"There's an interesting program on TV. Can I get a little bit done before the show comes on?"

"I don't have the proper equipment, but is there something I can do without it?"

"It's Friday. It's too late to finish it this week, but I can at least get started today."

When you catch yourself making excuses for not going ahead, you might try to come up with a new conclusion, one that allows you to do something that helps you at least get started, instead of giving you a reason to put everything off until later.

CHOOSING A PLAN OF ACTION

In the following chapters, we have brought together a smorgasbord of techniques to address the various aspects of procrastination that we have been discussing throughout the book. Some of the techniques may be familiar to you already, particularly if you've read books or attended seminars on time management. Other techniques will be new, and you'll need to spend some time thinking about them as you begin to put them into practice. Like all skills, they need to be used and refined over time. Though they may seem confusing or unnatural at first, with practice it will become easier to incorporate them into your life.

We suggest that you experiment with *one* technique at a time. Trying to put them *all* into practice immediately may make you feel overwhelmed, overworked, or discouraged. The result is likely to be that you will give up before you achieve any real progress.

One of the most important suggestions we can make is: *go slowly*. For many of you, there will be a temptation to move full steam ahead, to throw yourself whole-heartedly into this project, as you have done in so many other situations. Yet, as we have already said, trying to do too much is often part of the problem—so, SLOW DOWN. You won't stop procrastinating altogether tomorrow, or next week, or next month, no matter how much you want to or how hard you try.

There's another very important reason for changing slowly. Whether you like it or not, procrastinating has become a familiar way of life for you and for the people who live and work with you. In a sense, you have developed a routine. Change, even if for the better, introduces an element of the unknown; it is something different, something new that requires adaptation. If you change too suddenly, other people won't know how to deal with you and interpersonal conflicts may arise. You, too, may find it difficult to integrate sudden new behaviors with your old identity as a procrastinator, and this may lead to conflict within yourself. It is far better to change gradually, giving yourself and those around you the opportunity to adjust, bit by bit.

Some of you might want to consider doing these exercises with a friend. This can be helpful for a number of reasons. First, many procrastinators tell us that they are more likely to get things done if they make an agreement with someone else to do so. When you make a public statement, *someone else knows*, and your plans no longer exist solely in your own imagination. A public statement becomes a commitment to that other person, which you may then feel bound to honor. It may be harder to disappoint someone else than to disappoint yourself.

For other procrastinators, talking with another person helps make their own thoughts seem more *real.* When you daydream about something, it belongs to the nebulous realm of fantasy. Talking about your ideas is a step toward making them concrete, giving them form and substance, and bringing them to life. It may even help you clarify just what your ideas are.

Working with another person can also be an opportunity to obtain support for your efforts. When you are feeling down or discouraged with your progress—or lack of it—a friend can be an important source of encouragement and understanding. Support can keep us going when we most feel like giving up. If you work with a fellow procrastinator, you can help each other as you go and be reminded that you are not the *only* one who is struggling with this beast. For some people, this is the most important reassurance of all. Finally, working with a friend can be a lot more fun than approaching things by yourself.

Lest you begin to feel that you *must* work with someone, let us hasten to add that there are some people who work best alone. If you are one of them, it may make more sense for you to do this on your own. However, try to clarify whether you *truly* work best by yourself, or, you want to work alone because you are embarrassed or concerned about how others may judge you, or, you are too proud to admit that you could use some help. It may be hard to let someone else know about your struggles with procrastinating, but usually there is more to be gained than lost in creating some support for what you do.

If you do opt for working with someone else, remember it's important that you choose that person wisely. You want to talk with someone who can listen without judging you harshly and without ridiculing your efforts. Select someone who is not too involved with your everyday life. In general, friends are better to work with than family members, especially a spouse or parent, because friends have more emotional distance.

We strongly urge you to get a notebook that you can use for working on the exercises that follow, and to jot down any thoughts or reactions that you have along the way. Some people like to record specific incidents as they occur. Patterns and themes not easily identified at first may become more obvious when you can review a series of events. You can also observe patterns in your thinking and emotional responses if you include some notes about them, in addition to describing the event itself.

As you use the techniques we present, we suggest that you keep an eye out for feeling some resistance. It will probably crop up from time to time, and it can take many different forms. For example, even though you may begin to make some progress in handling your procrastination, you may feel disappointed or angry with yourself for not trying hard enough, not making progress fast enough, not accomplishing what you set out to do. Or, you may find yourself feeling that we are demanding too much of you, that these techniques require too much effort. Whatever form it takes, and whenever it appears, resistance can keep you stuck in one place like a car spinning its wheels.

People usually resist when something feels uncomfortable. But resistance can be turned into an ally. If you find yourself resisting these techniques, you can learn a lot by asking: What specifically do I feel uncomfortable about? Am I afraid of something? Am I confronting something that I usually try to push out of my mind?

Sometimes when people clarify what's behind their resistance they may see that they are automatically reacting with old patterns rather than responding only to the present situation. In addition, once people identify the issues involved in resistance, they often feel less overwhelmed or frightened and more able to proceed.

These techniques may appear simple, but the appearance is deceptive. The techniques *do* work, *if* you can use them. This, of course, is exactly what procrastinators have the greatest difficulty doing: putting into action things they know in their heads! When you get stuck, think back over the issues we raised in Part I. Are your fears getting in your way? Are you stopping because you are on the threshold of possible failure or success? Are you determined not to give in? Are you apprehensive about getting too close or being on your own? In spite of your fears, there are things you can do. To summarize:

1. Use only those techniques that work best for you.

2. Experiment with *one* technique at a time. Trying to do everything at once is part of the problem.

3. Use a procrastination notebook.

4. Go slowly. Change that occurs too quickly can be unsettling and may create new problems which you hadn't anticipated.

5. Expect setbacks. You won't stop procrastinating in a day or a week. Progress takes time.

6. Pay attention to resistance—it can teach you something important about yourself.

7. Remember: It's *your* procrastination. Nobody else can make you change it or can change it for you.

8

Setting and Achieving Goals

It is fairly apparent that procrastinators have difficulty achieving goals. For some of you, procrastination interferes to such an extent that you never accomplish the goals you've set. Others of you may ultimately attain your goals, but only after you've been through agonizing fits and starts.

It may not be as obvious that procrastinators also have difficulty *setting* goals, since many of them are busy setting goals all the time. They almost always set ambiguous goals, as, "I've got to get some work done today" or overly ambitious ones, as, "I want to be president of my own company someday." Goals such as these are sure to elude the procrastinator.

When we started out to write this book, we thought our goal was clear enough: we wanted to write a book on procrastination. We developed an outline and declared we would begin. Then it was time to write. Whenever we thought about getting down to work, we'd each say to ourselves, "I have to write the book." An invitation to socialize, the opportunity to do other kinds of work, the need for recreation—all these were weighed against the injunction, "I have to write the book." We even set aside certain hours during the week, but we still found writing the book very difficult to do.

Eventually we saw how sitting down each time to "write the book" was a very imposing demand. Each page seemed like a tiny drop in a huge bucket. Would they ever fit together into a cohesive form? We were taking such a broad view of our purpose that it was antithetical to making progress. We were setting ourselves up for trouble by the way we thought about our goal.

Finally we started to take our own advice. Instead of thinking about having to write a whole book, we focused on only one chapter at a time, trying to put the rest of it out of our minds. In the process, we began to say something different to ourselves when we anticipated our writing sessions, for example, "I have to spend two hours this afternoon working on the introduction to the goal-setting chapter." That seemed a more reasonable, reachable goal, and having it helped us to get to work.

THE BEHAVIORAL GOAL

We think it is helpful to define your goals in behavioral terms. Focusing on what you will be *doing* when you accomplish your objective gives you a place to start and helps you recognize when you've arrived at the end. A behavioral goal has the following characteristics: it is observable by you and others; it is specific and concrete; and it can be broken down into small steps. "I want to stop procrastinating" is a noble goal, but it is *not* a behavioral goal. You can't actually see yourself stop procrastinating—what would you look for? It is not concrete—stop procrastinating on what? It is difficult to break down into steps—how do you start out to stop procrastinating?

Let's look more closely at the elements of a behavioral goal.

Observable.   People can't see how you are feeling or know what you are thinking, but they can see what you do. For your goal to be observable by you and others, it must be defined as an *action*. Imagine a movie camera photographing you as you finish your goal. What action will you be taking when the camera records your accomplishments? If your goal is truly a behavioral one, you should be able to take a picture of yourself doing it.

For example, procrastinators often propose, "I'd like to feel less overwhelmed by all the work I have to do." It's an understandable desire, but it's not a behavioral goal. No one can observe you feeling less overwhelmed. And it's not a helpful statement, either. How do you know when you feel "less overwhelmed"? How much "less overwhelmed" would you have to feel to be relieved? To restate it as a behavioral goal, you may select one project you've been putting off and define its completion in behavioral terms. You may decide, "I'll mail ten résumés to prospective employers," or "I'll balance my checkbook," or "I'll make an appointment with the dentist." A camera could see you dropping the envelopes into the mailbox, sitting at your desk with your checkbook, or hanging up the phone after your conversation with the dentist. If you achieved any of these goals, you'd probably feel less overwhelmed, and you could know how it happened.

Specific and Concrete. Procrastinators are so prone to thinking in vague terms that they may find it very difficult to be specific. What *exactly* will you be doing when you accomplish your goal? When *specifically* will you do it? Who else *in particular* will be there?

We've often heard people state as a goal, "I'm going to reorganize my life." With a vague objective like this, a procrastinator is stymied. However, if you translate your goal into behavioral terms, you will have some clues about where to start to get better organized. You may decide to go through your files, keeping important papers and throwing out the rest. Getting organized might mean cleaning out a closet or hiring a secretary. Being specific about where you want to end up will facilitate your getting there.

Small Steps. The only way to achieve any goal, no matter how large or small, is step by step. As the old saying goes, "Life by the yard is very hard; life by the inch is a cinch."

A behavioral goal can be broken down into small, observable steps and, likewise, each of these steps should be observable and specific. You will end up with a series of mini-goals that you can attempt one by one. A project such as "I have to prepare my annual budget" can be overwhelming. Instead, the project could be divided into its component parts: locate last year's budget; list budget categories; estimate expenditures in each category; estimate income for each category; confer with administrative assistant

Setting and Achieving Goals

during Friday's meeting. As a series of steps, "preparing the annual budget," may seem more manageable.

Sometimes as you break a goal down, you discover that it's more complicated than you'd thought. Beth chose as a goal to write a report on the use of computer services for her company, a task she had put off for six months. The steps she anticipated were: 1) find the notes she'd already made; 2) outline the report; 3) write a rough draft; 4) revise the draft; 5) give it to her secretary for typing; 6) review the typed copy; and 7) distribute the report to division managers, with a short personal note to each one. But as she thought about these steps, Beth realized that she didn't have a clear conception of the focus of the report, and decided to talk to her boss before writing the outline. However, her boss was out of town for several days, so she wouldn't be able to see him right away. It also occurred to her that since six months had elapsed, it would be wise to double-check her information with the division managers. With these additional steps, Beth saw that her initial goal of distributing the report in three weeks was unrealistic. So she made a new three-week goal: to have the first draft of the report completed.

Breaking the goal down into smaller stages will help you clarify—for better or worse—the reality you face.

Focusing on the steps you'll take will also serve as a reminder that you have to travel down the road in order to reach your destination. Most procrastinators only think about "being there" and have a hard time "being en route." And many are surprised to find that the process of getting there and accomplishing each step as you go can be challenging and rewarding in its own right.

Procrastinators tend to be unrealistic about their goals because they often think in terms of an ideal situation, as if there were no limitations on their time or energy. As a way of establishing a more realistic goal, we ask procrastinators to consider what their *minimal* goal is. What is the *smallest* goal you could set that would give you some sense of progress and accomplishment? Is there part of a larger goal you could choose to work toward over a limited period of time? For example, your ideal goal may be to redecorate your house, but a minimal goal may be to reupholster the sofa.

Some of you may be reluctant to lower your sights even the least bit. Although it may feel like a blow to your pride to choose a minimal goal, we think that it could ultimately be more rewarding for you. You can build on real accomplishment by achieving your goal step by step, rather than by insisting on lofty goals and doing nothing.

A TWO-WEEK EXPERIMENT

We suggest that you pick out one goal to work toward during the next two weeks. See what you can learn about how you set up goals and how you handle them, when you make progress and when you procrastinate. It is important to examine both your successes and your setbacks. Think of it as a time for self-observation and learning. It is not an evaluation of how smart, responsible, or competent you are. Try to take the perspective of a researcher gathering data, not the role of a critic passing judgment. Use the following steps as a guide to accomplishing your goal.

Selecting a Goal

What are some things you would like to accomplish in the next two weeks? What would be your target date for each goal? Remember that a behavioral goal should be observable, specific, and able to complete in steps. Write down these goals and when you'd like to finish them.

Of the possible goals you've considered, select one—*and only one*—to use as the behavioral goal for your two-week experiment. It doesn't have to be the most significant goal of your life, or the hardest obstacle you face. Which goal you select is not as crucial as the process of defining and working toward a goal of your own choosing.

We realize that asking a procrastinator to select only one goal is like asking a dieter to eat only one potato chip. It's hard to limit yourself to just one, but having more than one is dangerous. For most procrastinators, trying to do everything is part of the problem.

To list the steps involved in breaking your behavioral goal down into its component parts, you can find your own method or use one of these common three: start with the first step and work forward; start with your last step and work backward; identify the main components of your goal and determine which steps are involved for each component. An example of how one procrastinator broke his two-week goal down into small steps is shown on page 136.

Write down your one behavioral goal, the steps involved, and when during the next two weeks you plan to take each step. Don't forget to consider other time commitments and obligations you have coming up in the next two weeks.

Goal:
Spend 2 Hours on Saturdays and Sundays
Cleaning and Reorganizing My Home Study
(total of 8 hours over 2 weekends)

A. Organize papers. 1) Sort through piles on the floor; throw away nonessentials without reading them! 2) Put all bills in a shoe box. 3) Put all correspondence to be answered in another shoe box. 4) Put all tax receipts in another shoe box. (Do I have enough shoe boxes?) 5) Buy file folders. 6) Sort through articles and clippings. 7) Make a file for those I want to save, and throw the rest away!

B. Clean the room. 1) Clean off desk. 2) Dust file and bookcase. 3) Empty wastebasket. 4) Put books that are lying around into bookshelf. 5) Vacuum.

Now that you've identified a behavioral goal and the steps you'll take toward it during the next two weeks, how do you get started? What is the very *first* step you will take? It should be something very small and very accomplishable, like finding last year's tax return, or buying a notebook, or getting empty shoe boxes. Exactly where and when will you begin? No matter how small an effort it is, you are moving in the right direction. "The journey of 1000 miles begins with a single step," as the saying goes.

Your two-week behavioral goal may seem clear and realistic to you. We suggest, however, that you do a reality check, and ask someone else for feedback. Then what seemed clear may still be too vague; what seemed realistic may still be too much; what seemed broken down may still be too global. In particular, consider with your friend if the goal you've selected is really your minimally acceptable goal.

Listen as objectively as you can to the feedback you get. If it makes sense to you, use it. You may even decide to revise your goal. Getting feedback assists you in thinking things through, but, of course, you don't have to follow someone's advice if it isn't suitable.

The Start-Up

Now you have selected a project you want to work on, and you've defined it so that it is clear and realistic. It's actually possible that you *can* get this done in the next two weeks. How does this prospect make you feel? What thoughts are going through your mind? Here are a few of the reactions we've heard from procrastinators as they've looked ahead to the prospect of an accomplishable goal: "I feel a sense of relief, because I finally have a handle on what I want to do." "I'm very anxious. I've committed myself to doing this and I wonder if I'll be able to do it. What if I fail again?" "This is scary! I want to run away and get out of here!" "I'm ready. I want to get started right now while I have the motivation and momentum." "This goal is too easy. It should be a cinch to do. But what if I don't get even this done?"

Notice you reactions as you anticipate your experiment. The thought of getting started is a trigger, a stimulus that sets off a whole chain of internal reactions—images, feelings, thoughts, expectations, and memories of past experiences.

Visualize Your Progress It may be helpful to visualize the specific steps and the exact circumstances of progress made toward your goal. You probably already use imagery in other situations—when you daydream about going on a date and how you'd like the evening to turn out, when you create an "instant replay" of an argument you've had and this time say all the things you didn't think of at the time. Imagery can be used to reduce stress and increase relaxation, to practice assertive behavior, to cope with anxiety, to aid physical healing, and to improve performance in academics and sports.

Imagine yourself taking your very first step, going through the motions you would actually make. Then see yourself continuing through each of the steps toward your goal. If your pessimism intrudes and you anticipate a snag, try to imagine yourself finding a way to cope with the problem. Eventually you'll watch yourself coming to the end of the process and accomplishing your goal. Imagery of this sort—best done when you are comfortable, alone, and relaxed—can prepare you for the real moment of action and make it easier for you to cross the threshold between thinking and doing.

Optimize Your Chances Even if you have a well-delineated behavioral goal and a manageable first step, where and when you attempt to begin can be crucial. The circumstances you set up can either greatly increase or disastrously decrease the probability of your succeeding.

Todd, a 20-year-old undergraduate student, selected as his behavioral goal to complete a term paper for an English literature course. His first step was to spend from 9–10 p.m. the next evening reading the required novel. So far so good. He planned to read the book in his room at the fraternity house. Not so good. The fraternity was an extremely social, distracting environment and, as 9 p.m. approached, Todd was having too good a time hanging around with the guys to leave and go into his room alone to read. He put it off until 9:30, then 10:00, and, at 10:30, he gave up because "it was too late by that time." Todd made his first step more difficult by trying to achieve it under less than optimal circumstances. He thought he would—and should—be able to overcome the social temptations, but he just made things harder for himself.

The next day, Todd revised his plans and decided to read the book in a campus library. In order to increase his chances of actually getting to the library, he arranged to go with Peter, a studious fraternity brother. Instead of going to the undergraduate library where he might run into friends and yield to social pressure again, he chose the law school library, where "people are really serious." Todd didn't change his first step, but he did alter the circumstances to maximize the chances that he would actually take it.

If you stop and think about it, you can exert a lot of control over the circumstances in which you function. Pick a time, place or person that will work *for* you instead of *against* you.

Stick To a Time Limit Stick to the limited period of time you have set to work on your goal. For example, you may decide to spend 30 minutes on your project. If you've stayed with it for that length of time you've been successful, regardless of how much you did, or how well you think it turned out. Your success is based on the amount of time you spend rather than on the amount or quality of work you accomplish. We're not suggesting that you work for 30 minutes *efficiently,* only that you spend 30 minutes working. The shorter the time, the easier it is to begin. We find that for most procrastinators an initial period of 15 minutes to a half-hour works best. If even 15 minutes feels like more than you can stand at first, set a limit of 10 minutes or even 5. With some some experimentation, you'll gradually learn what time limit is most effective for you.

It is absolutely necessary at first to *stop when you reach the end of your time limit.* You may think, "If I'm doing well, I should capitalize on it and keep up the momentum." But if you get carried away and work for 2 hours the first time, going well beyond your limit, the next time you'll expect that you should again work for 2 hours. That's a set-up for discouragement.

It's also better, in the long run, to stick to your limits because you're honoring an agreement you made with yourself. Doing exactly what you said you would do—no more and no less—builds trust and confidence in yourself. These are valuable feelings that many procrastinators have lost.

Don't Wait Until You Feel Like It   If you wait until you feel like starting, you may never get started. Many procrastinators expect to feel unafraid, totally confident, or completely prepared at the moment they take their first step. Kelly, a 33-year-old nurse said, "I keep thinking I should really be *ready* before I apply to go back to school. I should feel calm and completely together, not have any doubts about myself. Once I stop feeling afraid, I should have no problem going back." Kelly has been waiting for three years to feel "completely together." She's been out of school for a long time—how could she not be afraid?

Others expect that they should *want* to start, so they wait for desire to develop. There are some things, however, that are inherently unpleasant, tedious, or boring. Take taxes, for instance. We don't know a single person who looks forward to doing his or her taxes. Can you imagine anyone jumping up and down with joyful anticipation, "Oh boy! I can hardly wait to get to those tax forms! Just let me at all those receipts!" Do you know anyone who loves to go to the dentist or clean the kitchen floor? If you wait until you *want* to do these kinds of things, you'll probably wait forever—or at least until April 15, or until you need root canal, or until people start noticing how bad the kitchen smells.

If you think you have to feel a certain way before you can begin to do something, getting started can be a long time coming. You *can* start, even if you're not in the ideal mood or frame of mind.

The Follow-through

Once you do get started, how can you follow through beyond the first step to give yourself a chance to complete your goal? Procrastinators are all too familiar with the cycle of making some early efforts and then slowing down or giving up altogether. You may be a person who gets suffused with optimism at the beginning and then, at some point, gets stuck and stays stuck.

How can you keep from being disappointed by yet another incompleted project? Here are some guidelines for following through instead of giving up.

Watch Out for Your Excuses. Inevitably, many of the excuses you've identified in Chapter 7 will come up during your two-week experiment. If, for example, your next step is to call a business client to set up a meeting, you may catch yourself thinking, "She's probably already left for today. I'll call tomorrow."

Remember that an excuse is a red flag. It means that you're at a choice point: you can procrastinate or you can act. Ask yourself, "Do I want to procrastinate right now? Is procrastination in my best interests at this moment?"

Focus on One Step at a Time. In the process of writing this book, there were many times when we felt terribly depressed by thoughts such as "there's so much left to do," or "we'll never finish on time," or "what if it doesn't turn out well?" The task seemed enormous, and we felt overwhelmed. At these moments, one of us would say to the other, "Don't think so far ahead. Just take one step at a time." It diverted us from our fears of a disastrous future and brought us back to making a plan of action for the immediate present.

Several other procrastinators have told us that this statement has a soothing effect on them, like telling themselves, "Everything's going to be all right." Hearing it, believing it, they feel reassured somehow and are therefore more able to keep going.

Get Beyond the First Obstacle. Initially things may be going smoothly. Perhaps you've taken, with relative ease, some steps toward your goal. But almost certainly at some point you'll encounter a bump in the road. Maybe the person you want to talk to is not at work today, or you can't figure out how to solve a mathematical problem, or it rains on the first day of your new jogging program. Then you have reached a very difficult moment: the first obstacle.

Procrastinators are likely to become upset if the obstacle can't be overcome right away or if they imagine the problem can't be removed easily. Upon encountering the first trouble, they feel frustrated and think, "I can't deal with this." Or they may interpret an obstacle as a direct challenge to their incompetence and feel defeated if they can't find the correct solution quickly. Any snag, large or small, can become a source of frustration and humiliation.

The danger for procrastinators is not in withdrawing temporarily from working out the problem. At times, it may actually be wise to take time out to reassess your situation. The danger lies in abandoning *all* efforts and giving up altogether. Procrastinators feel so deflated by an obstacle that they have trouble returning to the problem and grappling with it a second or a third time. Unfortunately, obstacles are inevitable and if you can't overcome setbacks, you can't make progress.

When you encounter an obstacle, especially the first interference, remind yourself that this is *just an obstacle*. It is not an indictment that means you are stupid, incompetent, or unwanted. If you decide to pull back temporarily, set a specific time and place to approach the situation again. Identify as concretely as you can what action you will take at that time. Remember that you don't have to solve the problem all at once. You can leave it and come back to it again, several times if necessary. And, if you temporarily retreat from this obstacle, is there any other part of your goal that you can do? If it's raining outside, can you do indoor exercises? If someone you need is out of the office, can you make other calls? Although you might stop momentarily in one area, you don't have to stop completely.

Reward Yourself After You've Made Some Progress. The notion of giving yourself a reward may be somewhat foreign to many of you, because procrastinators are much more likely to punish themselves than to praise themselves. It's very sad to see that in almost every case procrastinators are highly skilled at beating themselves over the head but are not very good at being nice to themselves when they deserve it.

Roger, for example, was mad at himself at the end of his two-week experiment. He'd set out with the goal of paying three long overdue bills that had been plaguing him for months. He reported with bitterness that he'd only taken care of one of them—he'd covered his unpaid parking tickets, so that now he could re-register his car—but he still hadn't paid off his dentist or the credit card company. "I thought this time I could get out of the swamp, but no such luck."

Roger was unable to appreciate the benefits of what he had accomplished. By paying his tickets and registering his car, he stopped the penalties from accruing, and he could now drive around without having an anxiety attack every time he saw a police car. But, as is the case with most procrastinators, it never occurred to Roger to feel good about what he had done.

No matter how much progress procrastinators make toward a goal, they don't feel entitled to any satisfaction or reward until they have finished completely. Even when they do finally reach the end, they may not enjoy their accomplishment if they're mad at themselves for procrastinating somewhere along the way.

When you do make progress, even if you don't accomplish as much as you'd ideally like to, give yourself some reinforcement. A reward can be anything that you enjoy or that makes you feel good: dinner at a favorite restaurant, watching television, a weekend trip to the mountains, a game of racquetball, talking to a friend, or reading a book. A reward could also be praise from other people or private acknowledgment that you give to yourself.

Rewards are most effective when they occur just after the desired behavior. They work as "positive reinforcement," increasing the likelihood that the behavior will be repeated. In other words, the plan, "I'll go to a movie and then settle down to work," is not as effective as doing some work first, and going to the movie afterwards.

We suggest that you think about the things that are rewards for you, so that as you work toward your goal you'll be ready to reinforce your progress as soon as you make some. Self-reward is always more effective than self-criticism!

Be Flexible About Your Goal. As you progress toward your goal, you may discover that your initial reality checks weren't realistic enough. Perhaps you forgot to allot time for important commitments, like the theater director who set up an ambitious two-week goal, but forgot that her college roommate was coming for a visit. Or you may find as you go through your days that things take longer or are more complicated than you'd anticipated. You may be disrupted by circumstances beyond your control: your child becomes ill or your car breaks down. In situations like these, it may be necessary for you to alter your goal.

Revising your goal is not necessarily a sign of failure. It can be a response to realistic constraints, indicating that you are able to evaluate what is actually possible and adjust to it, instead of holding onto an impossible ideal.

It Doesn't Have to Be Perfect. If you are a perfectionist, you may get caught up in a struggle to do all things absolutely right, even when there is no real need for such a high standard. It's more important that your Christmas cards get sent out than that each person receive a unique, well-written personal note about how you are, what you've been doing all year, and your current philosophy of life.

If you can let go of your need for perfection at each step along the way, you'll probably be able to accomplish a lot more in the long run. As you're spinning your wheels, hoping for perfection, remind yourself, "It doesn't have to be perfect. It just has to be done!"

Looking Back

At the end of your two-week experiment, look back over what happened. This may be difficult for a lot of procrastinators who hate to be reminded of what they did—or didn't do. Some people feel that it's a waste of time to look backwards. Dan, a 47-year-old engineer, put it this way: "What's done is done. It's over, and I can't change it, so why should I spend my time thinking about it?"

If you actually finished your goal you may be reluctant to look carefully at how you got there. Some people are almost superstitious about it, worrying that if you examine a good thing too closely, you'll reveal the hidden flaws and then you won't feel good about it any more. "Even though I finished my project," said an accountant, "there were a lot of times along the way when I goofed off. I'd rather just hold onto my pride and not remember those bad times." She sounds ready to let her regret over her struggles outweigh the satisfaction of her success.

Setting and Achieving Goals

If you didn't accomplish your goal, you may be even more resistant to examining what happened. You may not want to add to your self-recriminations. If you are already critical of yourself for not finishing what you started, you may not want to give yourself more ammunition.

It will help in reviewing your experience to try to keep an open mind, to be *curious* rather than judgmental, *interested* rather than critical. Whether or not you completed your goal is less important than how you think about what happened. If you have begun to understand your successes and your setbacks, you are helping prepare yourself to procrastinate less the next time.

Let's start by looking at the steps you were able to take. How much did you accomplish toward your goal? Did you take your first step? Did you get some of the way toward your goal? Most of the way? Did you reach the end of your project?

We want to warn you that many procrastinators tend to underestimate how much they've done. Perhaps you took some steps that weren't part of your original plans, but they moved you along. These steps count. Perhaps you aren't giving yourself credit for some steps because they seem so small. These should count too. You may feel like you didn't do enough, but if you recount exactly what you have done, you may be pleasantly surprised. (It's also possible that as you review your steps you'll be unpleasantly surprised to find that you have fooled yourself into thinking that you did more than you actually accomplished. That's important to discover as well.)

We've heard a wide range of reactions from procrastinators at the end of their experiments: "I feel relieved because I got somewhere, but I'm disappointed that I didn't go all the way." "I did a hell of a lot more than I thought I'd do." "I was sneaky. I got to my goal, but not the way I planned. I took short cuts, and got around it. I don't feel good about it because I didn't stick to the plan." "I've failed again. I'll never get beyond this problem." "I was really off base in my planning." "I have a sense of accomplishment because I did what I said I would do—finally!"

How are you feeling as you look back on your own experience? Are you primarily pleased, or primarily disappointed? (As you may, by now, predict, no matter how much they've accomplished, most procrastinators are primarily disappointed.) Consider what happened for you that contributes to the way you feel about your progress. Are you disappointed because you didn't do anything, or disappointed because you didn't do everything? Are you wounded because you didn't accomplish a project that was really too big in the first place? Or are you relieved because you learned how to live with progress one step at a time?

In the past, you may have made the choice to procrastinate automatically, without even realizing it. Perhaps you accepted your excuses unquestioningly, or ran away from your goal on impulse. We hope that during your two-week experimental period, if nothing else, you procrastinated more consciously. Undoubtedly, there were times when you were tempted to put something off and wavered on the brink, debating whether to take the next step or avoid it, times when you could either move toward your goal or away from it. These "choice points" are important moments. The decisions we make at such times affect not only our performance, but also the way we feel about ourselves.

Try to recall one of those choice points in your recent experiment. If you can remember a time when you wavered and decided to move *toward* your goal, what helped you to take the plunge? What did you do or say to yourself that helped you to make progress?

Martin, a systems engineer, was a science fiction fan. Just at the time he'd planned to begin organizing the tools in his workshop, he started instead to read a terrific sci-fi book. Although tempted by the world of the future, he was also nagged by his guilt. "Finally, I saw that I wasn't enjoying the book because I was so conflicted. So I decided to spend ten minutes in my workshop and then return to my book. I was surprised that I actually rather liked straightening out the workshop, and I kept at it. When I went back to reading, I felt I'd earned it." Two things helped Martin move forward. First, he decided to take a small first step so that he wouldn't feel imprisoned in his workshop; second, he rewarded his progress by really enjoying his book.

Perhaps you can remember a time when you weren't so fortunate, a choice point when you decided to move *away* from your goal. What were the circumstances? What thoughts, feelings or images made it difficult for you to move ahead?

We offer as an example Elizabeth, a freelance writer who went to the movies instead of writing the article her editor was expecting. She explained, "I just felt restless and at loose ends and had to get out of the house." With some further thought, Elizabeth realized, "I was feeling sort of lonely. I didn't want to stay home by myself. At the movie, I was surrounded by other people, and that made me feel better." What was making her feel lonely on that particular day? She remembered that she was scheduled to have lunch with a friend who'd called and canceled. "I'd been looking forward to seeing him, and when he canceled I felt alone and isolated." It took a lot of hard thinking, but Elizabeth was able to see how procrastinating was her attempt to replace the social contact she'd missed. Had she realized that she was really looking for some companionship, perhaps she could have called another friend and arranged to spend the afternoon working together.

It can be difficult to identify exactly what you were thinking, feeling, and reacting to when you chose to move away from your goal. If you explore it in your own mind as Elizabeth did, asking yourself questions as a detective looking for clues, you may get some useful insight into your reasons for procrastinating.

Think back on how you handled the process of approaching your project, from defining your goal to getting started and following through. What *one* thing would you do differently next time? Like Todd, who discovered that the fraternity house was not conducive to studying and so decided instead to work in the library, what one change would you want to make that would increase your chances for success next time?

9

Learning How to Tell Time

On the surface, procrastination appears to be a rather straight-forward problem of poor time management. If you organized your time better and used it more efficiently, you wouldn't be procrastinating. So, many procrastinators turn to experts in time management for advice. You may have already read some of the extensive literature that exists in this area, and even seen the wisdom in the suggestions, but still had difficulty putting them into practice. If you could, you would. Why can't you?

Time is one of the great enigmas for procrastinators. This may sound odd at first—after all, procrastinators are preoccupied with time. They are always assessing how much they have left to do and how much time is left to do it in. A procrastinator plays games with time, trying to outsmart it: "I'll go to the movies tonight and still have my report ready for the noon meeting tomorrow." "I can do nothing now and use my time very efficiently later."

Yet for all of their experience at tampering with its constraints, procrastinators' views of time are quite unrealistic. They have a "wishful thinking" relationship with time—they hope to find more of it than there really is, almost as if time were a quantity that could be extended instead of being one that is fixed.

Perhaps it is this aspect of time—that it is fixed, measurable, and finite—that is so difficult for procrastinators to accept. Procrastinators, as we have observed, prefer to remain in the vague realms of potential and possibility and do not like to be concrete, measured, or limited. When they are ultimately caught short they are surprised, disappointed, and even offended. In order to implement the time management techniques in this and other books, you may have to confront your own wishful-thinking approach to time. Ask yourself if you really do know how to tell time. Most procrastinators don't.

Can you accurately predict how long things actually take to accomplish? Sometimes people underestimate, thinking, "This year my tax return is not as complicated as before, so it will only take a couple of hours," when in the past it has always taken two days. Sometimes procrastinators overestimate how much time is needed, putting off a project such as cleaning out the basement because they think, "I can't do that now—it will take forever." In both cases, the result is that they do nothing.

Do you know how much time is available for you to use? "I'll put off writing the outline for my sales presentation, and then I'll spend the whole weekend working on it," decided a computer sales representative. However, he didn't take into account the time he'd planned to spend with his family over the weekend.

Can you account for what happens to your time? "Time just slips away from me, and I don't know where it's gone or what I've done," lamented a woman who felt she didn't accomplish much and didn't know why.

In this chapter we will present several suggestions to improve your understanding and use of time. We've selected time management techniques that are specifically helpful for procrastinators, and we'll explain why. We've also anticipated some of the difficulties you may have in implementing these techniques and offered suggestions or perspectives that may make it easier to put them into practice.

THE UN-SCHEDULE

Psychologist Neil Fiore has developed a method of keeping track of time designed especially for procrastinators. He understands that many people set up schedules for themselves that they never fulfill, then become disappointed, and eventually give up. So Dr. Fiore recommends that procrastinators work not on the basis of a schedule of what they *should* do, but with an "un-schedule."

The un-schedule is a weekly calendar of all of your committed activities. It can help you accomplish your goal in two ways. First, in looking ahead to how much of your time is already committed, you will see the maximum amount of time you have left over to work toward your goal. Second, it helps you at the end of your week to look back and see where your time has actually gone.

Think about the next seven days, starting with tomorrow. Using the blank un-schedule on pages 150–151 as a model, write down all of the activities you can predict you will do in the coming week, however important or trivial they may seem. Mark on your un-schedule the hours when you most probably will be doing things you already know will occur in the next week. If you know exactly when you will be doing something, write it down in the appropriate box, e.g., a lunch meeting, Tuesday, 12–1 p.m. If you don't know exactly when you will do something, estimate the amount of time it will take, then mark it down on a day that you might do it. Include any special commitments you scheduled for the week, like an evening lecture or a movie date. In addition, mark off time for routine activities, such as going to the laundromat, that happen each week.

Consider the whole variety of activities in your life: work hours; scheduled meetings and appointments; classes and social events; time for regular exercise; time for meals including preparation and clean-up; time given to household chores such as cleaning, laundry, and shopping; time set aside to spend with your friends, spouse, or children; time that you spend sleeping. If you always watch the evening news, Monday night sports, or other favorite television programs, put them down as well. Anticipate the extra time you spend reading the newspaper on Sundays. Don't forget to include your commuting and travel time, too. You may want to consult your appointment book or calendar to remind yourself of your commitments. (And if you don't have a calendar to consult, this is a sure sign of trouble—go buy one!) On pages 152–153 is the un-schedule for Marsha, a teacher who is behind grading mid-term papers for her students.

Remember, we are not asking you to write down what you *should* be doing. Don't put down when you hope you'll get around to starting on your behavioral goal or when you think you'd like to

WEEKLY UN-SCHEDULE

Week of: _____

	Monday	Tuesday	Wednesday	Thursday	Friday	Saturday	Sunday
7 am							
8							
9							
10							
11							
12 noon							
1							
2							
3							

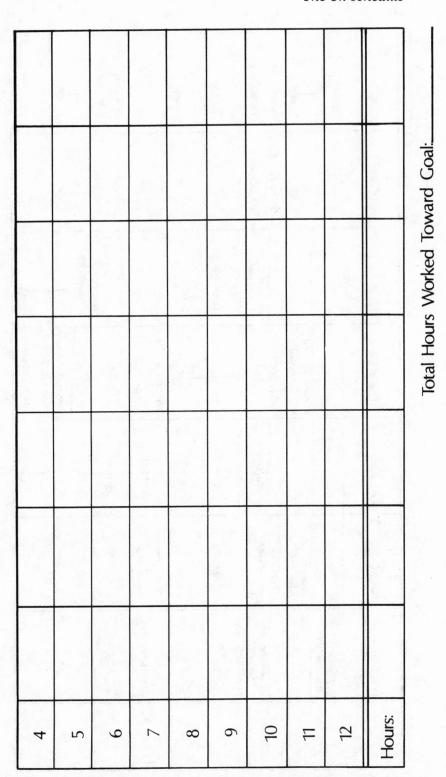

4								
5								
6								
7								
8								
9								
10								
11								
12								
Hours:								

Total Hours Worked Toward Goal: _____

WEEKLY UN-SCHEDULE

Week of: Sept 11-18

	Monday	Tuesday	Wednesday	Thursday	Friday	Saturday	Sunday
7am	Wake-up, shower, Breakfast with family				→	Sleep	Sleep
8		commute to dentist		commute to school		→	→
9	commute to school	Dentist appointment	commute to school	Office Hours	commute to school	shower & Breakfast	shower & Breakfast
10	prepare for lecture	→	Prepare for lecture	→	Prepare for lecture		Read Sunday Paper
11	Class		Class		Class		→
12 noon	lunch	Prep for lecture	lunch	Lunch with Jessica			
1	meet with the Dean	Class	office Hours	Class	To Errands – Bank, cleaners, grocery shopping	Clean House	work in garden
2		→	→	Commute home / Take Elisa to Piano lesson	→	→	→
3		office Hours					

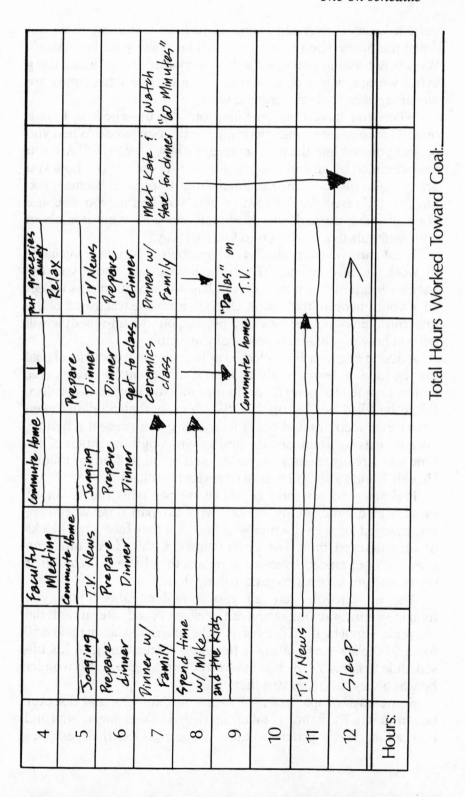

Total Hours Worked Toward Goal: _____

write a letter to your old friend. If you are a student, don't put down the times when you hope you'll be doing your homework. We are not asking you to promise yourself to try to do anything extra; we are only asking you to acknowledge what times are *already spoken for* in the coming week.

When you have finished filling out the un-schedule, look it over. This page represents your life for the next week. When you project yourself into the next seven days, how do you feel? Are you overwhelmed by all you are going to do? Anxious about how you are going to fill your uncommitted time? Depressed because you have so little free time? Examine how you feel as you visualize yourself going through this week, and consider what it is about your schedule that leads you to feel that way.

What can you learn about how much time you have available to work on any project? The un-schedule will show you the *maximum* amount of time you could use—the blank spaces reflect all of your uncommitted hours. Of course, no one will use all of the uncommitted hours to work on a project, but the un-schedule will tell you how much time is potentially available.

A design engineer had selected as his one-week behavioral goal that he have a design ready to submit to a client by week's end, and he planned to spend three hours a day working on his project. When he filled out his un-schedule, he saw that he didn't even have three uncommitted hours a day! Given his present schedule, his goal was unattainable. By underestimating how much of his time was already spoken for, he was setting himself up for failure. He either had to revise his goal or revise his schedule.

Perhaps you are one of those people who has a lot of unscheduled time. Many people who do part-time work, are unemployed, or are self-employed find that they face large blocks of unstructured time. For procrastinators, this "free" time can create a lot of anxiety, because it means they have to create their own structure in order to get anything done.

The un-schedule can tell you something about how you manage your time. One otherwise intelligent graduate student did not realize until he filled out his un-schedule that waking up at 8:50 for a 9:00 class was cutting it too close. Consistently, in his un-schedule as in his life, he had ignored commuting time. No wonder he was always late for everything!

Sometimes people examine their commitments and discover how much of their time is taken up with social engagements and recreation. These procrastinators have planned their excuses ahead of time, so that when the moment comes, they feel they are meeting their obligations, and they may not recognize that they're procrastinating. "I keep planning so many social events after work that I never even have to decide if I'm going to start on the writing of my own book or not," said a magazine editor. "I just barely have time to get where I'm going."

Look closely at your un-schedule. Is there anything missing from your life? Some procrastinators don't allow themselves any recreation. Amy, a real estate saleswoman, realized, "I haven't included any fun! I feel so guilty about all the work I have to do that I don't think I should take any time out for pleasure. No wonder I'm so tense all the time."

Some procrastinators schedule too much socializing and leave out time to be alone. Others withdraw from people and allow themselves too little social contact. What have you scheduled too little of? Time with your family? Physical activity? Leisurely reading? Most procrastinators have a tendency to deny themselves real pleasure. Even those who hop from one recreational event to another may not experience real pleasure in their frenetic activity. A freelance writer told us, "I finally stopped running around and went out to watch the sunset for the first time in a while. I remembered how much I like that time of day, and I'm going to try to do it more often. It really soothes me to watch the sky change color and darken, and it gives me a different perspective."

As you work on your behavioral goal or on any project, you can use the un-schedule to record your progress. After you have finished a half-hour of work toward your goal, block off half of the appropriate hour on your un-schedule. If you work for an hour, block off the entire box. (Some people who really enjoy charts use different colors to track progress on different activities.) Then add up the blocks to get the total amount of time you spent that week working toward your goal. For example, Marsha worked toward her goal for an hour on Monday, a half-hour on Wednesday, and two hours on Saturday and Sunday, for a total of 5½ hours. (See pages 156–157 for Marsha's completed un-schedule.)

Remember to record your progress *after* you have completed 30 minutes of work toward your goal. You may find that your life does not develop quite as you'd predicted, and so your blocks may appear at times you'd expected to use for something else.

Keeping track of your progress toward your goal in this simple way has several benefits. When you record progress *after* you've made it, you focus on what you *have* accomplished. Instead of

WEEKLY UN-SCHEDULE

Week of: Sept 11-18

	Monday	Tuesday	Wednesday	Thursday	Friday	Saturday	Sunday
7 am	Wake-up, Shower Breakfast with Family				→	Sleep	Sleep
8	commute to school	commute to dentist	commute to school	Commute to school		shower & Breakfast	shower & Breakfast
9	commute to school	Dentist appointment	commute to school	Office Hours	commute to school		Read Sunday Paper
10	Prepare for Lecture	Prep for Lecture	Prepare for Lecture		Prepare for lecture	/////	/////
11	Class		Class	Lunch with Jessica	Class	/////	/////
12 noon	Lunch	Prep for Lecture	Lunch				
1	meet with the Dean	Class	Office Hours	Class	Do Errands – Bank, cleaners, grocery shopping	clean House	work in garden
2	commute home	office Hours	Office Hours	Commute home			
3		office Hours		Take Elisa to Piano lesson			

	Day 1	Day 2	Day 3	Day 4	Day 5	Day 6	Day 7
4	[shaded]	Faculty Meeting	Commute home		Put Groceries away / Relax	Play Tennis	Barbeque Dinner
5	Jogging / Prepare dinner	commute home / TV News / Prepare dinner	Jogging / Prepare Dinner	Prepare dinner	TV News		
6	Dinner w/ Family			Dinner / get to class	Prepare Dinner		Watch "60 Minutes"
7	Spend time with mike and the kids			Ceramics Class	Dinner w/ family	Meet Kate & Steve for dinner	[shaded]
8			[shaded]				
9				Commute Home	"Dallas" on T.V.		
10							
11	T.V. News						
12	Sleep					Sleep	Sleep
Hours:	1	0	½	0	0	2	2

Total Hours Worked Toward Goal: 5½ hrs.

making a promise to yourself about when and how much you'll work, which can leave you feeling like a failure if you don't live up to it, you record what you have actually done, which is more likely to give you the experience of success. Monitoring your progress in this way helps you to see your glass as half-full, not half-empty, for a change.

Secondly, the darkened blocks serve as a *reward* for your productive behavior. The sooner after your thirty-minute work period you record your progress, the more reinforcing the blocks become. As the week goes by, and you watch the number of blocks increase, you may feel motivated to continue. "These marks work like gold stars in grade school," commented one procrastinator who found the un-schedule especially helpful. "I get a sense of satisfaction every time I fill in a block, and I feel like doing more."

Rewarding progress after thirty minutes of work is also a good way to recognize that even a half-hour of effort is worth while. The un-schedule can show you when you have small bits of time available and help you reward yourself for every half-hour you use toward your goal.

Keeping track of the number of hours you worked toward your goal is a method called "self-monitoring." Psychological research has shown that the very act of watching what you actually do gives you some incentive to do more.

Self-monitoring also helps procrastinators be more realistic. Counting up the number of hours you worked toward your goal is a very concrete activity. You can't fool yourself into believing that you've accomplished an enormous amount when you see that you spent one half-hour in your week on your goal. You also can't pretend that you haven't gotten anything done if you count up ten hours of effort. You may find that your feelings about what you've done don't match what the numbers tell you—you can work for 10 hours and still not feel accomplished or satisfied. But if you've made a record of those hours, at least you have something before you counter your disappointed feelings. Keeping track of work on projects is a concrete, realistic alternative to the procrastinator's tendency to remain vague and impressionistic. We think that using an un-schedule to monitor your projects and activities regularly is an enormous help in learning how to tell time more accurately.

TECHNIQUES TO IMPROVE YOUR TIMING

Practice Telling Time.   "I can read *War and Peace* in two nights." "I'll take a half day off to find a new apartment." "I can knock off my annual report in an hour." You can probably tell that these expectations are unrealistic. It's obvious that each of these activities will take a lot longer than the time allotted. Yet, to the student who is behind in his Russian literature class, to the harried school teacher who wants to move out of her parents' house, to the sales manager who hasn't compiled his yearly figures, these estimates seem possible. You have probably made some equally preposterous predictions about how long some task was going to take you and fully convinced yourself it was feasible.

One way to counter such wishful thinking is to compare your predictions about how long things take with what actually happens when you do them. For example, estimate how long it takes you from the time you hear the alarm in the morning to the time you leave your house, and then clock yourself. Or compare the number of pages of difficult material you read per hour versus your rate of reading an enjoyable novel. Or measure how long it takes you to drive across town. One procrastinator, a New York City businessman, planned his drives to Long Island using the timetable, "It takes 45 minutes without traffic." This is true, but had he ever driven to Long Island *without* traffic?

Learn to Use Little Bits of Time.   Alan Lakein made a great suggestion for procrastinators when he described the "Swiss cheese" method of time management in his book, *How to Get Control of Your Time and Your Life.* He recommends "poking holes" in a large task by using little bits of time instead of waiting for one large block of time. This technique can be an extremely helpful way for you to make a start on a project or to keep up some momentum once you have begun.

The significance of the "Swiss cheese" technique is that it advocates the value of any amount of time, no matter how small. The fact that your report will require 10 hours to prepare does not mean that you have to wait until you have a 10-hour block of time before you can start. There are a lot of crucial steps that you can take in just 15 minutes. If you're overwhelmed, you could make a list. If you've been avoiding the room where all your unfinished projects wait, you could just stand inside it for fifteen minutes, getting used to being there.

You may find small bits of time by surprise. If a colleague cancels an appointment that was supposed to last for a half-hour, you have just been given 30 minutes. If you finish your phone calls 10 minutes before you have to leave the office, those 10 minutes can be put to use.

The "Swiss-cheese" method has several advantages of particular benefit to procrastinators. For one thing, it's realistic. It is more likely that you can find 15 or 30 minutes here and there than a big block of free time. "I had so much paper work to catch up on," said a social worker, "that I thought I needed a whole day just to make a dent in it. Of course, I never had a whole day free, so I didn't do any of it, and I just fell further behind." If you're waiting for a large chunk of free time, you can wait forever.

In addition, setting a time limit for yourself is good practice for procrastinators. It helps you to counter the magical notion that one day when you have a lot of time you'll summon up all of your energy and just do it, until it's all done. This kind of time and this kind of effort rarely occur and even more rarely coincide.

Limiting your time working on a goal also makes it more tolerable. As difficult, unpleasant, or tedious as your desk may be, you can probably stand anything for 15 minutes. Horrible things can seem less horrible if you realize that getting started is not the beginning of an endless experience. And if you do manage to get even a little bit of a task accomplished, you're likely to feel good about it. Then the satisfaction you get from making progress can function as a reward. Believe it or not, you may be drawn to repeat the experience of working so that you'll feel good again.

This is a real contrast to the way you've probably been using work to punish yourself. If you've put something off, you may sentence yourself to solitary confinement for a whole weekend, in order to catch up. But the mere thought of such confinement can conjure up feelings of being chained to your desk while everyone else is watching football or going to the beach. The prospect of a lonely, arduous Sunday is hardly enticing, so you avoid it. Experience confirms what research has shown: Punishment is not a motivator. You're better off using a little carrot rather than a big stick.

Working in small amounts of time is an especially helpful technique when your procrastination is a sign that you're involved in a battle of wills, as we discussed in Chapter 3. If you put things off because you don't like feeling pushed around or controlled, your procrastination is saying, in effect, "You can't make me do this." Your sense of freedom and autonomy is somehow threatened if you go ahead and do the work. But if you decide that *you* will be the one to set your own time limits, that you will work for 10 minutes, or five minutes, *and no longer*, you can regain the sense of control you need and still move forward.

Using small bits of time is effective. A college professor was so pleased with this technique that she said, "I set my kitchen timer for an hour and use this method for all kinds of projects, from grading papers to cleaning closets. It gets me going, yet I know there's an end in sight!" Others are not so easily converted. If you don't see tangible results right away, you may discredit your initial steps, as if you'd taken none at all. You may find that doing a little at a time is inglorious. It's not as thrilling as being able to attack and conquer in one magnificent effort. A lawyer who had difficulty implementing this technique told us, "I still don't want to start anything unless I have enough time to finish it. I can see that thinking big is often counterproductive, but I do everything that way." The "all-or-nothing" view of life is a constant danger for procrastinators, and using small portions of time can be one antidote.

Expect Interruptions and Disruptions. According to Murphy's Law, "Anything that can go wrong, will go wrong." But many procrastinators don't believe that this rule of thumb will apply to them once they have finally made up their minds to get down to work.

Jack was scheduled for a job interview at 10 a.m. on Monday morning. He had to update his résumé to bring to the appointment, and he planned to do it over the weekend. After putting it off for two days, he finally started to revise the résumé on Sunday night. By the time he was ready to type it up, it was 9 p.m.

As Jack began to type the first lines, he saw with dismay that the words were faint on the page: He needed a new typewriter ribbon. At 9 p.m. on Sunday night, where could he get one? If he waited until Monday morning, would he have enough time to type the *vita* and make it to the interview? Frantically, he looked in the yellow pages for a store thath might be open late. No luck. Then, very upset and angry at himself, Jack started calling friends to see if he could borrow a typewriter. He found one, and had to drive over to his friend's house to do his résumé on an unfamiliar machine. He made a lot of errors, cursed the typewriter, and became increasingly frazzled. It was 1 a.m. before Jack finally got home with his new résumé, which was slightly smudged. Exhausted, he knew he wouldn't be alert for his interview.

Many of you can recall similar incidents when you've procrastinated and then been in a real jam because everything didn't go smoothly at the eleventh hour. Unexpected obstacles, like a phone call or a misplaced paper, can really throw you off balance. Why haven't you planned for the possibility that something could go wrong? Why assume that your effort is the only factor to consider? Once *you* finally overcome your own resistance and are ready to work, you may expect the rest of the world to cooperate.

Unfortunately, the world doesn't always take notice of your burst of resolve, and things go wrong at their usual rate. There *are* limits to what you can control. You can't get to the airport on time if there is a big traffic jam. You can't get your report to the Board if the Xerox machine breaks down. You can't study effectively all night if you're catching a cold. If you acknowledge in advance the possibility of random disaster, you are in a better position to take obstacles in stride instead of feeling either frantic or thwarted.

Delegate.   Delegating is a way to increase your efficiency. If you give some of your workload to someone else, then your burden is reduced and you are freed to concentrate on more important tasks. The process of delegating involves identifying tasks you alone don't have to do, finding the best person who could do it, making clear what needs to be done, and keeping track of how they're progressing.

Delegating sounds sensible and appealing. You'd think procrastinators would leap at the chance to lessen their burdens. But when we ask people to think specifically of a project they could actually give away, instead of feeling relieved, they usually object. Why?

"I should be able to do it all myself." Perhaps in your pursuit of perfection you believe that you should never have to ask for help. So you interpret delegating to mean that you have failed to meet your responsibility or that you are less competent. "I thought of hiring someone to clean my house while I was involved in an important court case," said an attorney, "but I know other women who are organized enough to do it all, and I should be, too."

We don't think delegating is a failure. It's a skill. The real failure occurs in stubbornly holding on to every item in your life so that you can't get half of them done.

"I'm the only one who can do this right." This is another perfectionistic pitfall. Although there may be some things that you—and only you—can do, is that really true of *everything* on your list of unfinished chores? Even if someone else wouldn't do it in quite your way, it would be better to have it done in a different manner than to leave it undone altogether. If you delegate, you will not have total control. You may have to stand that loss for the sake of accomplishment.

"Delegating is a cop-out." You may feel too guilty to ask for help. You may believe that because you've been Very Bad, you now have to be Very Good to make up for it. You may feel that you don't deserve to be helped, so you can't delegate or rely on others.

Refusing help is a good way to procrastinate yourself into martyrdom. "I was the only person on my committee who wasn't prepared for the meeting," reported a board member of a charitable organization. "I felt so terrible that I wouldn't talk to anyone about it. They did their work; why should they have to help me with mine? I wanted to be especially prepared the next time, but I wasn't so I didn't go to the meeting. Then I left the board."

This stoic and self-punitive approach does not increase your productivity; it only increases the pressure and, thus, your suffering. Adding pressure, as we have been saying, is adding problems.

"I might delegate the wrong thing to the wrong person." Even if you agree in principle that there are some matters you could shift to someone else, you may procrastinate in deciding what to delegate and to whom. It's best to delegate to someone who has the ability to help you, who doesn't hate you, and who isn't a procrastinator or a perfectionist. It also helps to release tasks that don't require your constant supervision, or you've defeated the purpose. But if you assume there is one right way to delegate, you will be unable to make a decision while you consider every possible angle, looking for the perfect solution. Anything you pass along will lighten your load, whether it's mundane or important.

"I'd run out of distractions." Imagine yourself getting help with many of the tasks that now bog you down. What then? Without the pressure of all those urgent demands, you'd have less standing between you and the really important things you've been avoiding. You'd be brought face to face with your fears. So if you are able to pare down your list of things to do, be forewarned that you may at first feel more anxiety than relief. But if you persevere, relief will probably come later.

Don't Spread Yourself Too Thinly. We knew a college student Greg, who took 18 course units, marched in the school band, played with an intercollegiate soccer team, and frequently traveled home to see his girlfriend. He'd squeeze in studying while he commuted home or between band practice and soccer practice. Although Greg claimed that school was his top priority, he behaved as if it were at the bottom of his list.

Clearly, if Greg really wanted to do better in school, he'd have to give something up. Perhaps drop band or soccer, and take fewer academic units. But when we suggested this to him, he refused. Greg wanted to do it all.

Is being too busy the same thing as procrastinating? It can be, if like Greg, you use your busyness to avoid something more important. In adding on commitments, not only are you setting the stage for procrastination, but you're also giving yourself a ready excuse: "I'm not really procrastinating, I'm just too busy to get everything done on time."

Take a hard look at your commitments (the un-schedule will be useful for this). Are you spread too thinly? Is this a set-up to procrastinate on something that matters? Aren't there things you really could give up? You may lose something in the process, but is it necessary for the sake of the greater goal?

We learned this lesson the hard way. While working full-time, we tried to write this book. Guess what happened? We couldn't do it! In addition to being teased mercilessly about procrastinating, we felt very bad that we weren't making more progress. Finally, with great reluctance, we decided to try working only part-time, and writing part-time. This proved to be successful. Although we missed our colleagues and our paychecks, we were able finally to turn out pages.

Identify Your Prime Time. If you promise yourself that you'll do 30 minutes of exercise each morning before work, but you're not really a morning person and you barely make it to work on time as it is, you're setting yourself up for failure. There is a natural rhythm to a day, and this rhythm is different for each of us. Think about when during the day you have the most mental energy, when you are most physically energetic, when you feel most sociable, and when you feel depleted. There's no point in planning to spend every night after work writing your novel, if all you have the energy for is a can of beer and reading someone else's novel.

You probably recognize the problem here for procrastinators: identifying your prime time means acknowledging that some of your time is less than prime. It's admitting that you can't work at top capacity all the time or whenever you think you should. It means realizing that you have human limits.

Enjoy Your "Free" Time.   It is ironic that procrastinators don't work, but they don't relax either. Even if you indulge in fun activities while you're procrastinating, chances are you're not enjoying them 100 percent because you know you're using them to avoid something else. Or, you may not even let yourself have these diversions because you feel unproductive and therefore undeserving. In either case, you're not having real fun.

Pleasure is so important in life. Try to plan for it, and give it to yourself, without guilt or desperation. Play time is necessary for everyone, no matter how degenerate you feel you are. If you deprive yourself of true relaxation, you will run out of energy the way a car runs out of gas. And you will steal leisure time by procrastinating.

10

Enlisting Support from Others

If we suggest that in your struggle to end procrastination you might get help from other people, what is your reaction? Does the idea of involving someone else sound like a weak-willed crutch, or does it perhaps conjure up the hope of being rescued?

Jack was shocked by the suggestion that he could consult other people about his procrastination. As administrative librarian for a large corporate bank, he felt his job required organization and efficiency. "I don't want anyone to help me or even to know that I'm not always up to date."

Alice had a very different reaction to the suggestion that she get some support. "I could ask my husband to help me. I have to analyze the computer output from a marketing survey and summarize the results for our weekly meeting, but I'm dreading it. If he sees how lost I am, maybe he'll take pity on me and do it for me. He's better at understanding statistics than I am anyway, and he hates to see me stay up all night." From the notion of getting help, Alice leapt to the hope of being rescued.

Finding creative ways to engage the support of others is not a statement of your weakness or incompetence, as Jack fears, nor is it a signal to back out completely and let someone else do your work for you, as Alice hopes to do. "Support" is a concept that is often misunderstood, by procrastinators and others alike.

For instance, the person who tells you to pull yourself together and get down to work may be trying to help you, but obviously doesn't understand your situation. If you *could* just "pull yourself together," you *would.* Support comes from someone who is predominantly on your side and tries to see things from your point of view. Supportive suggestions are ones that you can use to get yourself unstuck or that help you reach the very next point along the way.

Criticism and judgment are not supportive. They reinforce your own critical view of yourself and serve to hammer you down instead of buoying you up. A comment such as, "This is a poor piece of work" is critical and not supportive; however, "I think you have the capability to do better—what happened?" at least communicates some appreciation for your potential, and expresses interest in your plight.

Compliments are not necessarily supportive. You start a new job and your supervisor tells you, "You've come highly recommended and we're expecting big things from you, so let's see what you can do." Does this glowing speech feel like support or like pressure? Do you react with pride and confidence because you're so well-respected, or do you back away because you're afraid you won't live up to your reputation? Having great expectations put on you can be more of a burden than a motivator.

Unconditional praise is not really supportive either. You may develop the unrealistic idea that everything you do is terrific and should always be terrific. Hearing praise exclusively does not help you to accept whatever limitations you do have and to tolerate criticism when it does come.

Some procrastinators have told us that they do know how to get support from others. When they hit their last-minute frenzy, they latch onto anyone they can find to pitch in and help out. "At the last minute, I turn to everyone around me," said Daryl, an account executive for a drug company. "The weekend before my annual report is due, I have both my wife and my secretary typing at the office; my sales people are standing by their phones so that I can call them with any questions that might come up; my friend— a graphic artist—comes in to help me draw charts and tables; I even send my kids to their grandmother's house so that I can spend the whole weekend working with my crew." This arrangement may feel like support to Daryl, but he pays a price in the long run. He is resented for devoting everyone else's weekend to his project. It would be to everyone's benefit for you to enlist support *before* you get to the last-minute desperation stage, so that you can work with people without driving them crazy.

SETTING UP A SUPPORT SYSTEM

Choosing the Right People

When you're looking for support, you should give serious consideration to the question of who would be most helpful in which circumstances. We have a friend who is a terrific sounding board for our ideas. She has a tough intellectual mind and asks challenging questions that help us to clarify our thoughts—once we know what we're talking about. But if we were to discuss our ideas with her when they were just getting off the ground, her skepticism and her eye for contradictions could be devastating.

Another friend is always ready for fun. On any given evening, he knows where there are several interesting parties, what old movies are playing in town, or where to find a free concert. It's great to plan rewards with him—but he's not a good working partner, since he can't sit still long enough to get anything finished.

You must also think seriously about which people can help you because they have your best interests at heart and which people are unable to be wholeheartedly supportive. Sadly, we sometimes yearn for help from the very people who are least able to give it. You may crave support and encouragement from a parent, spouse, supervisor, or child—only to find repeatedly that neither is there. "Whenever I'm in trouble, I call my dad," said a business-woman who had always been close to her father. "If I'm in trouble at work, I think he'll know how to handle it. But instead, he criticizes me for having the problem in the first place. I probably shouldn't keep calling him, but each time I hope it will be different."

Whatever the reason some people can't help you—whether they are competitive, indifferent, or threatened, for example—their way of responding to you may set you back and increase the likelihood of your procrastinating. You'll need to learn from experience who is helpful to you and who is not.

Establishing
Communication

Once you've found people you can trust and rely upon, your next step may be to simply talk things over with them. Just having someone to listen to your side of the story can be a great support. But there are a number of other specific ways to get help for your procrastination through communication with the right person at the right time.

Make a Public Commitment. Tell someone what you're working on and when you want to complete it. You may take more seriously a commitment you've made to someone else than if you just think to yourself that you want to do something. It can work like telling a friend you're going on a diet—it's harder to eat dessert in front of someone who knows you're supposed to be abstaining. At the very least, going public with your intentions makes it very hard to avoid your goal in secret.

Make a Plan Together. Talking to another person forces you to put your thoughts into clear and concrete words and possibly receive necessary feedback. Once you state your goal openly, you may realize that you're trying to attempt too much, or you may discover that a plan that seemed overwhelming in your mind becomes more feasible as you explain it to a listener.

You can also benefit from hearing about how someone else has approached and solved a problem you're grappling with. We once interviewed a very prolific writer, comparing ideas about how to integrate writing into our other commitments. In contrast to our attempts to fit writing around the rest of our lives, he said, "I think of writing as my main priority. I work at it every day from 9 till 12 and I don't let myself be interrupted. I don't even answer the phone." We were startled. Not answer the phone? Actually let it ring when it could offer the possibility of a friendly chat, an invitation to escape, or a dire emergency? We could see from his clarity of purpose that we needed to change our perspective.

Another way to get helpful feedback on a situation is to discuss it with someone whose strengths are complementary to yours. If you're good at working out details, but have a hard time seeing the big picture, talk with someone who thinks in grand fashion. If you can creatively come up with several solutions to a problem, but you get bogged down trying to decide which would be best to implement, confer with a quick decision maker.

Keep in mind that even if you ask for help, you're not always obliged to take it. And don't be intimidated if this second party has an insight that you've overlooked. It's almost always easier to help someone else than to see your own issues clearly. When we work with groups of procrastinators, we ask people to formulate a goal and then to discuss their plans with two other people. Frequently, procrastinators can be very level-headed and realistic about the other person's project, while muddled and idealistic about their own. You might even try helping someone else think through a project of theirs to discover some of your own creative organizational and time-management skills.

Ask for Help When You're Stuck.   When you've procrastinated yourself into a bind, chances are you don't see a way out. Disheartened, you don't know what to do next, so you end up not doing anything. This is a good time to ask for help. But it is probably also a time when you feel so reprehensible that you're not sure you deserve to be helped. One procrastinator told us, "When I'm stuck, I hate myself so much that I don't even want to talk to other people, let alone ask them to help me. At these times I feel unfit for human contact." It is precisely when you have sunk to the depths of self-loathing that support can bring you the greatest relief. Someone else can be decent to you, even when you can't be decent to yourself. On the practical side, talking with someone else about your dilemma may help you to realize that all is not lost and enable you to find it within yourself to take some small step forward.

Working Together

Talking is great, but it has its limits. You still have to *do* something to make progress. There are several ways of working with other people that can help you do what has to be done. One of the most useful is to enlist a partner in a joint effort.

We weren't sure that either of us could write this book alone, but we were much more optimistic about doing it together. When two people are committed to the same goal, there is more incentive for both of you to live up to your commitments—if you don't, it's not only your life that's hurt, but someone else's, too.

It's also comforting to know that you're not the only one going through the agonies and deprivations of working hard. Our temptation to procrastinate would have been much more powerful had either of us been working by ourselves. On a beautiful sunny California day, when we were both sequestered indoors writing or rewriting, we each knew that there was at least one other person in the world who was not outside playing tennis or getting a suntan!

Having a partner also helps because you can create intermediate deadlines. If you set up regular meetings with your partner, it gives you some impetus to get to work—even if you wait until the night before the meeting to do it. Wanting to finish a chapter for a Thursday meeting is much more likely to inspire a trip to the library than is just thinking about having to work on it "sometime."

You can work with a partner as a co-equal, as we are co-authors, or you can engage a partner specifically as a check on your individual progress. A writer struggling with the draft of his first novel hired a friend to be his editor. He arranged weekly meetings with his "editor" so that he would feel the pressure to write something for his friend to read. You could also use your boss or supervisor as a partner by setting up a regular time to discuss your progress on a project. No matter how little you've actually accomplished, at the very least the meeting will be a consistent reminder for you. You'll have to do "some" thinking about the project in order to get through the meeting!

Parallel Play. As children develop, there is a period when they are toddlers during the which they engage in "parallel play." That is, they play *beside* each other with their own toys, rather than *with* each other. In the same way, you can arrange to work on your project with someone who works separately on his or her own task. For example, we know several people who hate to prepare their tax returns and get together every March for sessions they call "Tax Torture." Each person brings a large box filled with the forms, checks, receipts, and papers he or she needs. Then they all sit down together at a large table, moaning and groaning, but gradually get through the dreaded task.

You can arrange to work separately or together on all kinds of things that you've been postponing. One woman brought her ironing, which she hated to do, over to a friend's house, while the other woman wrote overdue thank-you notes for her wedding presents. An accountant arranged to meet a friend at the local library on Saturday mornings so that both could catch up on work they hadn't finished at their respective offices. They agreed that their offices and their homes would be more distracting environments.

Social Rewards. Sometimes progress is its own reward, but more often people are a better reward. One woman who worked at home told her husband to call one hour before he left his office. If she made a dent in her work by the time he arrived home, they would go out to dinner together. She spent the hour between the call and the dinner reading rather boring background material assigned by her company. Looking forward to going out gave her the incentive she needed to spend time on drudgery.

You can use social events as rewards at every step toward a goal: Call a friend after you've taken your first step and get some encouragement to continue; take a walk with someone when you need a break; go to the movies at the end of a long day; plan a holiday after you've completed a large project.

The whole process of using an alliance can be extremely effective for procrastinators: You commit yourself to a time to work; you have a reason to gather all the materials you'll need; you feel less isolated because you have a fellow sufferer; and you have someone to relax with when it's over.

But as useful as we think social support can be, there are also some potential dangers in relying on other people for help. There are some people who use social contact not as a reward for work accomplished, but for the purpose of procrastinating. They run around from one social activity to another, distracting themselves from their unfinished business. This kind of socializing is not a reward, it's a ruse. Further, the human contact it provides may not really be very satisfying, because there may be a sense of urgency in this frenetic activity. The pressure is on to have such a good time that regrets and twinges of guilt don't creep in. The procrastinator, while surrounded by people and engaged in activity, may still feel isolated and guilty.

Someone doing the job for you is not really a permanent solution either, though it may be a short-term boon. Perhaps you've had the experience of your parent finishing your home-work or preparing your school science project. You may have been bailed financially from a mess you'd procrastinated yourself into. Perhaps you were given a reprieve from a deadline that you'd feared was ironclad. In all of these cases, you probably felt great at the time. But that didn't stop you from procrastinating again. Ultimately, rescue adds to your sense of being weak. When you rely on someone else to do it for you, you never find out if you could have done it for yourself.

11

*Stress
and the
Procrastinator*

The issue of stress is an important one for procrastinators. Contrary to the myth that they are relaxed, easygoing, and lazy, we have seen that most procrastinators are in fact likely to be beset with fear, worry, and tension. For example, the stress inherent in the last-minute attempts to finish things is obvious. Just before a deadline, procrastinators may get "pumped up" for days of nonstop activity, consumed with the intensity of their drive to beat the clock. As pressure continues to mount, though, they may also become irritable, short-tempered, and relentless in pushing themselves and others to work faster and harder.

Stress is not, however, limited to such extreme circumstances. Consider the following examples.

Joan has fallen far behind in her college courses and doesn't want anyone to know. To hide her "terrible weakness," she uses her superior verbal skills to give an impression of being knowledgeable and confident. She puts a lot of effort into looking relaxed, and she works hard to smile, laugh, and to appear at ease. Behind this mask, however, Joan is tense. Her stomach is in knots, her shoulders are tight, and, at the end of the day, the muscles in her face often hurt. Because she is secretly terrified that at any moment she might be found out and exposed, she feels she must be careful to control even the smallest hint of uncertainty, anxiety, or fear.

Ed puts off small household tasks. Ellen, his wife of 35 years, constantly reminds him about a chore or repair that he hasn't done. Ed promises Ellen that he'll get around to it, but somehow he never does. After several more reminders, Ellen retreats into an irritated silence which is occasionally punctuated with pointed jokes and sarcastic comments about Ed's laziness. Each time this happens, Ed's stomach gets tight, his jaw tenses, and his hand curls into a fist. Sometimes just a glance from Ellen or the sight of an undone repair is enough to start Ed's blood boiling. But on the surface, Ed usually looks calm and unruffled. Few people would guess that this mild-mannered man is often seething with anger.

Larry is a journalist who agonizes over every word he writes. As a result, he repeatedly misses deadlines and his job is now in jeopardy. Whenever he sits down to write, he feels a tightness in his chest that constricts his breathing. His stomach often hurts. His mind wanders and he worries about how editors and readers will judge his words. To stave off rising panic, he may fix something to eat, pace back and forth, or try to watch TV. Gradually, Larry's worry turns into self-hate. He berates himself for his inability to produce anything, often yelling at himself out loud. "You dummy!" is one of his most-used phrases. He feels like hitting someone or lashing out and breaking something.

Although their life circumstances vary and their subjective experiences are quite different, all of the people above live with a high degree of stress that is directly related to their procrastination. Well before a deadline becomes imminent, they experience a build-up of tension that has serious effects on their lives. Procrastination can increase stress, and stress can increase procrastination. This cycle is hard to break, and can cause harm to your body, as well as to your ability to perform effectively. Making progress toward your goal can break the cycle and result in your feeling less nervous and depressed. Conversely, learning to manage stress more effectively can help you make progress. In order to understand more about breaking this cycle, let's first look at the signs of stress.

THE SIGNS OF STRESS

Think back to a time when you felt under a great deal of pressure. Recall the circumstances around the incident and remember how you felt. Can you identify any signs that might have been indications of the stress you were experiencing? Were there any changes in your behavior or attitude? Were there sensations in your body that were letting you know that you were feeling pressured?

Procrastinators we've talked to identify a number of different signs that are indicators of stress for them. Some signs are primarily physical. Others are behavioral or emotional. Here is a list of some of the more common signs procrastinators report.

Physical Signs
  a "knot," "butterflies," or pain in your stomach
  rapid heart beat, a "pounding heart"
  cold, clammy hands
  headache
  rapid breathing, hyperventilating
  tightness in neck or shoulders or both
  tension in the jaws (clamping or grinding teeth together)
  a weight or tightness in the chest
  lower back pain
  tendency toward illness (colds, flu)

Emotional and Behavioral Signs
  irritability
  fatigue, exhaustion (even upon awakening)
  trouble concentrating, sometimes even on small routine tasks
  mood swings
  increased alcohol or drug use
  changes in sleep, appetite, or sexual interest (marked increase
    or decrease)
  inability to relax, fidgeting
  inability to enjoy things that once brought you pleasure
  apathy, lethargy
  forgetfulness

Any one of these signs alone could be indicative of a number of different conditions—not just stress. However, alone or in combination, they do provide a general picture of how the procrastinator who is stressed may look and feel. Recognizing the signs of stress is the first step toward reducing it.

THE STRESS RESPONSE

We live in a world that is filled with stressors, that is, with demands on us to adapt and cope in order to survive. This is an age of fast-paced competitiveness, of crowded urban landscapes and rush-hour traffic jams. We are stressed all the time—we are constantly accommodating and responding to the changes and demands of our environment. Procrastinators are doubly stressed: Not only must they cope with environmental pressures, but also with the anxieties resulting from their delays. These external and internal stressors are not likely to disappear overnight, so it is important that we preserve our capacity to respond to them.

Stress researchers have emphasized that the stress response is an essential, adaptive mechanism that has long served a protective function for human and other animal species. They remind us that our cave-dwelling ancestors needed to be able to respond quickly to threats of danger. The threat may have been a bear or a mountain lion approaching the cave; it may have been a tree falling or a sudden rockslide. Crucial to their survival was the ability to quickly move from a relaxed state into a state of alertness. One had to be ready to do battle against the threat or to escape as swiftly as possible. Today, this response comes into play when a car swerves into our lane on the highway or when we suddenly awake, hearing strange noises in the middle of the night. This reaction is called the Fight-or-Flight response.

Once we perceive a threat, our bodies *automatically* make adjustments that are designed to maximize our ability to handle the danger. One of our most vital tools for survival is our capacity to think, so getting blood and oxygen to the brain is a major priority. Adrenalin is secreted into the bloodstream and our hearts immediately pump harder and faster, raising our blood pressure to send blood to the brain as rapidly as possible. The result is that blood is drained away from the extremities of our bodies, leaving our hands and feet cold, and digestive functions slow down as blood is diverted to places where it is most needed, in the head and vital organs. We breathe more rapidly in order to increase our intake of oxygen. Our muscles become tense and ready for action. The clotting response in our blood begins, ready to repair any wounds or injuries we might sustain.

Our response to threat is a non-specific one that affects every aspect of our physical functioning. Our cardiovascular, gastro-intestinal, skeletomuscular, and immune systems all make ad-justments, from the increased secretion of stomach acid and of steroids, to the constriction of the hair follicles of the skin (resulting in "goose bumps" or "chicken skin").

Hans Selye, an eminent stress researcher, found that our bodies respond this way not only to threats that are dangerous or unpleasant, but also to events that are desired or pleasurable, such as a job promotion, falling in love, or moving into a new home. On a purely *physical* level, there is very little difference between the state you experience when you are angry or afraid and that which you experience when you are elated or excited. In any of these situations, adrenalin is released into your bloodstream and the nonspecific stress response described above begins.

The difference in our experience of a situation lies in how we *label* the physical sensations that we feel. We might interpret this condition as pleasure, fear, anger, or anxiety, depending on the context in which it occurs. Your heart pounding wildly means one thing to you when you think about writing the speech you have to give; it means something entirely different when your favorite sports team has a chance to pull out from behind to win in the final seconds of the championship game.

So far we have been talking about our response to external events. But we are not simply passive organisms who react only when outside circumstances impinge upon us. We can think, which allows us to remember the past and to anticipate the future. Our capacity to imagine allows us to construct inner realities, private worlds of dreams and fantasies in which anything can come true. Sometimes these ideas spur us on toward accomplishment, some-times they are relaxing, and sometimes they are just plain fun. But there are also times when we imagine ourselves to be threatened or in danger, even when by all objective standards, there is no "real," life-threatening danger in sight. What is so threatening about writing a letter to an old friend? What is so traumatic about signing up for an exercise class or mowing the front lawn? What is so dangerous about going on an interview?

Obviously none of these activities present danger in the way that a mountain lion or someone pointing a gun at you would be a threat to your existence. Some people find writing letters or mowing the lawn fun, relaxing, or simply boring tasks that must be done. It's a question of interpretation, and of what danger that activity holds for you.

As a procrastinator, for example, you might see a letter as evidence of your writing ability (and therefore of your value as a friend and human being), so you believe it must be a witty, poetic, well-written little essay, full of interesting phrases and elegant grammatical structures. Or, the letter may be a reminder of how you've let the friendship go, and therefore is a testimonial to what a disloyal and uncaring "friend" you really are. In either case, you may feel open to devastating criticism, if not from someone else, then from the critic within you. Perhaps you've been nagged by someone to take an exercise class or mow the lawn. In your mind doing these activities might mean you'll be capitulating to someone else's demands. You would feel you had lost the battle and been stripped of your autonomy and independent will. That would be a dangerous matter indeed.

Our bodies are not very good at differentiating between "real" threats and situations that aren't truly dangerous but that we interpret as threats. If you see the performance evaluation from your boss as a threat to your self-esteem or well-being, there would be no difference between that performance evaluation and a mountain lion stalking through your living room, as far as your body is concerned. If you imagine your boss criticizing you for your lateness, saying that your work could have been better, and if you are worried that you could lose your job, your body prepares to meet that threat by mobilizing the stress response. Your muscles tense, your heart beats faster and your blood pressure rises. Perhaps you get a headache or your ulcer acts up. It doesn't matter whether the performance evaluation is tomorrow or six months from now. It doesn't matter whether your boss is really a push-over instead of a tyrant. If you *think* you are endangered, then for your body, the threat is real.

The Effects of Stress

Clearly, the stress response is a vital part of our capacity to survive and cope with threat. Why then is so much currently written about how bad stress is for you? We hear over and over again about how stress can lead to job burn-out. We hear that

"Type A Behavior" is bad for your heart. We are informed that there is a connection between stress and illness—not just coronary disease, but also arthritis, colitis, ulcers, cancer, and disorders of the immune system. People talk about stress as being one of the significant killers of the modern age. How can stress both protect and destroy at the same time?

The answer lies in the fact that the stress response we have described is helpful in the rapid mobilization of our defenses in acute situations. Its function is to help us overcome the stressor, by either fighting it or getting out of the way, so that we can return to the normal business of everyday living. The stress response is not meant to be prolonged into an ongoing part of our lives. Our bodies need time to recover from this protective effort, a chance to return to a state of rest and recuperation, in much the same way that a good night's sleep helps us recover from the efforts of one day and prepares us for the next.

All too often, however, we do not allow ourselves that time to rest. For example, after a long day at work you get in your car, thinking about the report that you haven't yet written for tomorrow's meeting, and you find yourself in the middle of rush-hour traffic. Thinking about the report adds to an already stressful situation. Or, when you finally have made a start on something you've been putting off, all you can think of is how bad, inadequate, or ridiculous your work is. You anticipate being criticized for your stupidity and laziness and your body continues to prepare itself for the battle that you constantly anticipate. No longer is the stress response something that is mobilized for specific moments of danger. It becomes a response that is constantly, chronically in action. It is this *frequent, repetitive* mobilization of our defensive reactions that is so wearing and destructive over time.*

---

*Selye has suggested that each of us is born with a certain capacity for adaptation. He calls this our "adaptation energy," and he believes that it is a genetically inherited, *finite* capacity to respond to stress. Some people "inherit" more adaptation energy than others, so their bodies are consequently able to tolerate greater demands before wearing down. Selye likens our adaptation energy to a monetary inheritance, which we can choose to squander recklessly or to invest wisely. If we squander our energy inheritance recklessly, driving ourselves relentlessly or "burning the candle at both ends," it will quickly be depleted, leaving us exhausted and burned-out. Thoughtful expenditure of effort, with periodic re-investments (such as taking time to do nothing or going on a relaxing vacation) can help extend the reserve of energy available to us over a longer period of time. Although we can recover from short-term expenditures

(*note continues on page 182*)

The duration of stress is not the only important factor that diminishes a person's ability to perform effectively. The *intensity* of stress is also a significant influence. Many people think that the more stressed or "psyched up" they are, the better they will do. For many procrastinators, "I work best under pressure" is a convincing argument for putting things off until the last minute. They believe that without the external pressure of a deadline or without the build-up of their own anxiety and internal pressure over time, they wouldn't do anything. And they're right—but only up to a point.

A person must experience *some* anxiety or physiological pressure in order just to get going. If we were not stressed at all, we'd be dead. At just a minimal level of activity we'd either be very relaxed, or asleep. You have to be alert in order to read a book, organize your desk, or write a letter. You need to be able to think quickly and clearly when you call a prospective client or meet with your boss. In other words, performance improves as anxiety increases.

However, this relationship does not continue on indefinitely. A substantial body of research confirms that there comes a point at which performance begins to decline as anxiety continues to rise. Perhaps you become restless—you can't sit still or think straight, you have a hard time breathing, and your head starts to hurt. When you try to read your book you can't concentrate even though the exam is tomorrow. Or, when you talk with the prospective client, you feel so anxious that you are stiff and tense, you miss a lot of what he says, and you can't think of what to say next.

The figure on page 183 roughly illustrates this curvilinear relationship between anxiety and performance:

There is, for each one of us, an *optimal* level of anxiety, a range within which we function best and our performance is maximized. This optimal range varies from person to person, as well as from situation to situation for a given individual. Performance on simple, routine tasks, for example, tends to be enhanced by high levels of anxiety, whereas complex tasks are best handled when anxiety is moderate. The challenge, of course, is to stay within your own optimal range.

(continued from page 181)

of effort by resting or relaxing, Selye believes that we can never regain the initial amount of adaptation energy with which we started. Our only choice in the matter is how fast we use it up.

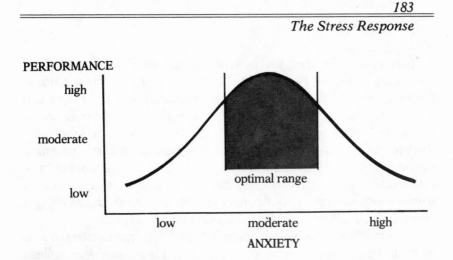

How the Procrastinator Experiences Stress

There are several ways in which procrastinators are especially prone to stress. The last-minute frenzy that is so common among procrastinators is typically a very high-stress situation. Whether you experience yourself as panicked with fear and worry or as flying high on the thrill of danger and risk, your body is mobilized for a full, all-out effort. You perform at top speed, aiming for maximum output in the shortest possible time. That is stress. Sometimes you may be so anxious and stressed that your performance is seriously impaired. At other times, the energy of the last-minute frenzy may allow you to pull through just in the nick of time. If you repeatedly get yourself into these full-alert, high-stress situations, you may, over the long haul, be exhausting yourself and wearing your body down.

Putting things off, too, often creates an internal build-up of pressure and stress. When you initially put something off, it may be of little consequence to you. As time passes and you still haven't gotten around to it, however, you begin to feel increasingly worse. The task nags at you, never leaving you in peace, seeming larger and less manageable as the days go by. In addition, you may become angry with yourself for not getting it done, as did Larry, the journalist we mentioned earlier. This kind of gradual intensification of pressure over time also mobilizes the stress response in your body, though probably at a more moderate level than during the last-minute frenzy. The longer you put things off and the more upset, anxious, or angry you become, the more stress you are contending with on a chronic, daily basis.

It may also be that the task or activity that is being avoided may in and of itself be a source of stress for the procrastinator—the favor you must do for someone you don't like, the tax return that's due, the doctoral or master's thesis that seems ominous. As we have seen, the tasks themselves are usually not inherently threatening, but the procrastinator has attributed some meaning to the activity or views it in such a way that it feels particularly unpleasant or dangerous. The task thus becomes a source of tremendous anxiety, and the mere thought of the dreaded thing is enough to mobilize the procrastinator's stress response.

A fourth way in which procrastinators may experience stress is in their relationships with other people. Like Joan, the college student who got behind on her coursework, some procrastinators worry about how other people will view them, so they try to look cheerful and confident in public, hiding their uncertainty and their fear. This kind of vigilance is highly stressful because it demands constant alertness, careful attention to the reactions of other people, and unceasing scrutiny of one's own behavior.

Relationships can also be stressful when other people become involved in the cycle of procrastination. Initially the other person may try to be supportive and help the procrastinator get going, but often the situation deteriorates into a power struggle, with attempts to pressure, cajole, entice, or shame the procrastinator into action. The other person may embody the procrastinator's internal critical voice—impatient, aggravated, angry, disappointed—and so become someone to be avoided or, at least, someone to be defended against. Over time, tension escalates, as it did between Ed and his wife Ellen, and the relationship evolves into another source of stress through apprehension, resentment, and threat. (We'll talk about managing relationships with other procrastinators in Chapter 12.)

Finally, some people procrastinate when stress from other aspects of their lives has become too great. One young professional woman who is generally responsible and attentive to her business affairs periodically finds herself putting things off—paying bills, getting her laundry done, or having her car serviced. Puzzled by her behavior, she thought about when these situations tended to occur, and she realized that she procrastinates at times when her job has been particularly demanding, and she feels exhausted and overextended. "I'm tired of being responsible," she said. "I want somebody to take over and let me rest!" In another situation, a salesman doing well at work put off personal things, such as tasks around the house and activities that were for his own enjoyment or well-being. His wife had recently moved out of their house and was planning to file for divorce. The separation was a tremendous stress for him, though he maintained a cheerful demeanor with friends and colleagues. This man's depression and the stress of the separation were evident in the difficulty he had doing things for himself.

Now let's consider the stresses in your life by going through a short exercise. Think about all the changes, both positive and negative, that you have gone through over the last 6–12 months. Recall the various situations you have had to cope with at home, on the job, with friends and family. How busy have you been? Have you had a lot of free time to fill? Are there new elements for you to adjust to—a new child, a different job or living situation, a romantic relationship, or a new school program? Have you experienced any losses—the death or illness of a loved one, marital separation or divorce, children leaving home, loss of a job, a move to a new city?

Think back over the signs of stress we listed at the beginning of the chapter. Have you experienced many of those signs over the last 6 months or so? How frequently do these signs appear? How severe are they? Are there one or two signs that are reliable indicators that you are stressed? Can you identify the first clue you get? Are there certain kinds of situations that almost always make you feel stressed? What are they? What about them is so stressful for you?

The benefits of asking yourself questions like these are, first, to become familiar with events or situations that are stressors *for you* and, second, to recognize your stress response when it occurs. Sometimes you'll be glad for the energy and alertness it provides for you, but there may be other times when you'll want to reduce the stress your feel.

Reducing Physical Tension

It is terribly important for procrastinators to learn how to relax physically. Psychological tension and anxiety are incompatible with physical relaxation. If your muscles are relaxed, you cannot be tense at the same time. One method of relaxing physically is to focus on your breathing. When we are stressed, our muscles tighten and our breathing becomes rapid and shallow. Sometimes we actually *forget* to breathe for a few seconds, or realize suddenly that we have been holding our breath during a tense moment. When you instead deliberately breathe slowly and deeply, muscles that have tensed up will soften and relax. You may be surprised how helpful a few slow, deep breaths can be at moments of high tension, panic, or anger!

If you wish, as you breathe slowly and easily, you can allow yourself to imagine being in a place that is soothing to you. Many people "go" to the ocean where they can "listen" to the sounds of waves on the beach and "smell" the saltiness of the sea air. Other people like to imagine themselves in the mountains, far from the demands of work and home as they walk along a ridge or through a forest. Some people recall a place that has been particularly comforting to them—lying in a hammock on the porch, sitting under a favorite tree from childhood. You can imagine whatever you want and enjoy it fully, as you let the tension gradually lessen and fade away.

These kinds of breathing techniques can be used at any time. They can help you relax a bit when you are at a moment of peak tension, and they can also be of benefit in helping you moderate the level of stress in your day-to-day life.

Another method of relaxing physically is to focus on various parts of your body one by one, first tensing that body part as much as you can, then relaxing it. This is the technique known as Progressive Relaxation, developed by Edmund Jacobsen in the 1920s. Jacobsen observed that people could achieve a greater degree of deep muscle relaxation if they tightened the muscles they wanted to relax *before* actually trying to relax them. Although Progressive Relaxation takes practice and some time to learn, most people are able to relax themselves quite rapidly after several weeks of daily practice. Here is how to use this technique:

Sit in a comfortable position, legs uncrossed.

Give yourself 10–15 minutes of quiet time to begin with—later you may only need 3–5 minutes.

Start by closing your eyes and breathing evenly.

Tense the selected body area (see list below); hold the tension tightly for about 5–10 seconds.

Relax the area you just tensed for 10–15 seconds. Let those muscles become soft, heavy, warm and loose. Breathe slowly and comfortably.

Progress slowly through each muscle group and repeat the tense-relax sequence a second time for any areas that are especially tight.

List of body parts with suggestions for tensing them:

1. Right hand and forearm. (Make a tight fist.)
2. Right upper arm. (Press arm against the side of your body.)
3. Left hand and forearm.
4. Left upper arm.
5. Forehead. (Raise eyebrows as high as possible, or frown deeply.)
6. Eyes and nose. (Squint hard and wrinkle up your nose.)
7. Mouth and jaw. (Clench teeth; force lips back or tightly together.)
8. Neck. (Push chin down and back—toward back of neck.)
9. Chest and shoulders. (Take a deep breath, hold it, and press shoulder blades down and together; or, shrug shoulders up to ears.)
10. Internal organs. (Tighten stomach, as if preparing to be punched in the abdomen. Also, tense pelvic area by squeezing buttocks tightly together.)
11. Right upper leg. (Tighten thigh.)
12. Right calf. (Point toes up toward your head.)
13. Right foot and toes. (Curl toes down and flex foot.)
14. Left upper leg, calf, and foot.

In addition to relaxing physically, you can reduce tension by changing your thoughts. Criticizing yourself, anticipating catastrophe, and focusing on faults, inadequacies and things left undone probably won't help you take action and will more likely increase your level of stress. When you find yourself thinking something that increases your stress, substitute some other phrase that helps relax you. For example, suppose you realize that you're thinking, "I've got to hurry. There's not much time left. I'll never make it!" You might interrupt that thought and say to yourself, "Calm down. Do what you can."

Doing something physically active on a regular basis is always good therapy for stress. (If you've been putting off getting exercise, this may be a hard one for you.) Physical activity stimulates the production of certain brain substances called endorphins, that are associated with a sense of well-being and calm. People who exercise regularly generally feel better about themselves. Exercise can be a useful way to release built-up tension and frustration, too. A good game of tennis or racquetball, swimming laps in the local pool, or even a brisk walk around the block often works wonders in letting go of the tension of tight muscles and anxieties.

Give yourself some time alone, time that's just for you. A 15- or 30-minute period without distractions, during which you don't have to achieve anything, can be a real comfort. If you don't have much time for yourself, or if you busy yourself with work and chores when you are alone, try taking a 15-minute period now and then to do absolutely nothing. This may be hard to do at first, but once you learn that it really is okay to do nothing, you'll probably find yourself cherishing private moments of quiet contemplation or rest—and your body will thank you for it.

Increasing Alertness

Some of you may find that there are times when you want to *increase* your pressure or anxiety rather than reduce it. You feel tired and are ready to fall asleep as soon as you open the book to study. Your body feels lethargic, and it takes all the energy you can muster just to turn on the TV set.

What is important in situations like these is to give yourself some short-term stimulation so that you can get started or make a small dent in what you want or have to do. You may not like it any better, and you may not become happily engrossed in your task, but if you can increase your physical alertness you can at least begin.

The best way we know of to increase your alertness is to wake up your body. If you find yourself sitting or lying down, not wanting to move, change your position. Stand up and stretch for a few minutes—reach for the ceiling, then bend over down toward the floor. Swing your arms in big circles; bend from side to side at the waist. Shake your hands as if you were rapidly flinging water off of them. Do a little running in place. Take a short, brisk walk. The important thing is to move. You aren't doing this for exercise, but to get your blood circulating and to get more oxygen up to your brain. You may only need two or three minutes to feel more alert.

Some people find that a shower helps them wake up and feel energized. If you don't want to take a shower, you could rinse your face with cool water, brush your teeth, brush your scalp, or lightly slap your skin all over your body until it tingles.

Once you are feeling a little more alert, you can at least make a start on what you want to do. If you have trouble maintaining your alertness as you work, you might find it useful to take short "wake-up breaks" every 15 minutes or half-hour to re-energize yourself again.

12

Living and Working with Procrastinators

We address this chapter to those of you whose lives are affected by someone else's procrastination, as well as to those procrastinators who want to understand the effects of their delay on others. Whether or not you are a procrastinator yourself, you may struggle with one in your life, trying vainly to motivate him or her into action, becoming more frustrated and disgusted each day. Or you may be struggling within yourself, living with the painful awareness that someone you care about is making a mess of his or her life, and not knowing how to help. Just as we have no simple solution for procrastinators who read this book, we have no simple answer for those of you who live and work with them. But we do have ideas about what helps and what doesn't.

THE CYCLE OF MUTUAL FRUSTRATION

I'm so fed up with Jamie not doing his homework. I've tried everything, and I'm absolutely at my wit's end. He's ruining his life! He can't see it, and I can, but he won't listen to me.

My company's productivity level is down because people won't complete assignments on time. I've singled out the worst cases, and told those people that if they don't shape up, they'll be in big trouble. But it doesn't do any good—they still drag their tails. It will cost the company money to hire and train new people, So I should try to solve the problem first rather than fire them. I don't know what to do.

You probably know that it can be very frustrating to live or work with a procrastinator. Their chronic lateness, their inaction, their not following through on commitments, can be difficult to understand if you are a nonprocrastinator who usually gets things done on time—and exasperating if you are a super-organized person who handles responsibilities with the utmost care and efficiency. They can also be hard to help if you're someone who struggles with the same problem.

With a procrastinator, it's easy to be drawn into a cycle doomed to frustration without ever realizing what is happening. Because procrastinators are so often indirect about what they are or aren't doing, you can be fooled into thinking that things are better or worse than they really are and that the reasons procrastinators give for their delay are the whole truth, when in fact, they are only part of the story. It's very hard to get a clear and realistic picture of what's going on, because the procrastinator either does not want, or is unable, to tell you. In either case, you are left to grope in the dark.

The cycle of mutual frustration has an infinite number of variations. However, the basic struggle always centers on one essential problem: You want the procrastinator to do something and he or she doesn't to do it. Let's take a closer look at what often happens.

Stage 1: Encouragement

When people first become aware that a procrastinator is having difficulty getting work done, they usually attempt to reassure and encourage the procrastinator with statements such as, "I know you can do it"; "Don't worry, there's still time"; "You just think it's harder than it really is; it won't be so bad once you start, you'll see." If you are a non-procrastinator, you may know that inaction doesn't lead anywhere. You know that you have to *do* something to get started, even if it is unpleasant, imperfect, or frightening at first. When a procrastinator is stuck, you may assume that with enough of your clear thinking and encouragement, he or she will finally see the logic in what you are saying, and will get going.

Unfortunately, the procrastinator usually does not hear your encouragement as support. Your insistence that a task isn't so difficult may be experienced as pressure, as an attempt to take control and force the procrastinator into action. If the procrastinator thinks you are being pushy, he or she is likely to feel resentful and push back, slowing down even more. Or, your reassurance may be experienced as pressure to perform well. This is particularly true for encouragement that reminds the procrastinator of his or her intelligence, competence, or skill, e.g., "You're so smart. I know you will do a terrific job." Deep down, even the most talented procrastinator may be afriad that he or she can't do the job. Feeling that you do not truly understand his or her plight, the procrastinator may *appear* reassured and encouraged, but internally may be more apprehensive than ever, knowing your reassurance is undeserved. You're just another person who's been fooled.

Consider the example of Craig who, at age 26, has returned to college for the third time and is currently struggling through his sophomore year. "I keep trying to believe what everyone tells me," he said. "They all say I have the brains to get through college, that if I just apply myself and work hard, I'll have no trouble doing well. But I don't really believe it. Everybody else seems to have forgotten I flunked out twice before. They just don't understand what it's like."

Other procrastinators will immediately reject any encouragement you offer. They may play the "Yes, but..." game, recognizing the validity of what you are saying, then coming up with six reasons why it won't work for them. "You're right, I ought to just make a start on the taxes, but I've got a lot of other things to do first." Or, "Narrowing the scope of this report probably *would* make it a lot easier to do. But I'd have to leave out a lot of important information and it just wouldn't be the same." Sometimes the procrastinator won't even acknowledge your attempt to help, and will instead leap directly into rejecting what you say. "This project is a lot more complicated than you think. It's easier to give advice than to put it into practice!"

Thus, whether the procrastinator reacts to your support with signs of reassurance, stymies you with a "Yes, but," or rejects your help altogether, the end result is that mere encouragement usually fails to get the procrastinator moving.

Stage 2: Disappointment

When it becomes clear that your initial efforts to be helpful and encouraging have not worked, it's easy to feel disappointed. Your disappointment may come from a feeling that the procrastinator has let you down somehow. *You've* put out a lot of effort to help, and your advice has gone unheeded. In your mind, perhaps, the procrastinator hasn't kept his or her side of the bargain which was implicit in your offer of help: "I'll give you my help and then you'll change. You'll start moving if you do as I suggest." This hidden *quid pro quo* may leave you feeling as though you've done all the work while the procrastinator has taken it easy.

You might also feel disappointed with yourself, thinking that the procrastinator would have been able to make progress if you had just done a better job of helping: You could have been more encouraging or thought of a more useful suggestion or you could have been more available to help. In essence, you are taking the burden of responsibility for the procrastinator's continued in-action on your own shoulders.

Whether their disappointment is with themselves, with the procrastinator, or a combination thereof, most people attempt to rectify the situation by trying even harder to help. They offer *more* encouragement and better advice, hoping that this will get the procrastinator moving, and thereby alleviate their disappointment.

It doesn't work.

The procrastinator, being exquisitely attuned to other people's reactions, will sense your disappointment and feel worse than ever. In addition to worrying about facing the task itself, he or she now must worry about letting *you* down. Soon, the procrastinator will silently begin to resent your investment in his or her progress—you become another expectation to live up to, another person to hide from. And ever so gradually, he or she will withdraw from you, attempting to shut out both your disappointment and your renewed efforts to help.

Stage 3: Irritation

Irritation often follows on the heels of disappointment. You begin to view the procrastinator's inaction as being willfully (perhaps even maliciously) motivated. This passivity may be incomprehensible to you, and you may feel stymied at every turn.

Irritation may derive from several different sources. You may, for example, be furious because the procrastinator who has rejected every effort you've made to help is still stuck, reciting the same tales of woe you heard at the outset. You've offered so much, but it's still not enough, still not accepted, still not appreciated. By now he or she may be angry at you too, telling you, directly or indirectly, to "get off my back." Frustration is also likely to mount when you have been trying to get the procrastinator to follow through on something that affects your welfare, too—a joint project at work, for example. Despite your initial patience and gentle reminders, he or she continues to put it off—leaving you understandably resentful. Finally, your frustration may evolve out of your feeling of helplessness as you watch the procrastinator head for self-imposed destruction. You've done all you could to help, and still the procrastinator delays, flirting with dismissal from school, loss of a job, financial ruin, legal retribution, or deterioration of physical health. Sometimes it's tempting to berate the procrastinator, lashing out with moralizing reproach. At least you can feel that you're doing *something*—even if it only makes things worse.

Stage 4: Stand-Off

At this point, both you and the procrastinator are caught in a deep rut. You are entrenched in the position of trying to get the procrastinator moving; the procrastinator is by now equally entrenched in the position of determined resistance. Tension can hang in the air like a thick cloud, with resentment brewing on both sides.

Over a long enough period of time, such a stand-off can destroy what was once a satisfying relationship and lead to the break-up of a marriage, a friendship, or a business partnership. Or, it can continue to haunt the relationship, reappearing periodically at moments of stress or disagreement. Sometimes the persons involved manage to salvage the relationship—the procrastinator eventually gets the task done, or you give up trying to force the issue. You manage to get through it this time—but not without pain and bitterness.

NEGOTIATING WITH A PROCRASTINATOR

How can you deal with a procrastinator so as to avoid, or at least minimize, the cycle of mutual frustration? How can you interact with a procrastinator and still maintain a relationship that is basically positive for you both?

Part of the answer depends on the nature of your relationship to the procrastinator. Your concerns will be quite different if the procrastinator you are dealing with is your employee, your boss, your child, your romantic partner, a close friend, or a casual acquaintance. But there are also some general considerations that can make life easier for both you and your procrastinator. First we'll identify some methods that *don't* work with *any* procrastinator.

What Doesn't Work

Saying, "Just Do It!" This phrase is the bane of the procrastinator's existence. Upon hearing it, he or she is likely to respond with a mix of resentment, frustration, anxiety, and self-deprecation. When you say "just do it," you emphasize the procrastinator's glaring inability to do what everyone else seems to be able to do, i.e., to get on with the responsibilities of life. The procrastinator will only feel worse about something that is already a depressing source of humiliation and fear, and find it even harder to take action.

Nagging and Being a Watchdog. This strategy puts you right in the middle of the cycle of mutual frustration and is doomed to fail. When you continually check up on the procrastinator's progress or remind him or her about what needs to be done, you invariably will be perceived as a watchdog—and be resented for it. The more you nag, the less the procrastinator will do. You may be placated with promises, but the procrastinator will feel so resentful of your watchfulness (however altruistically motivated) that he or she may slow down further just to get back at you.

Using Criticism, Ridicule, and Threats of Extreme or Exaggerated Consequences. The idea behind this strategy is that if you shame procrastinators enough, especially in public, they will stop delaying and start working. We've heard countless stories about parents and teachers who have announced in front of the class or in the presence of friends comments such as, "It's ridiculous to put off something that's so easy. Haven't you got your head screwed on right?" Such comments would be hurtful to anyone, and are especially so for procrastinators. Although you may succeed in humiliating them into taking some quick action, your success will be short-lived, because they will remember the indignity with a bitterness that will color all of your future interactions.

Similarly, threats of extreme or exaggerated consequence may result in momentary compliance, but in the long run will only alienate the person from you and paralyze him or her more severely. The father of one procrastinator continually warned, "If you don't start making more of an effort in school, you'll never get a job. And without a job you can't support a family. Nobody wants a loser—and that's what you'll be." The father started issuing these warnings when his son was in fourth grade. After hearing one, the son would dutifully spend more time looking at his books. But he wasn't reading; he was seething inside, thinking about how much he hated his father, and plotting ways to retaliate against him. He also began to worry that maybe his father was right after all— maybe he *was* a loser who wouldn't ever amount to anything. The son began to avoid schoolwork altogether.

Doing It Yourself. As we've mentioned in Chapter 10, you should never—except in rare cases—come to a procrastinator's rescue by doing the task yourself. It may be tempting to swoop in and take over, especially if you can see that there will be significant consequences if the procrastinator doesn't get it done. But in becoming the "magic solution" you perpetuate the procrastinator's problem. In the future, the procrastinator may continue to put things off, harboring the fantasy that you or someone else will come to the rescue at the last minute. What procrastinators need to learn is how to do things for themselves.

Saying "I Told You So!" If indeed things turn out the way you predicted, you may be tempted to remind the procrastinator that you were right. You want to say, "I told you so." But if you act on that impulse, what will happen? Will it help the procrastinator? Probably not. Whether or not he or she can admit it, the procrastinator already knows that you were right, and feels bad. Your saying, "I told you so!" is like rubbing salt into a wound. You may feel vindicated, but it will only further alienate the procrastinator from you.

Attitudes That Can Help

As we've said, there is no one guaranteed method for dealing with a procrastinator. Nevertheless, there are some general attitudes and specific responses that, when put into practice, can make life for you and your procrastinator a lot easier.

Maintain Your Individual Perspective.   It's easy to forget that you and your procrastinator are separate individuals. With time, you may begin to feel as though the procrastinator's problems were your own. You may develop a strong personal investment in the procrastinator's success, as if you need the procrastinator to perform well in order to feel good about yourself. If he or she doesn't, you feel lessened as a person—and eventually become frustrated, angry, and resentful.

Carol—at her wit's end with her 16-year-old son, Jamie—had lost the perspective that the two were separate people. She felt totally responsible for him. If Jamie didn't do well in school, it meant that she had failed as a mother in raising him. This attitude had been reinforced in PTA meetings where Carol would listen to teachers link troublemaking kids to their parents' negligence. She worried that other parents would think that she was irresponsible if she didn't force Jamie to do his homework.

Unfortunately, this kind of involvement will only make things worse for both you and your procrastinator. Even if Carol had succeeded in making Jamie sit with his school books for an hour a day, only Jamie himself could read the printed page and record it in his brain. You, too, must remind yourself that your power over your procrastinator is limited. You can try to influence your procrastinator to do what you want, but you can never make him or her take action. So if your previous efforts have been based on the idea that you can (or should be able to) force your procrastinator to act, you'll be more effective if shift your perspective.

Be Flexible About Your Strategy. This is a basic rule of thumb that is important in all personal interactions. All too often, when a strategy has failed to yield the desired results, people try the same thing over and over again, with increased insistence. It would be more helpful to do something that is fundamentally different from their previous efforts.

Carol tried many ways to get Jamie to stop procrastinating on his homework. For a time she nagged him: "Don't forget the science test you have on Friday, Jamie," "You should start on your paper before it's too late." Jamie usually responded by sulking, or by simply ignoring Carol altogether. When nagging didn't work, Carol tried to bribe him: "If you do an hour of homework every day for a month, I'll buy you a radio for your room." "Listen, you won't have to do the dishes if you'll finish your math problems before dinner." Not a chance. Next, Carol attempted to motivate Jamie with guilt. "After all that your father and I have done for you—can't you even do your school work? What an ungrateful child you are!" Still no success. Finally, Carol tried to threaten Jamie with moralistic doom: "You've got to learn how to discipline yourself, Jamie. How will you ever make it through life if you can't do basic math?"

What Carol failed to realize is that her "different" strategies are all variations of the same basic tactic: She is pushing Jamie to take action, whether it be by nagging, threatening, or bribing. It took time for Carol to see that everything she'd been doing was in one way or another aimed at convincing Jamie to do his homework— and nothing had come of it but conflict and resentment. Carol and Jamie are in a stand-off.

Eventually, Carol did do something quite novel. She decided she would stop pushing Jamie to study. Rather than pressuring him to do his homework, Carol said to him, "It's part of growing up to learn to make decisions for yourself. You have to decide how important school is to you." As part of her strategy, Carol no longer mentioned homework to Jamie or warned about the disastrous future that awaited him if he didn't start working. Even if her worst fear came true and Jamie never opened a book, Carol vowed to herself that she would hold her tongue and not pressure him about it.

This new stance was very different from Carol's previous nagging, threatening, and bribing. By taking this stance, Carol stepped out of a futile power struggle and let Jamie live his own life. She was delighted to find that after she made this shift in her own behavior, her relationship with Jamie became much friendlier. And Jamie, on his own, even gradually started to do his homework!

If you, like Carol, want to make a fundamental change in the way you interact with a procrastinator, here are some guidelines:

Think about what you've been trying to do to influence your procrastinator (nagging, bribing, pleading, threatening, etc.).

Identify the basic, implicit message you have been conveying ("Do your homework"). This will help you identify the thrust of your efforts, which most likely is an attempt to prod the procrastinator into action.

If your basic strategy hasn't worked, do something else—even if your old suggestions seemed rational to you. (Procrastinators are not always rational!) Change your fundamental position about solving the person's procrastination. For example, if you've been pushing your procrastinator to take action, stop pushing in *any* form.

Stick with your new game plan. Though it may be hard to hold your tongue at times, you must be consistent if you want things to change. Remember, the procrastinator may initially resist your new strategy. Changing old habits takes time.

Watch what happens. If you're still caught in a struggle with your procrastinator, then your new plan isn't working, either. Think about what you're now doing. Is it really just more of the same? If so, stop and try to find another way of interacting with your procrastinator.

Specific Techniques

With these general principles in mind, we'll now point out a few specific ways of interacting with a procrastinator that can help you avoid the notorious power struggle or stand-off.

Establish Clear Limits, Deadlines and Consequences. Sit down with your procrastinator and discuss what needs to be done and the date by which it must be completed. Also discuss what the consequences will be if the deadline is not met. Be *specific* and *concrete* so that both of you have the same understanding as to what is expected. You may even want to put your agreement in writing to be doubly sure that it's clear. As much as possible, let the procrastinator actively participate in setting the goal, deadline, and the consequences. This will give the procrastinator a sense of having some control in the situation, and may help to diminish his or her tendency to put things off in order to feel more powerful. What you want is a *mutual* agreement.

Sam and his wife, Theresa, discussed the back fence project that Sam had been putting off for three years. The existing fence was a rotting eyesore, and Sam had been meaning to tear it down and rebuild it with new lumber. Together, they decided that three months was a reasonable length of time for Sam to have built the new fence. Checking their calendar, they set June 17 as the deadline. They then agreed to the following consequences: On June 18, if the new fence wasn't completed, Theresa could hire someone to finish whatever remained to be done. The cost for this would come out of Sam's personal spending money. Since Sam loved to buy fishing gear, it meant that he would not be able to get new tackle, new poles, etc., until the cost of the fence was paid off.

Once the arrangement is set and the rewards and punishments are clear, leave it up to the procrastinator to meet the agreement. If he or she fails to do so, you can then follow through with the agreed-upon consequences. This is a much cleaner way to handle things—and it keeps you out of the watchdog role. After settling on their arrangement, Theresa had a concrete alternative to fall back on if Sam didn't live up to his promise. She felt less anxious knowing that one way or another, the fence would be rebuilt. And Sam, feeling less hounded by her, was more inclined to get out there and get started.

If your procrastinator is absolutely unwilling to discuss the issue with you, or you are unable to reach a joint agreement, you can establish some consequences unilaterally. In this case, be sure that you have the capability to enforce those consequences and that you do follow through if the procrastinator doesn't do the task. For example, if Sam had not been willing to work out an agreement for the fence, Theresa could have informed him that if he didn't do it by a certain date, she would hire someone else. Then, if Sam didn't finish the fence, she should stick to what she'd said and have it done, no matter how vehemently Sam protested. He might accuse her of being punitive toward him or of wasting money. But that's something you have to be willing to tolerate if you want to end the cycle of mutual frustration. If Theresa yields and gives Sam more time, he will know that her limits do not have to be taken seriously, and that will mean a stand-off somewhere down the line. In some situations, unfortunately, it's you or the procrastinator who must feel the pain.

Help the Procrastinator Set Small, Interim Goals. As we've said before, procrastinators tend to think about the final, end-point of a goal, but forget about the steps they'll have to take to get there. They also tend to be vague and unrealistic about time and often get caught short of it. As they scramble to do the task or project at the last minute, they find that there's more to do than they'd thought. Things are more complicated; they'd forgotten about certain steps that must be completed before proceeding.

One way to diminish this last-minute frenzy is to help the procrastinator set small mini-goals, a series of steps that need to be accomplished in order to reach the larger, final goal. Sam and Theresa identified four interim goals: tearing down the old fence; hauling away the materials; purchasing new lumber; starting the building of the new fence. They agreed to specific dates by which each of these interim goals would be accomplished. If Sam did not meet a deadline, Theresa could hire someone to do that specific task, and the cost would again come out of Sam's personal spending money.

Help the Procrastinator Be Concrete and Realistic About What He or She Needs to Do. Procrastinators hate to be specific about anything. As a result, they often set extremely unrealistic goals. They think about what they'd *like* to accomplish rather than about what is possible, given their limitations of time and energy and the disruptions that are likely to occur. The result is that they become discouraged when they are unable to follow through.

Sam's initial proposal to Theresa was, "I'll have the fence done by this weekend." But Sam hadn't given any thought to the fact that the coming week was going to be a hectic one in the office and he would probably have to work overtime. He hadn't considered that he and a friend had tickets to a Saturday afternoon baseball game. Finally, Sam had never really stopped to think about just what was involved in rebuilding the fence. It was only after thinking things through with Theresa that he realized there was no way he could have the new fence finished by the weekend. In the end, three months was a more realistic allotment of time.

To help a procrastinator be concrete and realistic about a job that needs to be done, you must first anticipate this tendency to be vague and overly confident or pessimistic about what's involved.

Be on the alert for phrases such as: "No problem—won't take any time at all," or "That's way too complicated—it will take me years to do it right!" Then, ask questions that help counter this global tendency. "What's actually involved in rebuilding the fence, Sam? Is it really just putting up new lumber?" or "How much free time do you have this week? Don't you have a presentation to make on Monday?" If nothing else, these questions will urge the procrastinator to stop and consider if his or her assessment of the situation makes any sense.

In all your interactions with procrastinators, try to function as a *consultant*, and not as a director. In other words, offer your support, be a sounding board, and help procrastinators be realistic, but don't try to decide things for them or judge their moral character.

Reward Progress Made Along the Way. Procrastinators usually don't think they've achieved anything until they've reached their final goal, which means that they derive no satisfaction from progress made along the way. All they can see is how much remains to be done. As you might imagine, this is a very discouraging state to be in.

Progress of any kind deserves to be recognized and rewarded. You can be positive without overdoing it—the latter will be perceived as pressure and will most likely come across as false. Better to say, "Hey, you got started. That's an important beginning," than, "Oh, how wonderful! You got started! It'll be smooth sailing from here on out!"

You can also participate in activities that reward the procrastinator at points along the way. Take your procrastinator out to lunch or dinner for accomplishing a difficult step; arrange an evening at the movies *after* he or she has spent two hours working; have the procrastinator take a break with you and go for a walk. (But don't let the break go on forever!) Your procrastinator will begin to value and appreciate what he or she has done, even before reaching the final goal. This is an invaluable lesson, because it makes working toward a goal a reinforcing experience rather than a demoralizing process fraught with frustration and despair.

Tell the Procrastinator Directly if You Do Get Angry. There will probably be times when the procrastinator's delaying irritates you or lets you down. Let the procrastinator know specifically what she or he has done to elicit this feeling in you, and discuss how the delay has affected you. You need to be clear, but you don't have to be punitive or brutal. You could say, for example, "Maria, you told me that you would compile a list of people to contact and have it for this meeting. You haven't done it, and it's holding up everything else we want to do. I feel very annoyed that you didn't do your part."

Try not to communicate your anger indirectly, through sarcastic comments, emotional withdrawal, or "loaded" nonverbal behaviors (facial expressions, loud sighs, a harsh tone of voice). The procrastinator will probably read the worst possible meaning into your indirect signals. Then, he or she is likely to retreat from you even further, and procrastinate all the more.

Let Procrastinators Know that They Are More to You Than Just Their Performance. If you really want to be of help to a procrastinator, let him or her know that you value other qualities besides productivity. What about his boundless generosity, her great sense of humor, or sensitivity to the personal dilemmas of other people? Your procrastinator may have a talent for cooking, an eye for design and color, a knack for repairing anything that isn't working.

Procrastinators can appreciate these qualities in other people, but they have trouble seeing the same qualities in themselves. They believe they *are* what they *do*. Their worth *as people* depends solely on how well they perform. You need to let procrastinators know that your caring and respect extend beyond their success or failure. It may take a while for the message to sink in, but it's one of the most important you can convey.

Consider Yourself. An important question to ask yourself is: What could happen to *you* if the procrastinator doesn't get around to doing something? Are there truly consequences of substance for you, or is it more that you would feel disappointed if the procrastinator didn't come through?

In some situations, the procrastinator's inaction may have a very real impact on your own life. For example, if the procrastinator is your business partner, you may stand to lose revenues and clients, be the target of a lawsuit, or damage your professional reputation in general. If your procrastinating spouse hasn't taken care of an important car repair, then your life may be in danger every time you drive. In these situations, you need to take care of yourself. First try to discuss things with the procrastinator to see if you can work out a solution together. If that fails you may have to take *unilateral* action—you either do the work yourself, hire somebody else to do it, or in extreme cases, sever the relationship altogether. You might dissolve the business partnership or fire an employee if you feel the procrastinator is too unreliable. You might decide to leave your marriage or break up a close relationship if you feel that the procrastinator's delays have caused more trouble than you can bear.

In other situations, you may feel uncomfortable as a result of the procrastinator's inaction—even though there may be no actual, concrete consequences for you. Perhaps you feel embarrassed by those delays or, like Carol, worry that other people will judge you on the basis of the procrastinator's behavior. You want the procrastinator to do well so that people will think well of you. Or, you may feel that it's wrong to procrastinate, that the person is betraying you by virtue of the fact that she or he isn't doing what you think they ought to do. It might be hard for you to accept that the procrastinator doesn't share your values and thus has no interest in living up to them.

PROCRASTINATORS YOU MAY KNOW

The people you know who procrastinate may occupy specific roles in your life: your child, your spouse, your boss, and your employee. Because the nature of each of these relationships is so different, there are unique issues involved in each kind that are important to consider in addition to the suggestions we've just made.

Your Child

It can be agonizing to be the parent of a child who is a chronic procrastinator. Perhaps, like Carol, you want your child to do better or work harder in school. Perhaps you're frustrated by your child's delaying on household chores and responsibilities. Perhaps you believe your adult child is wasting his or her life, doing nothing of value. These are some of the most common complaints we've heard from parents of procrastinators.

The biggest mistake that most parents of procrastinators make is that they nag. If your child is procrastinating because she or he is afraid of not doing well enough, your nagging will only add to his or her feeling of insecurity. It won't help your child learn to accept his or her limitations, deal with disappointments, or approach tasks more realistically. Incessant nagging will not help your child deal with the consequences of success, learning how to be outstanding and human at the same time, how to deal with competitive jealousy, how to say no to excessive demands. If your child is procrastinating as a way of rebelling against authority, nagging will intensify the rebellion, but it will not help your child develop a secure sense of autonomy. Nagging will not teach your child that it is possible to compromise with somebody and still respect oneself.

It is quite possible that in your desire to help your child, you may be forgetting a crucial fact of life: The most important developmental task of every child is to become *an autonomous adult*. In order to do this, all children must separate from their parents and find a way of defining themselves independently from other adults. Procrastination may be your child's attempt to separate from you. If you place high value on academics or on being responsible around the house, your child may delay on these things because they are important to you. Procrastination may be your child's way of saying, "I don't have to accept your values as my own." Even if your child initially began to procrastinate for other reasons, if you've been nagging him or her about it, he or she may *continue* to procrastinate to thwart you. This is often the case with adolescent children. They derive a sense of power from your inability to govern them. The more you press them to take action, the more they resist with continued procrastination, to prove that they are beyond your control. Your child's identity is at stake. If you let up on the pressure and allow your child to make some autonomous choices, he or she may not have to use procrastination to demonstrate independence.

Look over the general strategies we listed earlier in this chapter. For parents, two of these are the most important and the most difficult to put into practice: to let your procrastinator know that you value him or her *beyond* his or her performance, and to separate your life from your procrastinator's. Part of this difficulty for parents derives from the unique and complex nature of the parent-child bond. In no other relationships do there exist such expectations and dreams, nor such complete responsibility for another person.

Do you remember what hopes and dreams you had for your child when he or she was a tiny infant? You may have imagined a glorious future—he or she would be the lawyer you wish you had been, a concert pianist, or a doctor just like Uncle Jack. Be responsible and obedient. Get straight A's. Be a great ballplayer. Have lots of friends, a happy marriage, grandchildren. Your child would have all the advantages life could offer—good schools, a stimulating environment, financial and material comforts, the love and attention you might have missed as a kid, or the rules and limits you wished your parents had set for you.

After having been so emotionally invested in your child, it is difficult as a parent to separate yourself and your life from your procrastinator. It's hard to let go of that hope for the future, of that wish to see your child's life be something that pleases you. And yet, this is one of your most important tasks: To nurture and teach your child, and then, gradually, to let him or her make his or her own mistakes and to live with the consequences. Children need to learn what happens as a result of their procrastinating and decide for themselves whether the advantages of procrastination are worth its costs.

We do not wish to convey that by separating yourself from your procrastinator you should sever all emotional ties with your child. Regardless of how good or bad your relationship is, you will always occupy a special place in your child's life. Your love and approval (or lack of it) will have a special significance that cannot be replaced. For this reason, it is especially important that you let your child know that you give your love regardless of his or her performance—that you care about your child whether or not he or she comes in first place, has an IQ of 150, or procrastinates. Your child may not behave as if your approval matters, but deep down, everyone yearns to be loved and accepted. And your child yearns for that acceptance from *you.*

Your Spouse

Procrastination in a marriage can be anything from a petty annoyance to a major source of conflict and tension. Perhaps you've accepted this aspect of your spouse as a human imperfection you can live with, just as your spouse accepts your snoring, your squeezing the toothpaste in the middle of the tube, or your decision to take trumpet lessons and practice at home.

It is more likely, however, that your spouse's procrastination has had negative consequences for you as a couple and as individuals. It may be turning a formerly playful person into an anxious grump. It may be making your life more chaotic than you'd like, if for example, your checks bounce because your partner hasn't balanced the checkbook in three months, or if you had to cancel a planned vacation because your spouse waited too long to make travel arrangements. If your spouse's procrastination has interfered with a career, caused financial losses, or delayed important decisions, you may feel disappointed and frustrated with the circumstances. Worst of all, you may be losing a sense of trust and respect for your spouse. In any or all of these cases, you probably feel deprived, missing out on the fun you'd hoped to share together, and on the support you expected from your partner.

In addition to your own disappointments, it can be very painful to watch someone you love wrestling with the devil of procrastination. Living with it day by day, you see firsthand the price your spouse pays for putting things off—the restless nights, the fear of answering the phone or opening the mail, the apologies and fabrications, the wounded pride, the need to exert control in some other areas (over you, perhaps?). You may even be the only one who really sees the cost, especially if your partner maneuvers to cover up to the public. It is therefore for both of your sakes that you want to help find a solution to the problem of your spouse's procrastination.

Two suggestions that we discussed before in handling a procrastinator are especially important when the recalcitrant is your spouse. First, if you are angry or hurt by the effects of your husband's or wife's procrastination, communicate your feelings directly and as soon as possible. For example, Emily's husband Ben quit his job as an insurance agent to try to turn his hobby into a profession as a freelance photographer. Emily went along with the decision, agreeing to a one-year experimental period to test out Ben's new career. But she became increasingly frustrated as Ben hesitated to make the necessary contacts, to submit his photographs to dealers, or to hire an agent to represent him.

"I should have just told him that I was getting worried, then angry, then furious. Instead I didn't say anything until one day it all came to a head. Ben was working in his darkroom, and I thought, 'There he goes again, developing more pictures that no one will ever see.' So I burst into the room, letting the light in and ruining his pictures. He didn't speak to me for a week." Emily could probably have helped Ben instead of hurting both of them if she had let him know how upset she was from the start. And if he had been able to explain how afraid he was, how much he felt he was risking to show his work to other professionals, she might have had more compassion for him.

Critical comments, angry outbursts, a condescending or patronizing attitude, are all easy traps to fall into when you feel you've reached the end of your rope with a procrastinator. But not only do these arguments not help your spouse, they can be very damaging to your relationship. Find a time to discuss the problem when you are both in reasonable moods. You might even make an appointment. Emily could have said, "I'm getting concerned about your hesitation to show your pictures to anyone. We don't have to talk about it now if you don't want to, but maybe we can discuss it tomorrow. How about after dinner?"

Secondly, it is important that you remind your spouse of all the things you appreciate in him or her that have nothing whatsoever to do with the issue of procrastination. You can remind your spouse how much you love his spontaneous romantic side, the comfort she provides when you are down, the way he takes good care of your children. It can be very encouraging to a person to hear that in spite of procrastination, in spite of imperfections, limitations, and fears, your love will still be there.

At times, unfortunately, procrastination can seem to poison a whole relationship. It may seem much harder to have fun, feel loving, or be respectful anymore. Before you deadlock in a cold war or decide to throw in the towel, consider a few important issues.

First, how much direct bearing does your spouse's procrastination have on your own life? Does it have a clear and detrimental effect on you? Or are you upset with your spouse for procrastinating on something that would be beneficial for him or her, but does not have any direct consequences for you?

Wayne, for example, is impatiently waiting for Louise to follow through with her promise to lose 15 pounds. "Louise says she wants to lose weight, but she never does it," he complains. "She always has a good excuse for not starting a diet." At work, Louise puts off asking for the raise she thinks she deserves. Wayne is extremely frustrated with her reluctance, although he knows the additional salary would make no significant difference to their income or lifestyle.

Wayne has made a very common error. He has viewed Louise as an extension of himself, taking on her problems as his own.

Wayne's upset has more to do with his hopes and expectations for Louise than with any real consequences dealt him by her procrastination. He has trouble letting Louise be herself, with all of her imperfections, so he pushes her to change and she fights back. With a procrastinator this approach can only lead to trouble. Unless there is a clear and present way in which your spouse's procrastination diminishes the quality of your life, the problem does not belong to you. You can be supportive and caring, but your spouse's struggle with procrastination need not grow into a struggle between you.

A second important issue to consider is *why* procrastination has developed into such a struggle between the two of you. For some couples, procrastination has become a scapegoat that distracts them from more difficult issues, like sex, the children, or the way they treat each other. A woman who was terribly hurt when she discovered that her husband was having an extramarital affair began to procrastinate on the things she usually did for him. Instead of confronting her sense of betrayal or his dissatisfaction with their marriage, they fought about her procrastination. A man who felt unfulfilled in his job took his frustrations out by harping on every little thing his wife doesn't do right on time. He is focusing on her imperfections so that he doesn't have to look at himself.

Thirdly, consider for a moment if there isn't some way in which your spouse's procrastination suits you. If he or she were suddenly able to get everything done on time, to make quick solid decisions and act on them, to achieve all stated goals, where would you be then? Perhaps right now you feel you have a slight moral edge over your spouse, since he or she is so dilatory. Could you maintain that righteous standing relative to your spouse if procrastination were no longer such an obvious problem? You may also worry that if your spouse were to stop procrastinating and surge ahead, you would be left behind. If he or she managed to get into graduate school, be promoted, achieve recognition or notoriety, would you worry that this change would lead to new situations, new confidence—and less time for you?

As much as you would like procrastination to stop being such an interference in your life together, you may thus have some investment in keeping things the way they are. If you are somehow threatened by the prospect of your spouse being a more successful person, admit it to yourself and try to talk it over with your partner. Isn't it more appealing to think of working together on the consequences of success than to use procrastination to protect you from it?

Whether *you* can live a satisfying life with your procrastinator depends on the way in which he or she procrastinates, on the impact procrastination has on your life, on your own flexibility, and on the overall quality of your relationship. If your spouse continues to procrastinate in spite of your discussions and your efforts to help, you will then have to face some tough decisions. Consider what your life is presently like. Can you accept your spouse with the problem of procrastination, even though you are deeply affected by it?

Lauren had to confront this issue with her husband Allen. Allen was a notorious procrastinator who was laid off from his last job. Two years later, Allen still had made no serious efforts to find another job. During this time, Lauren supported the family with her job as a computer systems analyst. "I know Allen needed time to get over being laid off, but two years is too long. He's full of ideas about what he might do, but it doesn't pay the rent. Even though he's a good father for our two kids, I feel so resentful that I can hardly stand to be around him anymore. I want a husband, not another child!"

Lauren had to face up to her bottom-line needs. If nothing changed, could she continue to live with Allen as he was? You, too, may have to decide if your spouse's procrastination is so detrimental that your bottom-line needs are not being met. Is there some agreement or behavior that you absolutely insist upon in order to remain in the relationship, something so important that you feel you can't compromise on it for anyone?

Obviously, no one else can decide what's negotiable and what's non-negotiable for you in your relationship. You have to set your own bottom line. Emily decided that even if Ben never sold a single photograph, she would stop hounding him during his one-year experiment as a freelancer, and then they would decide together how to proceed. Wayne knew that he loved Louise whether she lost or gained 15 pounds. Another woman in Lauren's position might have been happy to have a househusband, and the marriage would have worked out very well. But for Lauren, the situation was intolerable. She told Allen that if he didn't make a serious attempt to find a job in six months, she would leave him. Seven months later, she moved out and eventually filed for divorce. "It was the hardest decision I've ever made," she recalled sadly. "I still loved him, but I couldn't live with him as long as he wasn't even trying to do what he said he would, and I couldn't get him to see how serious I was."

If you decide that your spouse must, in fact, do something different in order for you to remain in your relationship, *explain exactly what your bottom line is.* He or she may not realize how important the issue is for you. Give your spouse a chance to accommodate to what you need, before your relationship deteriorates beyond repair.

Your Employee

Whether your employee is late to work and to meetings, delays carrying out your instructions, misses deadlines, or puts off paperwork, his or her procrastination costs your business. Productivity is reduced, personnel problems may develop, and *you* may have to devote valuable time and energy to resolving the difficulties.

An employee may procrastinate for personal reasons—fears about performance and judgment, problems with authority figures and being controlled by others, feelings of insecurity and lack of self-confidence. But procrastination may also be related to the structure and operation of your organization. If procrastination is a widespread problem in your business, then those individuals with decision-making authority may need to examine how your institution is run. In one agency, 20 of 26 workers were delinquent on 30 or more case reports that were supposed to be submitted to their supervisors. When the employees were questioned about their delays, it became apparent that they felt no sense of pride or identification with the agency. Instead, they perceived themselves as having to do all the "dirty work" for a management staff they felt did not appreciate or value them. Procrastination had become an indirect expression of their grievances against management.

A difficulty that sometimes arises in hierarchical institutions is that employees lower than you in the hierarchy sometimes feel entitled to more power than they actually have. They may believe that they could do the job as well or better than you are doing it if only they had the chance. What this means is that although a boss wields formal power, his or her employees may try to equalize the imbalance of power by whatever means they can, procrastination is one possible strategy. If the organization is structured so that employees feel that their ideas will be given serious attention, they will probably perceive themselves as having some power in the organization. In this situation, procrastination *as an organizational problem* is less likely to occur. In a work environment that is highly rigid and authoritarian, however, employees often feel impotent, particularly if there are few avenues for the expression of dissatisfaction or for making constructive suggestions. In a situation like this, procratination may become a way to even the score.

If large numbers of your employees are procrastinating, then you should identify the problems in your current organizational structure and try to change them. If, on the other hand, procrastination is restricted to a few individuals, you might proceed differently.

You could begin by talking with the individual procrastinator about his or her specific behavior. You might bring it up during a scheduled performance review, or you could meet the employee specifically to discuss this issue. Whatever circumstances you choose, the objective for the meeting should be for you and the employee together to set clear objectives, definite deadlines, and follow-up procedures with appropriate positive or negative feedback and consequences. During your discussion, be careful not to make assumptions about why the employee is procrastinating. One of the most common, and erroneous, assumptions is that the employee is lazy, disorganized, or unmotivated.

Ask the employee to tell you about his or her procrastination.

Your method of handling the problem could depend on the reasons for the delay. If the person delays on written reports, for example, because of an exaggerated concern over whether his or her writing will be good enough, you might help the employee differentiate between what needs to be done perfectly and what simply needs to be done. If the employee seems to be worried that other colleagues might resent his or her efficiency or that timely reports would lead to additional responsibilities, you could talk with the employee about the realistic consequences of doing well in your company. And if the procrastinator indicates that they are unhappy in a specific job, you could discuss alternative job assignments or responsibilities, or point them to the human resources department or employee assistance program.

Many procrastinators bring to their jobs personal issues with power and authority that have little to do with you or the way your organization is run. They are worried about being pushed around or humiliated by others, and therefore insist on doing things on their terms so they won't feel weak or compromised. Unfortunately, these procrastinators will probably have difficulty talking about such issues with you. As an important authority figure, you control much of their fate within the organization, and they'll be loathe to tell you that you're the object of their fears or resentment. However, you can help these procrastinators get back on the right track professionally—in spite of their personal issues—by giving them a role in the decision-making process whenever possible.

Of course, whatever the reason an employee procrastinates, the bottom line for you as a manager is to reduce delaying behavior. Some of the general techniques that we described earlier in this chapter are of particular relevance to the workplace, including setting clear limits and deadlines, clarifying concrete and specific goals, and rewarding progress along the way. It is especially important in this area to let the procrastinator know that you value him or her for more than simply what he or she produces. When a procrastinator feels valued as a *person*, his or her performance is likely to improve markedly.

Procrastination among one or more of your employees may be a sign that you are not using your human resources most effectively. Like all employees, procrastinators have strengths and weaknesses. An employee may be one of the best salesmen you have and one of the worst report writers you've ever hired. Is there any way to capitalize on the strengths and talents of those employees whose procrastination is currently a drain on your organization? Could you, for example, team a procrastinator who has great ideas with another employee who is a meticulous memo and report writer, but not a very innovative thinker? Procrastinators are people who are not utilizing their full potential. The challenge for you as a manager is to see how creative you can be in maximizing the hidden assets of your procrastinating employees.

Your Boss

"My editor drives me nuts!" said a magazine writer who interviewed us for a story on procrastination. "He's a consummate procrastinator. All month long it's, 'I'll get to your article soon,' but he doesn't read it until a day or two before our monthly deadline. Then I have to do a rush job on the revisions to have it ready in time. The entire office staff goes crazy trying to get everything done, and it could all be avoided if our boss would just do his job sooner!"

This writer exemplifies the plight of the employee who must contend with a boss who procrastinates. You may know that something is due—the layout for the next issue, the company report, the budget proposal, an upcoming business trip agenda—

but when you try to specify what needs to be done and by when, your boss remains elusive. You are left in limbo, aware of the approaching deadline, but unclear about what you need to do to meet it. Or, you may have fulfilled your responsibility, like the magazine writer above, only to have your boss put off his or her job. It can be very frustrating when your boss sits on your work—not giving you the information or feedback that you need; delaying turning your report over to the appropriate person; putting off an important decision which would determine what you'll do next. In all of these situations, you are left hanging, uncertain about what to expect or how to proceed.

Another consequence of having a boss who procrastinates is the last-minute frenzy. Like our magazine writer, you and other subordinates may get caught up in a flurry of activity just prior to deadlines. You suddenly find yourself without a moment to spare, working overtime and weekends, cancelling personal plans so that you can do your part to stave off a major professional disaster. Your blood pressure shoots skyward, you feel tense and irritable, your family and friends are upset because you're unavailable and preoccupied. In short, your life is hell. And to make it all worse, in the back of your mind you know that all this chaos could have been avoided had your boss acted when he or she was supposed to.

To add insult to injury, it is very common for subordinates to be blamed for a missed deadline or last-minute rush, when in fact it was their supervisor's fault. Unfortunately, some bosses are not about to admit that it was their procrastination that resulted in a crisis. When they have to account to *their* superiors, they attribute the situation to others like yourself. It's not fair, but it happens.

In many respects, working with a procrastinating boss is more difficult than dealing with a child, spouse, or employee who procrastinates. You have little power or leverage over your boss and you may have to get along with him or her to keep your job. If you have a comfortable relationship with your boss, then without being accusatory, describe to your boss how his or her procrastination affects you, how it makes your job more difficult. Some procrastinators have no idea that their delaying creates problems for others, and once they are told, will attempt to improve—especially if the problem is presented in a nonjudgmental way. One of the best ways to do this is to convey the message, "Please help me. *I've* got a problem." By emphasizing *your* difficulty, you take the heat off your boss while inviting him or her to help you solve the problem. He or she is less likely to feel threatened or criticized by you, so the potential for a power struggle is reduced.

Many bosses are not, however, easy to talk to. Some of them resent hearing anything of a remotely critical nature from a subordinate, and become more defensive toward the employee as a result. With such a person, you may jeopardize your job by speaking too freely. Other bosses are so preoccupied that they practically ignore what their subordinates are telling them. With a boss like this, you might feel as though you're talking to a brick wall—and have about as much impact.

If you can't talk with your boss, or if talking doesn't do any good, then face it: Your boss isn't likely to change. You've got to do what you can to take care of yourself under the circumstances. One thing you can do is to anticipate those last-minute flurries of activity, even if you don't like them. Expect to work frantically just before a deadline, and to do overtime. Let your friends and family know ahead of time that you may not be able to spend much time with them. Don't get baseball or opera tickets for a time when you're likely to be burning the candle at both ends. Canceling social arrangements at the last minute will make you feel more deprived and resentful than ever about having to work. In other words, try to make the last-minute rush as predictable as possible. This may give you just enough predictability to save your sanity.

Another tactic is to get as much information from your boss as you can about a project or deadline that involves you. This will allow you to make as much progress as possible before the last-minute crunch. You can solicit information from your boss in several ways. You can ask him or her directly—for example, "Janet, the deadline for our next issue is coming up in two weeks and I need your comments on my article so I can start revising it." If you are given an evasive answer such as, "OK, I'll get around to it soon," you can matter-of-factly press for a more specific date. "I'd like to plan time in my schedule for this, so can you tell me what day this week you'll have it back to me?" If you still receive a vague reply, you can try the "Broken Record Technique" that is taught in many assertiveness training courses. You simply say the same thing over and over again until you get the response you want. For example, "I know it may be difficult, but I'd really like to get your comments by Friday." If your boss becomes more and more irritated as you try to pin him or her down, don't press your luck. Remember, you can ask for what you want, but you won't always get it. Even so, if you get an answer 10 percent of the time, or you obtain more information to go on than before, it's still better than nothing!

The second way to get information from your boss is to play dumb. This is a strategy that professional negotiators often use. It can be especially useful if your boss is vague, because it indirectly pressures the person to be more definitive while leaving them "in charge." "I'm sorry, Pete. I'm not sure I understand what's involved in this project. When exactly is the deadline? And what exactly do we have to come up with by that date?" When done in a sincere and earnest manner, such a tactic is usually successful. In fact, while explaining it more systematically to you, your boss may realize that the project won't be as easy as he initially thought. You may get more information for yourself, and your boss may get the message that it's time to get moving. And, just as important, your boss saves face by remaining in the role of the authority giving help.

Another technique to use with your boss is to offer assistance in doing some of the work for him or her. You can do the work and suggest it as a first draft, an outline of the steps and target days for completion, a description of the issues involved in the subject, etc. The main goal is to help your boss complete a task that will benefit both of you. Although you may not get direct credit for your work, you can remind your boss about it when you ask for your next raise or promotion.

These, then, are some suggestions for what you can do to make life bearable with a boss who procrastinates. But what if your boss's procrastination is so stressful or disruptive for you that you feel you just can't take it any more? As in so many other situations, you have to decide for yourself what is bottom line. How much are you willing to tolerate? Have you developed an ulcer or other physical symptoms from the constant stress of your job? Have you started to abuse drugs or alcohol? Is your marriage on the verge of breaking up because you're so frustrated over your work?

If you conclude that the costs of working with your boss are too great, then you may need to consider requesting a transfer to another department or supervisor. As a last resort, you can look elsewhere for a job. It's certainly not an appealing alternative, but it may be better than battling an impossible situation and being miserable while you do it.

To Our Fellow Procrastinators

Finally, we've come all the way from start to finish. As we reflect back on the process of creating this book, we are reminded of the many steps along the way: the initial excitement of authorship, the hard work of starting over again, and the welcome relief and pride in bringing our work to completion. It hasn't been easy, but we did it.

We hope that our thoughts will help you make a start—to act instead of waiting, to persevere instead of giving up. It is possible, with self-knowledge and patience, to take the small steps that will carry you through to the finish.

We wish you well.

Further Readings

Beery, R. G. "Fear of Failure in the Student Experience." *Personnel and Guidance Journal* 54 (1975), pp. 190–203.

Bliss, E. C. *Getting Things Done.* New York: Bantam Books, 1978.

Burns, D. *Feeling Good.* New York: William Morrow and Company, Inc., 1980.

Campbell, D. *If You Don't Know Where You're Going, You'll Probably End up Somewhere Else.* Niles, IL: Argus Communications, 1974.

Davis, M., E. R. Eshelman, and M. McKay. *The Relaxation and Stress Reduction Workbook.* Richmond, CA: New Harbinger Publications, 1980.

Friedman, M. *Overcoming the Fear of Success.* New York: Seaview Books, 1980.

Knaus, W. J. *Do it Now: How to Stop Procrastinating.* Englewood Cliffs, NJ: Prentice-Hall, 1979.

Lakein, A. L. *How to Get Control of Your Time and Your Life.* New York: Peter Wyden, 1973.

Mackenzie, A. and K. C. Waldo. *About Time! A Woman's Guide to Time Management.* New York: McGraw-Hill, 1981.

Miller, A. *Prisoners of Childhood.* New York: Basic Books, Inc., 1981.

Porat, F. *Creative Procrastination.* San Francisco: Harper and Row, 1980.

Scott, D. *How to Put More Time in Your Life.* New York: Signet, 1981.

Selye, H. *Stress Without Distress.* New York: Signet, 1974.

Siegelman, E. Y. *Personal Risk: Mastering Change in Love and Work.* New York: Harper and Row, 1983.

Index

A

Ability, vs. performance, 21–23
Adaptation energy, 181n–182n
Adrenalin, 178, 179
Agreements, mutual, 201
Alertness, increase of, 188–189
Anxiety, vs. performance, 182, 183
Attachment fears, 70–79
Attitudes, with procrastinators,
    198–200
    See also Family attitudes
Authority, rebellion against, 46–47,
    51–53
Authority figures, 15
Autonomy issue, 49–60
    for children, 58–59
    secrecy and, 53–56
    self-worth and, 50

B

Beery, Richard, 20–21
Behavioral goals, 132–146
    elements of, 132–134
    follow-through of, 140–143

review of, 143–146
selection of, 135–136
start-up of, 137–139
Bosses, as procrastinators, 214–217
Breathing techniques, 186
Bribery, 199
Brief Therapy Center of the Mental
    Research Institute, 106n
Burns, David, 23

C

Childhood experiences, 12–15, 58–59
Children:
    autonomy issue for, 58–59
    as procrastinators, 205–207
Clinging, by family, 97–100
Comfort zone, 61–63
Commitment:
    fear of, 25–26, 32–33
    public, 170
Communication, 170–171
Competition, 11, 26
    retreat from, 32–33

secrecy and, 54–55
Compliments, 168
Compulsiveness, 35
Consequences, 6–7, 28–29, 38–39,
    105–106, 118–119, 200–201
Control:
    by family, 94–97
    need for, 44–49
Criticism, 197
    See also Self-criticism

D

Deadlines, 138–39, 200–201
Delegating, 162–163
    See also Support system
Dependency. *See* Separation fears
Distancing, in families, 100–102
Doubting, by family, 88, 92–94

E

Employees, as procrastinators,
    212–214
Encouragement, procrastinator's
    view of, 192–194
Endorphins, 187
Ethical problems, 112
Excuses, 124–127, 140
Exercise, 187–188

F

Failure, fear of, 19–29
Failure models, 84–86
Family attitudes, 86–104

clinging, 97–100
controlling, 94–97
distancing, 100–102
doubting, 88, 92–94
pressuring, 87–88, 89–92
self-esteem and, 102–104
See also Children; Parents;
    Spouses
Family background, 13–15, 28, 79–80
Fears:
    attachment, 70–79
    commitment, 25–26, 32–33
    failure, 19–29
    improvement, 107–108
    loss, 77–79
    punishment, 38–39
    separation, 63–70
    success, 29–42
Feedback, 136
Fight-or-Flight response, 178–180
Finances, procrastination in, 122
Fiore, Neil, 148–149
Fisch, Richard, 106n
Flexibility, 199–200
Friends. *See* Support system
Frustration cycle, 191–196
    disappointment, 194
    encouragement, 192–194
    irritation, 195
    stand-off, 195–196

G

Gender, 33–34
Goals, 131–146
    elements of, 132–134
    follow-through of, 140–143
    interim, 202
    realistic, 202–203
    review of, 143–146
    selection of, 135–136

start-up of, 137–139
two-week experiment with,
135–146
Guilt:
as barrier to success, 35–36
over procrastination, 9, 145, 199

H

Household procrastination, 121
*How to Get Control of Your Time and
Your Life*, 159
Husbands, as procrastinators,
207–212

I

Identity, 108–114
blank slate, 111
lovable clown, 109
miracle worker, 110–111
saint, 109–110
Imagery, 137, 186
Improvement, dangers of, 106–108
Inventory, 117–130

J

Jacobsen, Edmund, 186

L

Lakein, Alan, 159
Leisure time, 154–155, 165
Limits, 200–201
Loss, fear of, 77–79

M

Marriage, procrastination in, 207–212
Mental Research Institute, 106n
Models, 84–86
Moral problems, 112
Muscle relaxation, 186–187
Mutual frustration cycle, 191–196
disappointment, 194
encouragement, 192–194
irritation, 195
stand-off, 195–196

N

Nagging, 196–197, 205–206
Negotiating, 196–205
ineffective methods of, 196–198
helpful attitudes in, 198–200
useful techniques for, 200–205
Notebook, 129

P

Parallel play, 172–173
Parents:
clinging by, 97–100
conflict with, 76
controlling by, 94–97
distancing by, 100–102
doubts of, 88, 92–94
as models, 84–85
pressuring by, 87–88, 89–92
of procrastinators, 205–207
rebellion against, 52–53, 58–59
self-esteem and, 102–104
Partners, 171–172
Perfectionism, 23–28, 94, 143
Performance:
vs. ability, 21–23

vs. anxiety, 182, 183
Personal care, procrastination in, 122
Physical tension, reduction of,
    185–188
Planning, 127–130, 170–171
Praise, 168
Pressuring:
    encouragement vs., 192–194
    by family, 87–88, 89–92
Procrastination:
    areas of, 120–123
    choosing plan for, 127–130
    consequences of, 6–7, 28–29,
    38–39, 105–106, 118–119, 200–201
    cycle of, 7–11
    excuses for, 124–127
    as an identity, 108–114
    reviewing incidents of, 117–120
    roots of, 11–15, 56–60
    style of, 123–124
Procrastination inventory, 117–130
Procrastinators, 191–217
    bosses as, 214–217
    children as, 205–207
    employees as, 212–214
    mutual frustration cycle and,
    191–196
    negotiating with, 196–205
    spouses as, 207–212
Procrastinator's Code, 16–17
Progressive Relaxation, 186
Public commitment, 170
Punishment, fear of, 38–39
    See also Consequences

R

Recreation, 154–155, 165
Relationship fears:
    attachment, 70–79
    comfort zones and, 61–63
    separation, 63–70
    stress and, 184

Relaxation exercises, 185–188
Revenge, 48–49
Rewards, 141–142, 203
    social, 173
Ridicule, 197
Role models, 84–86
Rules, rebellion against, 45–46

S

School, procrastination in, 121
School history, 13–15
Secrecy, 53–56
Segal, Lynn, 106n
Self-criticism, 112–114
Self-esteem, and family, 102–104
Self-monitoring. *See* Un-schedule
Self-worth equation, 21–22, 50
Selye, Hans, 179, 181n–182n
Separation fears, 63–70
Social life, 154–155
Social relationships, procrastination
    in, 122
Social rewards, 173
Spouses, as procrastinators, 207–212
Stress, 175–189
    effects of, 180–182
    examples of, 175–176
    intensity of, 182
    physical response to, 178–180
    relaxation exercises for, 185–188
    signs of, 177–178
    sources of, 183–185
Stress response, 178–189
Success, 11–12
    family doubts and, 88, 92–94
    family pressures and, 87–88,
    89–92
    fear of, 29–42
    guilt and, 35–36

personal risks of, 34–42
support for, 88
women and, 33–34
Success models, 84–86
Support system, 167–174
attitudes of, 198–200
communication in, 170–171
selection of, 169
techniques for, 200–205
working in, 171–173
See also Delegating
Survivor guilt, 35–36
"Swiss cheese" method of time
management, 159–161

T

Teachers, as models, 85
Tension reduction, 185–188
Threats, 197
Time, 147–165
estimating of, 159
leisure, 154–155, 165
prime, 164–165
"Swiss cheese" method of
managing, 159–161
un-schedule of, 148–158
Time limits, 138–139, 200–201
Type A Behavior, 181

U

Un-schedule, 148–158

V

Visualization, 137

W

Wake-up breaks, 189
Watzlawick, Paul, 106n
Weakland, John, 106n
Wives, as procrastinators, 207–212
Women, and fear of success, 33–34
Work, procrastination at, 121
See also Bosses; Employees
Workaholics, 34–35